Vendetta

The Kennedys

Also by the same author:

JFK: The Second Plot

VENDETTA
THE KENNEDYS

MATTHEW SMITH
Foreword by JIM MARRS

MAINSTREAM
PUBLISHING

EDINBURGH AND LONDON

The moral right of the author has been asserted

First published in Great Britain in 1993 by
MAINSTREAM PUBLISHING COMPANY (EDINBURGH) LTD
7 Albany Street
Edinburgh EH1 3UG

ISBN 1 85158 553 2

A catalogue record for this book is available from the British Library

Typeset in Berkeley Old Style Book by Saxon Graphics Ltd, Derby
Printed in Great Britain by Butler and Tanner Ltd, Frome

I dedicate this book
to my wife, Margaret

Contents

ACKNOWLEDGMENTS

I AM INDEBTED to that noted researcher and archivist, Mary Ferrell, who kindly undertook the task of reading my manuscript, and Jim Marrs, whose name is synonymous with Kennedy research, who interrupted his busy programme to write a foreword to this book. Chris Longbottom's assistance in pinpointing often obscure and invariably useful documents and literature was invaluable to me, and I greatly appreciate his efforts on my behalf, also.

My work has been enriched by the discussions I have had with a number of people during the preparation of this book and I record, with thanks, the help of Professor Philip H. Melanson, whose work on the Robert Kennedy murder has been outstanding; William Baillie, who worked for the FBI when Robert Kennedy was killed and who is now a lecturer; John Miner, ex-Assistant District Attorney in Los Angeles during the period in which Marilyn Monroe was murdered; and Colonel L. Fletcher Prouty, USAF (Ret.), whose expert knowledge of the CIA and the relationship between intelligence services and the military is well known. I want to express my gratitude to Jon Kimche, also, for his patience and kind help.

The sterling investigatory work carried out on my behalf by Wayne January and John Craig in regard to the Hank Gordon information merits my very special thanks. In this connection I am also grateful to J. Gary Shaw for his assistance. I am also, of course, deeply appreciative of the fact that Hank Gordon chose to reveal his important information to me. Though I preserve Gordon's true identity, he agreed to meet Mary Ferrell in order that she could verify the information he gave me, and I am grateful to him and to Mary Ferrell for that meeting and for the confirmation she was able to give.

Finally, I must express gratitude to my family for their help and support during the time I have been an absentee from my household, and particularly to my wife, Margaret, my tower of strength.

FOREWORD

by Jim Marrs

IN CLASSES, CONFERENCES and lectures all across the United States regarding the assassination of President John F. Kennedy, one question inevitably is asked – 'Was the assassination connected to the assassination of his brother, Robert F. Kennedy?' In recent years other names, such as Dr Martin Luther King and the actress Marilyn Monroe, have also been brought up in discussions of the deaths of the two Kennedy brothers. It's as if there is a natural tendency to lump these deaths of the 1960s together in some as-yet-undiscovered plot.

Serious researchers of the Kennedy assassinations have long believed that some connection existed between the violent ends of the brothers. But, belief is not knowledge. And, especially in these deaths, firm knowledge is hard to obtain. Official obfuscation, and even deceit, have prevented a truthful and meaningful investigation of these deaths. That fact alone should tell us much.

While a wide array of groups had the ability to send assassins against the Kennedys, including Fidel Castro agents, Mafia hitmen, CIA rogues and KGB operatives, the question of who had the power to subvert official investigations of the US government narrows the field considerably. Under the American legal system, anyone who helps a felon cover up his crime is considered an accessory after the fact and treated as just as guilty as the one who committed the crime. Therefore, at least in the case of the assassination of President Kennedy, we can say without fear of contradiction that his successor Lyndon B. Johnson and FBI Director J. Edgar Hoover are guilty parties in his death – if not for allowing or ordering the assassination, certainly for the demonstrable cover-up which took place in its aftermath.

This, of course, means that anyone seriously studying these two assassinations must take a hard look at the upper echelons of power in America. And it is there that the conscientious student will find all

11

the tell-tale signs of a government within the government, or, as Mr Smith has chosen to call it, the Consortium. This Consortium is difficult to penetrate, combining as it does three of the most secret-filled organisations in the United States – organised crime, the intelligence community and the military. All operate under a code of silence with harsh punishments (including death) to violators and all operate on a strict 'need-to-know' basis, ensuring that even direct participants in schemes often cannot truthfully say what happened or how.

But small, and often circumstantial, bits of information can shed light on the Consortium's activities when put together and viewed in its entirety. For example, the rough draft of National Security Action Memorandum No. 273 – issued under President Johnson just four days after Kennedy's death, reversing JFK's pullout orders for Vietnam – was released from the LBJ Library in Austin, Texas, in January 1991. It is dated 21 November 1963. While other interpretations are possible – for instance that Kennedy was countermanding himself the day before he was killed – the most direct interpretation is that this document reversing JFK's Vietnam policies was being prepared within the government the day before his death and while Kennedy was in Texas on a goodwill tour. It is this sort of evidence which leads open-minded researchers to the idea that someone knew of Kennedy's fate in advance. Other evidence of such advance knowledge can be found in the stories of Joseph Milteer, FBI clerk William S. Walter and LBJ's former mistress Madeleine Brown. The evidence continues to pile up.

The laxity and malfeasance of the Los Angeles Police in regard to the Robert Kennedy shooting are now common knowledge among the legion of researchers in the USA. And it is now generally accepted that Marilyn Monroe's death, quite apart from being a suicide as officially claimed, instead may have been a pre-assassination assassination attempt on both Kennedy brothers. There seems to be little doubt that she was murdered and the only question is who was responsible – either the Kennedy faction or the anti-Kennedy faction. The smart money seems to be on the anti-Kennedy faction. And this faction – an integral part of the Consortium according to Mr Smith – had deep roots in my native state of Texas. The anti-Kennedy sentiment so prevalent in Texas is reflected today by the widespread dislike and distrust of President Bill Clinton here.

One other idea to be considered is that the Consortium which ordered a vendetta against the Kennedys may be broader and stronger than any of us imagine. In the 1940s and 50s, after crime boss Charles 'Lucky' Luciano had created a national crime syndicate in the United States, few Americans knew of its existence. FBI Director Hoover constantly denied such a group existed. Today we face a similar situation. Luciano spent the rest of his life travelling through Europe and South America establishing an international crime syndicate. It may have been this syndicate – with members in Britain, France, Italy and the Caribbean – that provided the means of assassination to the Consortium mentioned here. A syndicate of this sort would yield power on an international scale, power unanswerable to national laws and a power which is little known, little understood and, therefore, rarely observed by the average man on the street. And, just like Hoover in the past, it is a power which goes unacknowledged at the highest levels of the world's governments.

While the case for a 'vendetta' against the Kennedy family is far from established, Matthew Smith has, at least, set the perimeters and laid out the basic evidence. And his scenario is well worth considering, especially since the alternative – namely that all of these deaths were simply isolated incidents of accidental misfortune or the handiwork of a lone, somewhat deranged misfit with no connections to anyone with a vendetta against the Kennedys – has been thoroughly demolished over the years by the available evidence.

*

Fort Worth, Texas

(*Jim Marrs is the author of the* New York Times *bestseller* Crossfire: The Plot that Killed Kennedy.)

INTRODUCTION

IT WAS ALL over in a decade. The Kennedy brothers arrived on the presidential scene and were quickly disposed of. When President John F. Kennedy was assassinated the world greeted the news with stunned disbelief. When Robert Kennedy was killed there was a different kind of disbelief. On the face of it there was a tragic coincidence involved in a second brother from the same family meeting his death at the hand of an assassin. When Mary Jo Kopechne died at Chappaquiddick, and Edward Kennedy's political future hung in the balance, there was talk of a curse on the Kennedy family.

The notion of a curse betrayed the fact that people had recognised a pattern in the tragedies which overtook the Kennedys. But there was no curse. To those responsible, it was convenient that people talked of such things, for it concealed what had really happened. Some added the names of Joe Jr, who died on a dangerous bombing mission during the Second World War, and Kathleen, who died also in a plane crash in Europe, but this only served to distort the pattern. The pattern related to the three brothers, all of whom had presidential aspirations, one of whom reached the White House, one of whom stood at its portals and one whose chances were denied him. They had brought something new to American politics, something stirring and exciting. It was a promise of better things for the poor and underprivileged, for the sick and the elderly. It brought a new, fresh look at what was happening in the United States and a sane approach to domestic and international problems.

When Robert Kennedy was murdered I was not the only one who caught my breath and wondered what I was going to hear next. But the newspapers told the story of Sirhan Sirhan shooting the Senator, and there seemed no doubt that there was no connection with the killing of his brother in Dallas. 'An open and shut case,' said Los Angeles police, and there appeared to be no 'inside story'. As with the assassination of President Kennedy, it was left to researchers and those who investigated privately to ferret out what had really happened. When the Chappaquiddick incident occurred the following year, the published story this time left many unanswered questions, but, again, it was left to researchers and journalists to probe for the answers.

When I viewed the trail of disaster which had overtaken the Kennedy brothers I believed I saw a pattern, but I would be lying if I said that I instantly knew what was afoot. It was some time afterwards, when disturbing notions surfaced about how the actress Marilyn Monroe had really died that the pattern began to crystallise. When I began to look into the reality of such a pattern I found there were other researchers who connected the deaths of John and Robert. It was not until my research for this book was well under way that I found there had been one or two others, also, who had investigated the Marilyn Monroe death from the viewpoint that it was the Kennedys who were the targets of her murderers. When I eventually managed to piece together some kind of picture of who was behind the crimes, I found that, once again, I was not alone in identifying the existence of a secret, powerful force which controlled America and which, some had detected, had influence which extended to many other countries in the world.

My study seeks to establish the existence of the vendetta carried out by this secret force against the Kennedy brothers and to show the links between the crimes its members perpetrated to achieve their objectives. That it is restricted to that does not mean that I do not acknowledge this force's other, wider activities. This, however, would be the subject of another, far greater study. It is sufficient to identify the strand of activity which has deprived the United States of its most innovative, insightful and compassionate leaders, in the hope that those whose responsibility it is will finally institute an intensive and thorough investigation into the crimes involved and the pattern we expose.

Matthew Smith,
Sheffield, England

CHAPTER ONE

A Kennedy for King

*'My father always told me that all businessmen were
sons-of-bitches but I never believed it till now.'*
John F. Kennedy

JOSEPH P. KENNEDY was certainly an ambitious man. There were few
things he really wanted to achieve which he did not accomplish on his
way to becoming one of America's richest men. The Presidency was
one of those things which eluded him.

Joe was born in September 1888, the son of Patrick J. and Mary
Kennedy. Patrick was the owner of a saloon and liquor business, and,
notwithstanding the claims made by Joseph P. of impoverishment in
his young life, Patrick and Mary were well off and the poverty Joe
claimed was a figment of his imagination, designed to create a 'rags-
to-riches' image for himself. In 1914 he married Rose Fitzgerald, the
catch of Boston, daughter of John F. Fitzgerald, Boston's mayor. Joe
Kennedy was some catch himself, however, having become America's
youngest bank president at the age of 25, the year before he was
married. It mattered not that it was a small bank: Joe was President of
it and that made him top dog. It reflected well Joe's philosophy of life.
Losing was not for him. Even being second was no good. He had to be
first, he had to win whatever fight he got into, whatever race he
entered. He had to succeed whatever the task he set himself.

Joe and Rose had nine children. Joe Jr was the eldest and John F. the second in the family. They were followed by Rosemary, Kathleen, Eunice, Patricia, Jean, Robert F. and, in 1932, Edward. To say this was a close-knit family was to understate the allegiance they showed for each other. This was the family destined to capture the imagination of the American people. A kind of royalty, possessing style, they were set apart: a new and truly American aristocracy. Though Joe and Rose, for the most part, led separate lives, the children were well provided for. Joe was the biggest influence on them, encouraging competition and demanding their best performances. He applied the same rules to them as he applied to himself: whatever they undertook they had to come out best. They had to reach first place; second would not do.

In the United States in which Joe had grown up, the acquisition of wealth brought power. The greater the wealth, the greater the power. So much so that the collaboration of a group of wealthy people could result in causes – good or bad – failing or succeeding, politicians rising as stars or disappearing out of sight, regardless of their talent, and governments being shaken up to order, according to the dispositions of the group. Joseph P. Kennedy was one who did not flinch at using the power his money brought to gain what he wanted for himself. In a country where it might be said that this was par for the course, this did not necessarily make him a bad person. It was expected that the wealthy would take advantage of their wealth and, anyway, whether he was seen as 'good' or 'bad' much depended on whether one agreed with the objectives of such a man. It is a matter for the record, nonetheless, that Joe Kennedy was unscrupulous if need be when it came to fighting a battle, and he seldom lost.

Joe, however, did not seek collaborations with other wealthy men. They could get on and collaborate with one another to exert their influence, but Joe, unaccepted by the mainstream people of wealth, was essentially a loner. This did not stop him from exerting enormous influence all by himself, however, and when the extent of his power is assessed, it serves to indicate what frightening power was wielded by alliances of such men. Joseph P. Kennedy, the outsider, gave no impression of pining for acceptance by his moneyed peers. 'Big businessmen are the most overrated people in the country,' he said. He did not even work in partnerships but frequently worked with others to achieve his own ends, though his reputation among those with whom he did business did not rank high. John F. Kennedy, when campaigning for the Presidency, was introduced in New York to an important man in the liquor industry who had bought the business he owned from Joe Kennedy. 'I was amazed to hear such warm praise from anyone who has done business with my father!' he quipped.

Joe bore all the appearances of being a far-sighted speculator, and so he was. He made a fortune from cornering the market in Scotch whiskies and Gordon's gin, timing his move for the point at which Prohibition was abolished. Many believed this followed a fortune he had already made from bootlegging. He forayed into the motion-picture business and came out with a six-million-dollar profit. When others were driven to ruin in the Wall Street Crash he not only survived, he came out ahead. '. . . He rode the market down and grew rich out of the depression,' said one newspaper. In the thirties, what would be termed today insider dealings on the stock market were identified and declared illegal, but not before Joe had made another fortune from them. This kind of operation earned him the reputation of one who thrived on the misfortunes of others. Joe Kennedy made one fortune after another. There is a story told of how, when *Fortune* magazine ran an article on him in 1957 estimating his wealth somewhere between $200 and $400 million, his wife, Rose, asked, 'Why didn't you tell me you had all that money?' Answered Joe, 'How could I tell you? I didn't know it myself.'

Though the term may not have been fashionable in his day, Joe Kennedy was a womaniser. It seems that Rose Kennedy knew and preferred to ignore it in favour of preserving family unity and holding on to her husband. Joe, for his part, always returned to Rose, even when, in his Hollywood days, the other woman was the celebrated actress Gloria Swanson. Years later, Joe was to say of his infatuation with the actress, 'She wrecked my business, wrecked my health and damn near wrecked my life.'

At the time of the Wall Street Crash, the perceptive Joe saw the real power in the country transferring from the financiers of Wall Street to the politicians of Washington. In the early thirties he attached himself to the campaign being fought for the New Deal and the election of Franklin Delano Roosevelt to the Presidency. FDR's success at the polls did not, however, win for Joe the cabinet post he expected. As Louis McHenry Howe, one of Roosevelt's closest political advisers expressed it, 'FDR ran a campaign to drive the money-changers out of the temple.' To have invited a 'money-changer' into the White House would have been damaging to the New Deal. Instead, he appointed Joe Kennedy chairman of a commission to oversee the implementation of the new Securities Exchange Act, which was designed to eradicate the outlandish wheeling and dealing evident on Wall Street. Joe having been one of the biggest exponents of such activities, the appointment staggered the administration. It was seen as setting the fox to guard the chicken coop. Joe Kennedy was spectacularly successful in carrying out his appointment, however, and critics were confounded. The clean-up on Wall Street proved one of the outstanding achievements of the New Deal, and Joe had arrived in politics.

In support of Roosevelt's bid for a second term, Joe Kennedy wrote – he had it ghosted – a book, *I'm for Roosevelt*, which defended the doctrine of the New Deal, argued for a planned economy and condemned 'irresponsible wealth'. In 1937, when he had completed his work with the Securities Exchange Commission, a grateful FDR called upon him to take on the Maritime Commission. This time Joe tried hard to wriggle out of the appointment, arguing that his term with the Securities Exchange Commission had cost him $100,000, which was an immense sum of money in the mid-thirties. 'If it's all the same to you, let some other patriot take it on the chin for a while. I'm fed up,' he said. The President won the day, however, and Joe found himself faced with the thorny task of revitalising the US Merchant Marine. It might have been a simple case of the right man at the wrong time, but Joe Kennedy soon found himself in great difficulty, at loggerheads with the unions at a time when the labour movement was gaining both strength and popularity. Joe's approach became destructive to the New Deal and he was relieved of his task.

Roosevelt by now knew that Joe's sights were set on the White House. A national poll showed him then running fifth in the league of likely candidates to succeed FDR. Roosevelt, however, had his eyes on an unprecedented third term of office and he was well aware of the threat Joe's tenacity, combined with his power and influence, rated. It is likely that this was in the President's mind when he appointed

Joseph P. Kennedy the United States Ambassador to London, Britain being far enough away from the US political scene. Joe was enormously flattered, since to him this was a crown which would forever establish him among his peers. The appointment both flabbergasted the American Establishment and annoyed the British, however. The somewhat abrasive Joe was no diplomat, as he was to prove. Moreover he saw the appointment as a stepping-stone to the Presidency, which only served to alienate Roosevelt. Joe gave the impression that he was in London to promote his own interests rather than those of the President.

Outspoken in his support of Prime Minister Neville Chamberlain and his policy of appeasement, this was to be Joe's downfall. That Roosevelt also associated himself with the appeasement policy, sending a congratulatory cable to Chamberlain on the signing of the Munich Pact, was soon, diplomatically, forgotten, as was the speech the President would make in Boston promising, 'Your boys are not going to be sent into any foreign wars.' But Joe went much further than Roosevelt, almost to the point of interfering in British affairs. He was suspected of being pro-Hitler, and it would be no great surprise if the claim were true that Churchill, who strongly disliked Joe, had his phone tapped and opened his mail during the war. Diarist Harold Ickes, recording the Ambassador's personal report to Roosevelt in the spring of 1940, indicated how little Joe knew of the British. '. . . Kennedy was saying that Germany would win,' he wrote, 'that everything in France and England would go to hell, and that his one interest was in saving his money for his children.' It seems that money, and the making of it, was by no means forgotten to Joe while he was in Britain. It appears he used the influence of the Embassy to secure scarce and much needed cargo space for shipping 200,000 cases of whisky back home during the darkest days of the war.

The Ambassador was suspicious that Britain would 'engineer' an incident designed to bring America into the conflict. He had no confidence that Britain could win the war, and his views, well known in Berlin, were no doubt of great comfort to the Hitler regime. During the bombing of London he left the Embassy to seek safety, taking up residence outside the capital, which did not endear him to Londoners. This same man would later strongly oppose America's Lease-Lend programme for Britain.

Ambassador Kennedy paid a visit home to the United States in late 1940. It was believed that he made the trip home to counter Franklin D. Roosevelt's intentions to run for a third term in the White House, though a shroud of mystery fell over certain aspects of the visit. Joe, it seems, was dramatically summoned to a talk with FDR and afterwards quickly endorsed the President's third-term bid. It was later speculated that Roosevelt offered a deal in return for Joe's endorsement, in which he would nominate the Ambassador for the Presidency in 1944.* In the event FDR ran for a fourth term.

It was during his October 1940 trip home that Joe gave an interview to a *Boston Globe* journalist in which it was claimed he made indiscreet remarks about Winston Churchill's affection for brandy, King George's speech defect and Queen Elizabeth's dress sense, remarks he said he believed he was making off the record. On or off the record he was also quoted as saying, 'Democracy is finished in England . . . She's fighting for self-preservation.' Joe Kennedy denied his statements but to no avail. He had no alternative but to tender his resignation, and it was promptly accepted. Fifty-two-year-old Joe Kennedy's foray into politics was ended. His political reputation was in tatters. Nonetheless he proceeded to make another fortune – this time in real estate – during the war.

Joe now directed his political aspirations towards his eldest son, Joe Jr. If he could not have the Presidency for himself he would have it for his son, he determined. Joe Jr was the model of his father. When Joe Sr was away from home Joe Jr presided at table and it was demanded of the family that they show him the same respect and obedience as their father. Joe Jr, after his Harvard days, was sent by his father to England to study under Harold Laski at the London School of Economics. Though this was, at first glance, a curious choice for Joe Sr to make, since Laski was renowned the world over as a socialist thinker, it may have represented a certain shrewdness on father Joe's part, for Laski was a friend of Roosevelt and there was liaison between the brilliant Laski and the New Dealers. Laski liked and respected young Joe, and they got on well together.

*According to Stewart Alsop writing in the *Saturday Evening Post*, 13 August 1960

In 1940 Joe Jr, a delegate at the Democratic National Convention, came out in opposition to Franklin D. Roosevelt, which might easily be seen as an expression of his father's attitude towards the President at that time. Joe Jr's philosophy of life and ideologies closely reflected those of his father. At Harvard he joined a 'keep America out of the war' group and went on record as favouring bartering with a Hitler-dominated Europe rather than going to war on Britain's side. Young Joe did go to war, however. He became a pilot and, in 1944, gave up his leave to undertake a special mission. Sending a message to his father assuring him it was not dangerous, he piloted a 'drone' B17 Flying Fortress, packed with explosives from which it was planned he and his co-pilot would parachute to safety while the plane, guided on its last stage by a remote facility, went on to crash into a V-2 rocket-launching site in Normandy. Sadly the plane exploded before the pilots ejected and they were both killed. Father Joe was devastated. He was felled by the news and grieved for many years the loss of his first-born.

So it befell Jack Kennedy to step into his brother Joe's shoes in the political arena. It was expected of him and there was no dispute of this on his part. Whatever his secret dreams for the future might have been the tragic loss of his hero brother changed everything. Jack had not been thought of as a potential politician in the family. His father said of him, 'Jack was rather shy, withdrawn and quiet. His mother and I couldn't think of him as a politician. We were sure he'd be a teacher or a writer.'

Educated at Chaote, an exclusive boarding school, at Princeton for a brief spell and, like his brother Joe, at Harvard, Jack did, in fact, after his discharge from the Navy, spend some time in journalism as a special correspondent for the William Randolph Hearst newspapers. His father's name opened many doors for him and, interestingly enough, he covered the first post-VE election in Britain when the Conservatives – and Winston Churchill – were ignominiously defeated by Labour. But he was not to settle into journalism.

Ever since his youth, Jack suffered much from bad health, and had had considerable experience of handling pain. In addition to childhood illnesses – scarlet fever, chicken pox, appendicitis, jaundice, hepatitis, whooping cough and measles – he had a back condition with which he lived all his life. Referred to as a 'war injury', it certainly may have been worsened during his time in the Navy, when he did his best not to let it impede his active life, but – though the family concealed the exact nature of the problem and its origin – it seems it was something he was born with, and the defect of one of his legs being very slightly shorter than the other exacerbated the problem.

In view of his health record it is surprising that Jack Kennedy was ever accepted for service in the Navy. It was also a great credit to him that he rejected the desk job to which he was assigned in favour of active service. Jack's wartime exploits have been well chronicled. The PT-109 affair, over which he was heralded as a hero, was possibly a mixture of heroism, misfortune and, perhaps, incompetence. Whatever the facts of the matter, Jack came in for a drubbing from the disbelievers for ever letting the small, easily navigable boat in his command get into the path of a Japanese destroyer. In the incident two men lost their lives but there would have been a greater death toll had it not been for Jack Kennedy's heroic actions. In the murky waters he relentlessly drove his crew on in their search for a shore. The shore they found was in Japanese hands and it was due entirely to Jack's tireless efforts that he and his men avoided capture. He it was, too, who organised their escape and safe return to base.

When his second son came to making his bid for election to Congress in 1946, Joe Kennedy poured money into the campaign as if it was water. The family were in evidence everywhere working for Jack, who had also enlisted the help of old school and Navy pals as campaign organisers. The astute Joe did not rely entirely upon them, however, making sure their ranks were well augmented by hardened pros. And although Francis – later Judge – Morrissey was listed officially as Campaign Manager, it was well known that he fronted for father Joe. Joe had a finger on everything.

At first Jack Kennedy's candidature was not taken seriously by the others standing in the election. They soon changed their minds, however, accusing Joe of attempting to buy the election for his son. What an incredible campaign it was. The social highlight was a reception at the Hotel Commander in Cambridge at which Jack, his brothers and sisters and his father stood in the long reception line. The event was notable for being the only time Joe Kennedy appeared publicly at any of JFK's campaigns. Although this consolidated his appeal to the well-to-do—those on the social register—Jack by no means neglected the huge Irish-American population and the Italian-American voters. It was a funny thing that when the name Joseph Russo appeared on the list of candidates, a name calculated to attract the Italian voters, it was quickly followed by a registration from another Joseph Russo. The story circulated that Joe Kennedy was determined to reduce the impact of the original candidate and split his vote by having the second Russo stand. Every trick in the book was used. JFK's picture appeared on billboards, posters, stickers and in the newspapers. There was a trolley-car campaign and he was promoted on radio. Everywhere. And added to the promotion which was bought came the highly desired news stories. Needless to say, Joe Kennedy was also directing the publicity campaign. Extraordinary sums of money were involved in implanting the name and the face of Jack Kennedy in the minds of the electors. JFK biographer, J. M. Burns, reported a story in which '. . . the old man claimed that with the money he was spending he could elect his chauffeur to Congress.' This was no slur on his son. Joe simply did not spend money like that without being acutely aware of it. He was leaving nothing to chance. He was prepared to pay for both belt and braces. But in the minds of some he need not have bothered. Joe Kane, Joe Kennedy's cousin who was drafted in to tutor young Jack in political matters, was quoted as saying, 'Jack could have gone to Congress like everyone else for ten cents.'

Election to Congress would be a formality depending on the outcome of the vote on Primary day. John F. Kennedy polled a massive 22,183 votes, almost double the number cast for his chief rival, whose name, incidentally, was not Russo.

John F. Kennedy's time in Congress was relatively uneventful, and he could hardly be classed among the most skilled and distinguished of politicians when he decided to run for the Senate. He had been faithful to his electorate, however, and had acquitted himself tolerably well in a job he had, at the outset, not really wanted. But above all he had been learning during this period, and he was about to take the bit between his teeth. In his battle for the Senate, Jack Kennedy was to have a formidable opponent, the experienced, well-respected Bostonian, Henry Cabot Lodge Jr.

As the battle wagons rolled out, Joe Kennedy again assumed command, but this time much more the shadowy figure behind the scenes. Victor Lasky, in his book, *JFK: The Man and the Myth*, quoted one campaign worker as saying:

> There would often be conferences in the morning in the father's apartment. The father was always very much in the background, away from public view. I don't know how much direct influence he had on Jack . . . I remember [him] bawling Jack out for hurting himself. You don't argue with Joe Kennedy.*

This time it was to be 27-year-old Bobby Kennedy who held the title Campaign Manager but, as Lasky put it, '. . . the elder Kennedy, ensconced in a suite at the Ritz-Carlton, called the signals, hired the experts and paid the bills.' From time to time who *really* was in command showed between the cracks to those around. When staff running the campaign could not be pinned down for a decision, workers turned to Joe—and got decisions.

At one point in the campaign an extraordinary, fleeting insight was obtained into how JFK saw his father in relation to his hard, sometimes bitter, campaigning. Help had been enlisted from Gardner 'Pat' Jackson, known as a New Dealer, but he and Joe Kennedy clashed head on and a fearful row ensued. 'I hear my father gave you a bad time,' said JFK. 'How do you explain your father, Jack?' asked Jackson. JFK pondered awhile and then said, 'I guess there isn't a motive in it which I think you'd respect, except love of family . . .' He pondered a little more and produced the tailpiece, '. . . although sometimes I think it's pride.'

The whole Kennedy parade was put into top gear. The family trooped out again and assumed battle stations, sisters Eunice, Patricia and Jean joining the men in campaigning. Even mother Rose was prevailed upon to play a significant part in the proceedings. The Kennedy tea-parties were top-ranking social events, and the ladies

*Victor Lasky, *JFK: The Man and the Myth*, Macmillan, New York, 1963

turned out in droves to pass down the reception lines. 'Whoever heard of reception lines in politics, as though to meet the King and Queen?' asked one reporter. But they were enormously successful. 'Every woman,' someone said, 'either wants to mother him or to marry him.' There was no denying Jack's 'little boy lost' appearance – he was a bit on the skinny side and looked as though he would have profited from a good haircut – had a magnetic effect on the ladies. 'What is there about Jack Kennedy,' commented one notable Republican, 'that makes every Catholic girl in Boston think it's a holy crusade to get him elected?' The tea-parties were very successful.

This is not to say that other aspects of the campaign were not equally effective, and, as a change from tea, the programme, 'Coffee with the Kennedys' headed up the television drive. There was no doubt that the huge sums of money being spent in every direction on the campaign had the desired effect, and the Kennedy family, acting as a team, presented an act which was extremely hard to follow. Henry Cabot Lodge Jr, a man much respected and with everything going for him by normal standards, was defeated by a mere 70,000 votes. But the Kennedy machine had triumphed.

During the period of the election campaign, Jack Kennedy had been keeping company with the beautiful and accomplished Jacqueline Bouvier on the odd occasions when he could get away. Although they had met before, the relationship did not develop until after they were dinner guests at the Georgetown home of Charles Bartlett, a *Chattanooga Times* journalist. Their engagement was announced in June 1953, inappropriately coinciding with the *Saturday Evening Post* article 'The Senate's Gay Young Bachelor'. They were married in Newport on 12 September 1953 by Archbishop (later Cardinal) Cushing. Nine hundred guests were invited, and religious differences were put aside for the occasion.

The marriage must have been a successful one if the stresses to which it was subjected were any guide. Jack was completely immersed in politics, his whole being consumed by his total commitment to his work, while Jackie made no secret to her friends of how much it all bored her. Her husband spent a great deal of time away from home, which was another consequence of the demands his work made on their marriage. 'Politics was sort of my enemy . . . It was like being married to a whirlwind,' she once said. When they were together there were stresses of other kinds. Their tastes in food, music and other cultural pursuits differed considerably. And early in their marriage Jackie became greatly aware of the severity of Jack's health problems.

Jack Kennedy suffered incredible pain from his back condition. A plate had been inserted into his spine after the war and the wound had never successfully healed. In desperation, he agreed to two operations, only one of which was ever admitted to by the family. The operations left him slim hope of survival. Twice the family were summoned when he was believed to be close to death. The greatest complications arose from the fact that Jack Kennedy also suffered from Addison's Disease, though this was not advertised. Happily the young man's patience and forbearance, the skill of his team of doctors and the prayers of his family brought the outcome they sought. The metal plate was finally removed and Jack recovered.

In the months following the surgery, Jack suffered from deep depression. Writing of the time in the *American Weekly* sometime later, he told how a letter from a 90-year-old fellow sufferer, who had little hope of ever being able to leave her bed, helped him to sort out his problems. Full of hope and good humour, in spite of her afflictions, she wrote, 'Don't waste away feeling sorry for yourself, young man. Keep busy. Do all the things you never had time to do . . .' The young Senator responded by writing his Pulitzer prize-winning book, *Profiles in Courage*.

After an eight-month absence from his work, JFK returned to a hero's welcome. Almost immediately after his return, he was being spoken of as a possible candidate for the Vice-Presidency, as running mate to Adlai Stevenson, the 'Man from Libertyville', as he was known, in the up-coming 1956 Presidential election. Kennedy was greatly excited at the prospect of running for the office, which may have accounted for him once turning up at a New York photographer's studio with socks which did not match. Father Joe did not share his son's enthusiasm, since he could not see Stevenson beating Eisenhower and didn't want Jack to be associated with a failure. Quite untypically, Joe took Rose and gracefully repaired to the French Riviera while Jack got on with it, which might reasonably inspire questions of a 'did-he-fall-or-was-he-pushed' nature. Stevenson, not renowned for his decisiveness, kept Kennedy waiting and waiting, unreasonably, until the last minute, when he announced that he would allow his running mate to be chosen by the delegates. This was carrying indecisiveness to the extreme and Jack Kennedy was furious. He failed to obtain the nomination by a cat's whisker and, in a brief speech, smiling in defeat, he asked for the nomination of his rival, Senator Estes Kefauver, to be made unanimous by the delegates. The delegates roared their appreciation and John F. Kennedy left the Convention with a greatly enhanced reputation.

As it happened, father Joe was right: Stevenson lost the election to General Dwight Eisenhower, and his son had had a lucky escape. Had he been at the side of the failed Stevenson it would have been extremely unlikely that he would have received the party's nomination for the 1960 Presidential election. The 1956 Democratic Convention had been to the Senator for Massachusetts a pivot upon which his future—and indeed the history of the world—would turn. John F. Kennedy was on the threshold of national politics. It was but one giant step to the race for the Presidency.

CHAPTER TWO

A Man for his Time

'Methought I heard a voice cry, "Sleep no more!" '
Shakespeare, *Macbeth*

SENATOR JOHN F. KENNEDY'S campaign for the Presidency was carefully planned and meticulously executed. Even his greatest political enemies conceded this. For JFK the campaign began soon after his 'lucky escape' from running as Vice-Presidential candidate on the losing Adlai Stevenson ticket in 1956. Though he lost the nomination for running for the Vice-Presidency, he emerged in the 1956 Democratic Convention as a nationally known figure and he determined to build his campaign for the Presidency on that.

By 1957 the fact that he had Presidential ambitions was no secret in Washington. 'When you see a Senator doing much speaking outside his own state it means one of two things,' the *Saturday Evening Post* recorded a fellow Senator saying. 'He needs the money or he's got his eye on higher office.' No one could think of JFK needing money. Looking back at the trend during his early campaigning, two things concerning his father could be easily detected. The first was that Joe, as would be expected, was behind his son all the way, for as much effort as it took and as much money as it cost. But the other was that the Ambassador, as he had become known, had the enormous good sense to realise that his own political record – especially as it related to wartime Europe – was a liability to his son's ambitions, and he became more and more adept at standing back in the shadows. There is no doubt that had father Joe insisted on standing at his son's side during the electioneering, JFK's chances would have evaporated. After all, his eventual majority was less than 120,000 votes from the massive 69 million votes cast throughout the United States.

It is interesting, therefore, to reflect that Jack Kennedy was unlikely to make any move of importance during the campaign without, at some point, stepping back into the shadows to consult with his father. Had his close supporters known – those who had abiding faith in their candidate – he would have been perceived as receiving true and wise counselling. Most others, however, would have suspected some kind of diabolical plotting. His enemies would have been sure of it, and Jack had plenty of enemies. But by the time electioneering started, Joe had mastered the art of appearing to disappear. During the campaign, when Jack received news that Martin Luther King's father had announced his support for him, adding that he had originally planned to vote against him because of his religion, his first reaction was, 'That was a hell of an intolerant statement, wasn't it? Imagine Martin Luther King with a father like that.' There was a pause and a grin followed by, 'Well, we all have our fathers, don't we?' John F. Kennedy had his work cut out to persuade people in certain quarters that he did not play Trilby to his father's Svengali.

Behind the scenes, Joe Kennedy was mindful of the need for top-of-the-line publicity for his son. It was his ambition that by the time of the Democratic Convention of 1960, Jack would be known to everyone. He said, '. . . there won't be a place in America where he isn't familiar.' Jack, he would later assert, 'is the greatest attraction in the country today . . . Why is it that when his picture is on the cover of *Life* or *Redbook* that they will sell a record number of copies?' Similarly he scored heavily on television, being much in demand on panel shows, and it was a daily event to find his name in the newspapers. The ladies continued to find him irresistible. 'The effect he has on women voters is almost naughty,' said the *New York Times's* James Reston. Said Joe Kennedy, 'You advertise the fact that Jack will be at a dinner and you will break all records for attendance. He can draw more people to a fund-raising dinner than Cary Grant or Jimmy

Stewart.' Joe knew what he was talking about. When Jack agreed to address the Social Science Foundation of the University of Denver they had to replan the venue for the meeting. Before the event they had to think again and move it to an even bigger hall—at the City Auditorium—to accommodate the 8,000 who attended. 'The party leaders around the country realise that to win they have to nominate him,' said Joe, and at the Convention the nomination for JFK to run as the Democratic Candidate for the Presidency was won on the first ballot. He had a runaway success. His long-drawn-out campaign, which started soon after the 1956 Convention—much too early, some had thought—had paid off handsomely. 'To run early and hard is the only way I know,' said JFK. Now all he had to do was persuade the people of America to vote for him in a 'young man's clash' with Republican Richard Nixon. Veteran Adlai Stevenson summed up the problems in his candidature saying that he had three strikes against him before he started. He was, '. . . young, rich and Roman Catholic'.

The Kennedy family were marshalled once again for the forthcoming electoral battle and a brilliant team of vigorous young pros was assembled to take the bandwagon into every part of the United States. And some bandwagon it was. The success with which the campaign met might even have been thought to have tumbled to JFK's feet, but it was not so. Every inch of the progress he made had to be fought for. The long hours, the late nights and early mornings, the constant movement and hustle; it was wearing, even to the youthful members of the team. Even Jackie, heavily pregnant with John Jr, played her part in a telephone campaign. Not a trick was missed and there was little doubt that any trick in danger of being missed was spotted by the vigilant Joe, whether he be close at hand or far from the scene of action.

Though all the expected ballyhoo was present, the Kennedy campaign machine generated a kind of electioneering which was different from the usual as it inexorably ground on towards voting day. But the slogans were much as expected, save for the odd eyecatcher like the ever-so-slightly naughty, 'Let's put a New John in the White House'. As for JFK himself, his right hand was blistered and swollen from countless handshakes. Though there were detractors, the reactions of people in the main reflected the findings of the pollsters* at his 1958 Senate re-election campaign. They thought of him as honest, full of personality, looking good and speaking well. He came across as courageous, a hard worker, of good family, knowledgeable and intelligent. As Sorensen puts it:

> His magnetic appeal to youth–the phenomenon of female 'jumpers', 'leapers', 'touchers' and 'screamers' in the crowds along his route–the recurrent risks they took darting between his moving motorcycle escorts to grasp his hand (including one woman who nearly dislocated his shoulder holding on as though frozen)–the sound of thousands upon thousands of milling, yelling fans–the sea of outstretched hands along airport fences and barricades–all this surprised and amused him without instilling a speck of overconfidence or conceit.[†]

But he was not to be taken in by such performances. Sorensen pointed out that, 'Much of the yelling and jumping . . . came from (those too young to vote).' And not all of those who leaped at him in his motorcades were friendly. A woman, feeling the effects of too much drink, ran to the car and threw a glass of whisky in his face. Wiping off the whisky, he politely handed back the tumbler saying, 'Here's your glass.' When the counting was over his margin was incredibly small. In terms of a Presidential election it was a cat's whisker. But he made it. Against all the odds, the taunts of being too young, too rich and an unacceptable Roman Catholic, he made it.

For JFK the Presidency was not a bed of roses. His abbreviated term– less than three years–might suggest a short and, therefore, superficial encounter with the Office to those unacquainted with history. In terms of events both at home and abroad, the volume of Presidential business in which he became involved and the way he gave himself totally and utterly to the demands of government, it was better thought of as a long, long Presidency and an in-depth encounter with the needs of the nation, for so much was packed into the 34 months in which he served as Head of State. It was a tenacious, youthful administration, as tough as nails when it was demanded, otherwise

*The pollsters' calculations of Kennedy's public appeal, 1958
†Theodore C. Sorensen, *Kennedy*, Hodder and Stoughton, London, 1965

stylish, gentle where individuals were concerned, efficient, and strong in facing up to unpopular issues. This, however, is not to say it did not make mistakes.

The Bay of Pigs invasion in April 1961 undoubtedly involved JFK in the biggest blunders he would ever make. It presented him with no-win alternatives: it was an embarrassment, a quagmire from which there was no escape. And, of course, we can all see now that the President should have completely scrapped the plan. It is entirely possible that the Bay of Pigs affair exposed the only glimpse there existed of a President suffering from youth and inexperience. But that should not be taken for granted. After all, the plan had been hatched during his predecessor's Presidency and it was reasonable to assume that Eisenhower would have considered the detail of such proposals with great care. Unhappily, it was later to be shown that there appeared to be discrepancies between what Eisenhower had agreed and the decisions which were taken by the CIA.

Kennedy had hardly moved into the White House before the plan for Cuban exiles to invade Cuba was placed before him. Though he had a great deal of confidence in plans formulated in his predecessor's time in office, this did not, in any sense, absolve him from making the decisions which were now his to make. Eisenhower, no doubt mindful of the dangers of having militant communists only 70 miles from the US coast since Castro had seized control in Cuba, was well aware that the revolutionary had significant opposition both inside his country and outside, in the form of exiles, many thousands of whom had sought refuge in the United States. The exiles lived for the day when their country would be rid of Castro and communism, and they were spoiling to return to their homeland in strength to achieve their ambition. Eisenhower agreed to a plan under which a band of guerillas would be recruited, trained and armed to return to Cuba as an 'army of liberation'. It seems that the CIA, whose agents were to be responsible for the recruitment, training and arming of such a band in camps set up in Guatemala, had other ideas about what the plan should be, however. Apparently unknown to Eisenhower, they enlisted a greater number of men than had been envisaged and trained them as a conventional army.

The scheme had been in progress for about a year before it was inherited by President Kennedy, and by then it was in the final stages of completion. Kennedy was told that the success of the plan depended on Castro's military weakness and that to delay would allow the Cuban revolutionary army time to be equipped by Russia. Crated MIG fighters, for instance, were expected to be delivered, shortly to be followed by pilots who were under training in the Soviet Union. Allen Dulles, Head of the CIA, pressed the issue by publicly speaking of a 'group of fine young men who asked nothing other than the opportunity to try to restore a free government to their country . . . [They were] ready to risk their lives . . .' Were they to receive '. . . no sympathy, no support, no aid from the United States'? Besides other considerations, the existence of the camps in Guatemala was well known and they had already become an embarrassment. The CIA told Kennedy that it was now or never.

Of course Kennedy could have killed off the plan, though he was not much enamoured with the idea of having 1,400 Cuban exiles spreading the word that he had gone 'soft' on Cuba. And he could not see why he should take exception to the idea of Cubans fighting against Cubans. Assured that the plan, which had been approved by the Joint Chiefs of Staff, had high prospects of success, he permitted it to go ahead with the crucial proviso that there should be no overt US military participation. The President was assured that such involvement would be unnecessary anyway: the Cuban exiles were self-sufficient. At a press conference prior to the operation he said:

> . . . there will not be, under any conditions, any intervention in Cuba by United States armed forces, and this government will do everything it possibly can—and I think it can meet its responsibilities—to make sure that there are no Americans involved in any actions inside Cuba . . . the basic issue in Cuba is not one between the United States and Cuba; it is between the Cubans themselves. And I intend to see that we adhere to that principle . . . this administration's attitude is so understood and shared by the anti-Castro exiles from Cuba in this country.

Whether it ever *was* understood by the exiles under arms is another matter. At best due to poor liaison between the CIA and the exiles, it is doubtful whether they realised they were on their own. The operation continued to be planned assuming the availability of US military support, or at least on the basis that the President could be pressured into changing his mind if the need should arise for military assistance.

The landings took place on Monday, 17 April 1961. Unbelievably, air attacks intended to destroy Castro's planes had been carried out two days beforehand – the 'first air strike' – which were singularly unsuccessful, and Castro was thus alerted to the danger ahead. The plan appeared to smack of recklessness since it was unlikely that he was unaware of the purpose of the camps in Guatemala. In accordance with a cover story put out, the CIA expected the world to believe that the first air strike was the work of Castro's own pilots who were revolting against him and defecting. Since this story was quickly disposed of, the world was shocked at America's deception over the matter, and Kennedy ordered a second air strike, planned for invasion day – the Monday morning – to be cancelled.

Whatever had gone wrong with intelligence coming out of Cuba, the CIA had a seriously flawed picture of Castro's military strength and capacity for counter-attack. They would have done well to have consulted British Intelligence on the subject for they, at that time, were in possession of more accurate data. Castro, even without the expected MIGs, had jet fighters at the ready, and quickly fielded an army estimated at close to 20,000 troops to repel the 1,400 insurgents. The CIA had also seriously misjudged the willingness of the Cuban people to rebel and take up arms in support of the exile force. They simply did not rally in the way expected. The exiles, fighting on the beaches of the Bay of Pigs, the chosen landing point, soon ran short of ammunition and they found themselves in a desperate plight since two of the four supply ships carrying replenishments were sunk and the other two were driven away. The exiles' 'air force' consisted of 16 elderly B-26 aircraft, which were no match for Castro's jets. The B-26s also had the critical disadvantage of having to fly so far to their engagement that fuel supplies permitted them only one hour's combat when they arrived. It was an unmitigated disaster.

Much has been made of claims that John F. Kennedy was beseeched to provide air cover which could have rescued the invading forces and that he refused, callously abandoning those fighting on the shores of the Bay of Pigs – including numerous CIA agents – to their fate. The 'facts' presented seem to vary according to the viewpoint of the presenter. The CIA and the exiles claimed the President had promised such aid and that he reneged on his word. In an account given by Kennedy biographer Theodore C. Sorensen, one of the President's closest aides, he recalls that one of the supply ships which had been driven off returned with supplies but by then the night was well through and the cover of darkness was rapidly being lost:

> . . . The Cuban crew threatened to mutiny unless provided with a US Navy destroyer escort and jet cover. With the hard-pressed exiles on the beaches pleading for supplies, the convoy commander requested the CIA in Washington to seek the Navy's help; but CIA headquarters, unable to keep fully abreast of the situation on the beach and apparently unaware of the desperate need for ammunition in particular, instead called off the convoy without consulting the President.*

That, it was claimed, was the only request for air cover formally made from the area and it never reached the President.

This did not mean that the CIA and the Joint Chiefs did not pressure Kennedy to change his mind and throw US military might behind the exiles. On the same night as the beleaguered crew of the supply ship demanded air cover, a meeting took place between Kennedy, CIA chiefs and the Joint Chiefs in the Cabinet Room. The President's argument was that if he decided that it was right for the US to engage in an all-out war with Cuba he would not enter it 'by default' as an ad hoc appendage to an attack made by a small exile force. Under the pressure to which he was subjected, however (Sorensen recounts), Kennedy did go as far as agreeing to allow unmarked Navy jets to protect the old B-26s as they made their run to provide air cover to the exiles next morning. Whether because of a time-zone error or some other misunderstanding, the Navy planes took off one hour after the B-26s and the need for protection soon disappeared as they were either shot down or returned to base. As far as Kennedy's refusal to throw US forces into the fray was concerned, he had made it abundantly clear at the outset that he would not agree to such action. Such a decision would clearly have been foolish, carrying risks of escalation into a world war.

Though the invasion may have been gallantly executed, the planning for it—based on poor intelligence—was flawed. Blood ran

*Theodore C. Sorensen, *Kennedy*, Hodder and Stoughton, London, 1965

freely in the Bay of Pigs, both that of the exiles and of the CIA 'monitors'. It seems that neither the exiles who survived, nor the CIA agents who lost friends and colleagues, nor for that matter the Chiefs of Staff were ever likely to forget the event or forgive the President whom they blamed for the fiasco. For his part, whatever it was—or wasn't—the President generously accepted responsibility for the failed plan.

From the time of his inauguration, President Kennedy had had to learn to spar with the Soviets. Another legacy inherited from the Eisenhower period provided ongoing, worrying problems over which to spar. This was to develop into the Berlin crisis, which strained the Western Alliance—probably Khrushchev's principal aim—and which culminated in the raising of the Berlin Wall on 13 August 1961. Kennedy spoke of the drawn-out negotiations as a 'test of nerve and will'. In this matter he was short of neither. His resounding rallying speech at the Berlin Wall has been quoted and requoted and now survives the existence of the Wall itself.

At home Kennedy was preoccupied with the needs of ordinary people whose livelihoods were under threat. In the 15 years 1947–1962, the number of workers had increased by almost 12 million, whereas the number of jobs for them had increased by only ten million. Recession and high unemployment were on the cards and the solution lay, not in papering over the cracks, but in long-term planning, re-education and new investment. In the case of the latter, dramatic injections of new capital were achieved by means of significant tax benefits to those who expanded, buying new plant and equipment, and to those who replaced old and worn plant with new. The two-and-a-half-billion-dollar drop in business revenue in 1962 was responsible for half of the $40 billion investment in new plant and machinery in 1963. But there were other worrying factors which would accelerate the problem. The developing effects of automation and computerisation had not escaped the President's notice, and, as in a number of other nations which had been involved in the Second World War, the post-war baby boom was working through to the point where 23 million new job-seekers would flood the labour market. Changes in taxation alone could not solve all America's unemployment problems, and Kennedy launched a whole series of programmes designed to contribute to a solution. To trade expansion he added vocational training, youth employment and literacy training projects as well as the first ever programme for Manpower Development and assistance. Specific hardship was combated in programmes for depressed areas and the hard-hit farming industry was assisted in the Rural Area Development programmes. One Area Redevelopment Act, passed in 1961, was aimed at moving industry into the worst-hit areas, while worker relocation, often unpopular and impractical, was encouraged within limits. A new Public Works programme in 1962 provided more sorely needed jobs. Late in Kennedy's term in office, extreme hardship noted in some areas resulted in an anti-poverty bill which was finally approved in 1964 under Johnson's leadership.

Unemployment and poverty had a meaning at an altogether different level for America's Negro population. Their problems were rooted in segregationalism and racial discrimination, no form of which, to Kennedy, was morally defensible or socially tolerable. The President, both realistic and compassionate, recognised that the time had come for action on these matters. In speeches he showed his awareness of their problems:

> The Negro baby born in America today, regardless of the section of the nation in which he is born, has about one-half as much chance of completing high school as a white baby born in the same place on the same day, one-third as much chance of completing college, one-third as much chance of becoming a professional man, twice as much chance of becoming unemployed, about one-seventh as much chance of earning $10,000 a year, a life expectancy which is seven years shorter, and the prospects of earning only half as much.

Kennedy approached the problem of racism broadly in two ways. One was through legislation and executive action. The other was through his personal powers of persuasion. The first piece of legislation dealt with a ban on poll taxes in Federal elections. This effectively extended the franchise to huge numbers of Negroes and also to poorer white people. There was then a long period of waiting until the resistance to change in both the House and the Senate gave way to further legislative progress. This came in the form of a Civil Rights Bill which sought to end discrimination in hotels, restaurants, stores and other places of public accommodation, and provided authority to the Attorney General to seek desegregation of public education where students' and parents' efforts were frustrated. Said JFK:

> I . . . ask every member of Congress to set aside sectional and political ties, and to look at this issue from the viewpoint of the nation. I ask you to look into your hearts – not in search of charity, for the Negro neither wants nor needs condescension – but for the one plain, proud and priceless quality that unites us all as Americans: a sense of justice.

While the time may have arrived for such a bill to pass through Congress, it should not be supposed that all Americans were yet ready to stand behind it. 'I am not sure that I am the most popular political figure . . . today in the South,' said the President, 'but that is all right.' With some his stance on the issue had taken him much further than lost popularity. It was attracting hatred. In private he confided to a Negro leader, '. . . this issue could cost me [the next] election, but,' he added, 'we're not turning back.' He knew that, merely by becoming law, a bill did not change deep-seated attitudes, and to get this one off the ground it would have to be acted upon. But he had foreseen this. The legislation, he said:

> . . . will not solve all our problems of race relations. The bill must be supplemented by action in every branch of government at the Federal, state and local level. It must be supplemented as well by enlightened private citizens, private businesses and private labor and civic organisations.

President Kennedy's time in office was punctuated throughout by efforts to restore the dignity of Negro people. He sought to support their rights by invoking the laws of the land and relying on the Attorney General, his brother Robert, to see they were pressed home. He listened to the Negroes' leaders; he honoured them with his presence in just the same way as any other branch of society; he appointed five Federal judges from their number; and he sought gains for them through an Executive Order which combined established Committees on Government Contracts and Employment into a single President's Committee on Equal Employment Opportunity, with sanctions covering 20 million employees. Changes began to be made in industries where previously Negroes had been employed only to sweep floors and carry out other menial tasks. Jobs became available where the rule had been they need not apply. Under Kennedy, administration officials refused to speak before segregated audiences and US Employment Offices were instructed to refuse to handle 'whites-only' job vacancies. Employee unions and recreation clubs were told that if they practised discrimination they would be 'de-recognised'. Kennedy, aware of the Negroes' housing and poverty problems, was known to intervene personally on behalf of individuals. And when racial issues bludgeoned their way into the headlines, the President gave them his personal attention. Such was the case with events at Mississippi and at Alabama.

In Mississippi, James Meredith had applied to enrol in the state university at Oxford. It was an application which had to be fought inch by inch through the courts until it eventually reached the US Supreme Court. The Supreme Court ordered that Meredith promptly be admitted and that those who sought to reject him should cease their resistance. When this was not complied with, an appeal court found both the Governor of the state and the Lieutenant Governor guilty of contempt. A first-class crisis then existed, the likes of which had not been seen since the Civil War, for the judges called upon the Federal government to enforce the order of the Supreme Court. Thus it was required of President Kennedy and Attorney General Robert Kennedy that they meet the demand made upon the government, though it should be noted that it was the government with which the state officials had seen fit to enter into conflict. It was Robert Kennedy, as Attorney General, whose job it was to enforce the law, but the President, also, followed the progress of the confrontation from start to finish. The flat refusal to accept the authority of the courts started with defiance and finished with bloodshed and virtual war. Two were killed and large numbers of marshals were injured by gunfire, with many more injured in other ways. The President spoke on national television, appealing to those involved to comply with the law and restore order, and explaining his position:

> Our nation is founded on the principle that observance of the law is the eternal safeguard of liberty . . . Even among law-abiding men, few laws are universally loved, but they are uniformly respected and not resisted.

Americans are free to disagree with the law, but not to disobey it . . . My obligation . . . is to implement the orders of the court with whatever means are necessary, and with as little force and civil disorder as the circumstances permit.

In his discourse, he recounted the events which had brought about the conflict and paid tribute to Mississippi's proud record of patriotic courage. He then concluded:

You have a great tradition to uphold, a tradition of honor and courage . . . Let us preserve both the law and the peace, and then, healing those wounds that are within, we can turn to the greater crises that are without, and stand united as one people in our pledge to man's freedom.

The President's plea went largely unheeded. Of the thousands who had assembled to oppose the law, few were actually involved with the university and many were racists who had rallied from various parts of Mississippi and other Southern states for what they saw as a showdown. Their guns and firebombs were supplemented by rocks and bricks, clubs, piping, bottles and anything else they could lay hands on. Vehicles were destroyed and buildings burned, and a fire engine and bulldozer were stolen to use in battering entry to an administration building. The Kennedys followed a soft line after a discussion on the telephone with the Governor in which he mooted the means of complying with the court order. This, however, allowed the mob to force the pace. As the violence increased the President responded with strength and blamed himself for not having used greater force earlier, for when he reviewed the circumstances, he felt that by so doing he could have saved at least one of the two lives lost. Nonetheless, his approach was commendable. The court order was not carried out before some 20,000 troops arrived to bolster the local National Guard, marshals and other law-enforcement officers.

Alabama provided the next great test for President Kennedy. Birmingham, Alabama, was said by Martin Luther King to be '. . . the most thoroughly segregated big city in the United States', and it had become a target for non-violent resistance by civil rights groups. All through Kennedy's Presidency there was growing impatience on the part of the Negroes and demonstrations took place all over the United States. But Birmingham, Alabama, might be said to have been the centre of the increasing unrest. Early in April 1963, a campaign organised by Martin Luther King was set into motion. The demonstrations, which included parades, sit-ins, boycotts and the presentation of petitions, were met with violence from the police, who used clubs and fire-hoses against the demonstrators. They also set dogs upon them. Mass arrests followed and more than 3,000 Negro men, women and children, including Martin Luther King himself, were jailed. King's wife, fearful for his life, telephoned a sympathetic John F. Kennedy, who monitored events carefully. There were limits to what the President could do since no Federal law was being broken at this time. (The Civil Rights Bill dealing with segregation, for instance, had not yet become law.) The ferocity of police action in Birmingham shocked America—indeed the world—and this made the issues involved national rather than local. Kennedy played a cool hand and his actions were conciliatory which, unfortunately, pleased neither side. It was not until May that persuasion appeared to prevail, the city's more responsible leaders seeing reason. The Negroes then suspended their operation, and it appeared that moderation was, at last, about to break out in Birmingham. Three days later, however, a Negro home and hotel were aggressively bombed and the streets were filled with rioters. The President promptly despatched 3,000 troops to bases near Birmingham, and consequently the rioting subsided and the tensions eased. Alabama's Governor George Wallace challenged the legal basis for the deployment of troops but the President flatly asserted his authority and stood his ground. An uneasy peace followed. The battle was won but the war was by no means over.

Alabama was the last remaining state in the United States which did not have a desegregated state university, and both John and Robert Kennedy, from the time of the Mississippi confrontation, were waiting, watching and preparing for the showdown which approached like a ticking time-bomb. In a classic instance of being forewarned and, therefore, forearmed, augmenting his soft approach with steel, the President manoeuvred the situation to a successful conclusion. In Alabama, his state of preparedness proving the vital factor, the court order was satisfied and the university—which had been willing all along—received its first Negro students.

Arguing the need for their defence, the Soviets had been arming Cuba for some time. US intelligence watched carefully as Castro's forces acquired greater and greater strength, and there were many in the US, some in positions of power and influence and some in positions of authority, who were nervous and apprehensive about the build-up of arms in the US's backyard. Continued surveillance produced reports that armaments which were classified offensive rather than defensive were present in Cuba, and the President was informed. President Kennedy opted for classifying such reports as 'hearsay', and placed his reliance on CIA and other intelligence sources. Besides, U2 spy planes were carrying out regular fortnightly flights over Cuba and there seemed no cause for alarm.

But information continued to be received from a variety of sources that missiles incompatible with defence purposes were in Cuba, the trouble being that the sources—mainly civilians who could not tell one kind of missile from another, and sometimes Cuban patriots known to be anxious to find reasons for America to invade their homeland—were unreliable. Such stories had even been coming in since before the time when defensive weapons started to be supplied to Cuba. It was not, therefore, until August 1962 that White House officials began to take a close interest in what was happening on the island.

By late August, U2 surveillance planes were bringing back photographs which confirmed that Soviet medium-range and intermediate-range ballistic missiles were being installed in Cuba, and further intelligence revealed that many more were to be delivered. There was no doubt that they were to be equipped with nuclear warheads which would be some 20 times more powerful than the Hiroshima bomb. The White House experts, who had accepted that they could not object to defensive weaponry being supplied to Castro's Cuba, reasonably paled at the notion that their communist neighbour was in the process of becoming a vast nuclear arsenal capable of devastating large parts of the United States and Latin America, too. Furthermore, the Soviets, who were supplying the missile installations, were clearly carrying out the whole operation by stealth and deception.

This created the greatest crisis ever known in the history of the United States, and brought the entire world to the brink of nuclear war. The hour-by-hour build-up to the crisis which, in all, covered 13 days in October of 1962 has been described in detail by historians both opposing and favouring the President's handling of it. The 'quarantine' imposed on the Soviet shipping carrying the deadly cargoes, combined with the threat of air strikes, the invasion of Cuba and escalation to a possible nuclear war resulted in what became known as the 'eyeball-to-eyeball' confrontation between Kennedy and Khrushchev, and the world held its breath while it was in progress.

The crisis had the effect of uniting the country behind the President. Kennedy's political enemies abandoned their rancorous criticism, and factions disappeared in favour of a closing of ranks to facilitate all energies to be directed towards bringing the emergency to a successful conclusion. Abroad, the Allies were, at first, simply horrified and quite critical of the position adopted by the President. Documents released in Britain in 1993 showed that even Kennedy's good friend Harold Macmillan felt that the President was '. . . risking too much for too little', and suggested a solution be sought in a 'trade off' of nuclear missiles. Europeans had, of course, long since accepted that they had no alternative than to live cheek by jowl with enemy missiles and felt that nuclear warheads in Cuba rated no greater threat than the dangers to which they were already daily subjected.

But, in fact, the move towards introducing a nuclear arsenal to Cuba represented a perilous shift in the balance of power which– particularly if such advantages were allowed to be obtained by stealth and deception – could tip the scales in favour of setting Communism on the road to world domination. A further strong concern was that during the Cuban revolution, Fidel Castro had not impressed America nor had he revealed himself as a stable leader. The idea of him controlling such awesome power was quite unacceptable to the United States. The Allies fell in behind President Kennedy and provided the solid front he needed.

When Khrushchev backed down the sigh of relief could be heard across the entire world. The Soviet leader retained his dignity by exacting an agreement from Kennedy that the United States would not invade Cuba, and John F. Kennedy emerged as the youngest version the world has known of a wise elder statesman. Had Kennedy betrayed any sign of weakness during the confrontation the Soviets would have pressed their advantage, an advantage which would have been greatly enhanced by an immediate loss of confidence among the Allies. The strength and tenacity demonstrated by the President provided a stern rebuff for the Soviets and this was amplified by the confidence shown by the Allies. The Cuban Missiles Crisis was undoubtedly a turning point in the Cold War, and Harold Macmillan expressed it well when he said that John F. Kennedy had earned his place in history by this one act alone.

Thus among the many problems which beset John F. Kennedy during his time in office, Cuba was predominant, first in the Bay of Pigs affair and then in the Missiles Crisis. In international affairs it was the closing of borders to East Germany, the raising of the Berlin Wall and the Berlin question in general which constituted a running sore. Kennedy, however, had a jewel of enormous worth to show for his efforts to limit the arms race: obtaining East–West agreement in a treaty banning nuclear testing in the environment.

There is no doubt that President Kennedy achieved a great deal, not just for America and the Allies, but for the whole world, in successfully negotiating the first ever nuclear test-ban treaty. The day after the treaty was initialled, he spoke to the American nation:

> I speak to you tonight in a spirit of hope . . . [Since] the advent of nuclear weapons, all mankind has been struggling to escape from the darkening prospect of mass destruction on earth.
> . . . Yesterday a shaft of light cut into the darkness . . .
> This treaty is not the millennium . . . But it is an important first step – a step toward peace, a step toward reason, a step away from war . . . This treaty is for all of us. It is particularly for our children and our grandchildren, and they have no lobby here in Washington . . .
> According to the ancient Chinese proverb, 'A journey of a thousand miles must begin with a single step' . . . Let us take that first step.

This is not to say that his sentiments were echoed by all in the Senate. A stiff battle lay ahead before the Senate gave its approval to the treaty. But President Kennedy demonstrated his enormous political skills in the task of obtaining the support he needed from Senators who had expressed their doubts, uncertainties and, in some cases, their opposition. His spectacular success in enlisting their support and approval for the treaty provided welcome reassurance that, when the chips were down, politicians were prepared to put aside party issues in order to cast a vote for reason. In this case it was a vote for all Americans, for mankind, for peace.

John F. Kennedy's patient behind-the-scenes efforts talking to groups and explaining details to individuals resulted in 'a welcome culmination' to his efforts, as he modestly expressed it. The first small step he claimed the treaty to represent, might justly be considered to have been the foundation on which all subsequent treaties were built. It was Kennedy's greatest achievement and he rightly obtained deeper satisfaction from this than any other of his Presidential accomplishments.

In domestic affairs he had also achieved great things. His feelings for the poor and for the United States Negro demonstrated a compassion and a willingness to stand up and be counted which would never be forgotten.

But during his time in office, John F. Kennedy, with his brother Robert, seen forever by the President's side, also succeeded in making deadly and dangerous enemies. The President would be the first to meet their wrath. It was 1963, and he was to visit the Lone Star State of Texas in November . . .

CHAPTER THREE

An Unofficial Government

> 'On that day . . . when crime dons the apparel of
> innocence, it is innocence that is called upon to justify
> its existence.'
>
> Albert Camus

MORE AND MORE, the people liked the President, and his following
came from those in every age group. He was, after all, a war hero and
in the fifties and sixties, that counted for a great deal. Seen as the
herald of a new era in politics, his image was that of a dashing,
attractive, clean-cut American boy who understood the problems of
the times—those at home and those abroad—and knew what to do
about them. His appeal was that of a man of vision, a man of courage
and, perhaps above all, a man of compassion. But these were not the
feelings of all Americans. Like all other Presidents, he had his
opposition, and JFK had particularly strong opposition, much of
which derived from the family background he brought to the
Presidency: the rest he earned for himself with his words and with his
actions, since no President could please all of the people all of the
time.

There were many who knew little of John F. Kennedy's background when he became President. What they learnt as time went by
did not alter their enthusiasm for him or their willingness to judge
him on his merits. There were others who knew a great deal about the

Kennedy family and their reactions were divided. Many thought of the Kennedy family as a new kind of – specifically American – royalty, and had a great deal of respect for the buccaneering Ambassador. Others despised them and were appalled that the son of such a family could become President, and as President become one of the most powerful men in the world. The country's captains of industry, financial experts and professional people were distributed across both camps and among these people were those who knew the most about the Kennedys. They had watched the power and wealth of the family grow over the space of a generation. Some of them had rubbed shoulders with them. Stories of Joe's stockmarket coups, his ruthlessness in business and his clout in politics were legend. In some circles he was celebrated, but there is no doubt that the elder Kennedy also made many enemies. They had followed his rise to the rank of Ambassador to the Court of St James and they were well aware of his Presidential aspirations. They had witnessed his fall and experienced no regret. Yes, Joe had many enemies and, in the way of things, this enmity tended to be something bequeathed. When John F. Kennedy reached the Presidency he reached it largely under the auspices of his father. This is not to say that he could not have become President without his father's help. It is merely to state the fact that he *did not* become President without his father's help. To many, Joe had 'put' him there. And there was a feeling among them that the hand of Joe would clearly be seen in his son's Presidency.

Among the country's most powerful men, there were those to whom John F. Kennedy had entered the Presidential park with three strikes against him. Just as surely as the leopard could not change his spots, the son could not fail to be a reflection of the father. Having a Kennedy boy in the White House was having the Kennedy family in the White House. Besides all this, the family wealth combined with his personal wealth made him untouchable. He would never be subjected to the pressures which derived from dependence upon sources of essential cash for electioneering purposes, a feature which, to most voters, was an enormous plus. As his Presidency would show, he was his own man, but there were those whose prejudice would only allow them to go as far as conceding he was his family's man. The move to appoint his brother Robert to the office of Attorney General only served to confirm to those who thought that way that they were right. And, over and above all this, there were others who, though they did not suffer from a prejudice against the family, were nervous because the appointment of John F. Kennedy to the White House marked a distinct shift in American politics.

The appointment of Robert Kennedy as Attorney General can be seen as a smart move on JFK's part. He needed someone standing beside him in this key role who was utterly loyal, totally dependable and capable of great courage: someone in whom, in the loneliness of the Great Office, he could confide. He could not share the Presidency with anyone. But Bobby, representing his strong right arm, allowed him the confidence he needed for a term of office which was to prove eventful, to say the least, both at home and in world affairs. There was no doubt, however, that the appointment of his brother unnerved many of his opponents and worried many of his supporters, too. It gave the impression that the critics were right: the Kennedy family had moved into the White House.

Robert Kennedy became identified with many of JFK's policies, his achievements and his failures. He was party to many of the President's decisions on foreign affairs and on domestic issues. Because of this he earned the enmity of those who hated JFK, one special group of whom were the mobsters, though here, it must be said, Robert was only adding to the hatred he already attracted as a consequence of his zealous work on the Senate Rackets Committee. The influence of the individual gangster of the ilk of John Dillinger and Al Capone, who carried out their reigns of terror in their own 'territories', had long since gone. Things had changed and not for the better. Crime was organised now and the syndicates co-operated with one another across America. Crime was run in the manner, and on the scale, of big business, and very big business it was. J. Edgar Hoover, Director of the FBI, whose preoccupation this development this should have been, was still arguing it had never happened and was giving priority to the fight against communism. Since communism by this time was no longer the menace it had been, with membership of the American Communist Party significantly in decline, it befell the Attorney General to enlighten Hoover, so that the energies of the FBI could be brought to bear upon the real 'enemy within'. As Arthur Schlesinger Jr put it:

[Robert] Kennedy was determined to stop the drain of power in America to obscure forces beyond moral and legal accountability. In insisting on the spreading threat of organised crime, he offended J. Edgar Hoover doubly—by dismissing the cherished Red menace and by raising a question the director had done his best for 40 years to ignore.*

It was, perhaps, not surprising that neither Robert Kennedy nor the President had a friend in J. Edgar Hoover.†

Robert Kennedy turned his attention and all his energies to combating organised crime, and it was not long before the mobsters were acutely aware of what was happening. He continued the work he had begun during his time on the Rackets Committee in pressing for the conviction of the notorious Jimmy Hoffa, who was President of the enormously powerful Teamster's Union, though with great difficulty since, as Hoffa himself expressed it, he 'had a way with juries'. Undeterred, Robert Kennedy piled on the pressure and, inspired by the Attorney General's example, a national offensive against the syndicates began.

> Under Kennedy's pressure the national government took on organised crime as it had never done before. In New York, Robert Morgenthau, the Federal attorney, successfully prosecuted one syndicate leader after another. The Patriarca gang in Rhode Island and the De Cavalcante gang in New Jersey were smashed. Convictions of racketeers by the Organised Crime Section and the Tax Division steadily increased—96 in 1961, 101 in 1962, 373 in 1963. So long as John Kennedy sat in the White House, giving his Attorney General absolute backing, the underworld knew that the heat was on.*†

In many parts of the United States, law enforcement officers who, as a consequence of suffering frustration after frustration in trying to secure convictions against the mobsters, had virtually given up, renewed their efforts and now met with success. The underworld was in retreat as it had never been before. This great achievement, which

---

* Arthur M. Schlesinger Jr, *Robert Kennedy and His Times*, Andre Deutsch, London, 1978
† In his book, *The Secret Life of J. Edgar Hoover* (Gollancz, 1993), Anthony Summers has sought to expose J. Edgar Hoover as a corrupt, despotic fraud, a homosexual and a friend to certain underworld figures. If Summers is right, this would explain Hoover's reluctance to fight—or even acknowledge the existence of—organised crime
‡ Prosecutions dropped by a massive 83 per cent after the assassination of President John F. Kennedy

brought the acclaim of the people, naturally attracted the hatred of the Mafia, whose members came under fire or the threat of fire. Included in their number were many who had thrown their weight behind John F. Kennedy in his campaign for the Presidency, believing they had ways of 'reaching' and manipulating him. Too late, they realised their mistake, and poured out their venom on the Kennedy brothers.

When reference is made to the military-industrial complex, a tacit acknowledgment is made that the US military – the Pentagon – had a relationship with those who designed and manufactured weaponry and other armaments not common to all countries. Until the Second World War, the United States was never seen as a world military force. It was during the war that it achieved such status, and the years following the conflict saw America periodically flexing its military muscle, the action in Korea providing a notable example of this. As year followed year, the men in the Pentagon became stronger and stronger, and this did not escape notice. It was the inspiration for the highly popular novel, *Seven Days in May*, written by Fletcher Knebel and Charles W. Bentley, the scenario for which featured highly placed generals plotting to assume supreme power in the United States. The book was dynamite in Washington, where it served as a stern warning to politicians in particular that military influence and power was becoming top heavy and that there might be those in the Pentagon who were inclined to be dissatisfied with playing a subservient role in decision-making.

John F. Kennedy knew what Knebel and Bentley were talking about. He had listened to the warning publicly delivered by his predecessor, President Dwight D. Eisenhower, just before he left office, 'Beware the military-industrial complex.' He was well aware of the dangers in the situation and, apparently, expressed his misgivings in a conversation with Khrushchev, who said as much in his memoirs. When *Seven Days in May* was made into a movie, it is said that it was at the suggestion of JFK, who vacated the White House one weekend to allow the film crew to go in. The film had a wider audience and the message was driven home.

During John F. Kennedy's term of office, there was frequent conflict between the Pentagon and the White House. The military was extremely unhappy that the President did not throw his weight behind the Cuban exiles in their attempt to stage a counter-revolution at the Bay of Pigs. The generals pressed for him to do so, along with the CIA who had hatched the scheme in conjunction with the Chiefs of Staff. At the time of the Missiles Crisis, again, the advice he met with was to unleash the power of America's military might against the Cubans and, if necessary, the Russians also. The signing of the nuclear test-ban treaty with the Soviets was seen as the next best thing to an act of treason by some, a deliberate undermining of American initiative. The decision to withdraw 1,000 'advisers' from Vietnam was probably the very last straw to the generals, who saw the United States being committed to a policy of disengagement everywhere. To them the President's actions were ignominious. The United States, who possessed the greatest, most awe-inspiring capacity for war in the world, was being made to appear retiring and weak in resolution.

It goes without saying that if Kennedy's policies made the generals unhappy, then those who headed the armaments industry were at least equally unhappy. A nation at peace did not make for a thriving armaments industry. Besides, arms and ammunition deteriorated and the rate of obsolescence was greater than it had ever been. Aircraft, for instance, were notorious for becoming obsolete before ever leaving the drawing board. And if the armaments people were disenchanted then the oil barons, whose revenues were always affected by an outbreak of peace, were also piqued since, in war, nothing moved or worked without their product. The oil barons had other deep worries in addition to this. Shifts in US influence abroad made them nervous about their overseas oil interests which were vulnerable to nationalisation. At home, another cause of nervousness was that the President had decided it was time to review the special tax benefits the industry enjoyed, the 'oil depletion allowances'. It was the latter which struck to their hearts.

When the Bay of Pigs débâcle was over, it was not just the military who nursed resentments. The CIA was seen by the world to be wearing egg on its face, and those involved in the planning and execution of the operation were livid. They blamed Kennedy. They felt that the Chief had 'dropped them in the mire' by refusing the support they needed to make the offensive successful. True, they had assured him they would not need such support and, true, before it started the President had made it abundantly clear that he was not prepared to plunge America into this enterprise which, ostensibly, was Cuban against Cuban. This did not stop them feeling badly let down, however. As far as Kennedy was concerned America's contribution to the Cuban exiles' incursion was limited to the planning of the operation, the arming, training, housing, clothing and feeding of the 1,400 Cuban participants, all of this through the CIA. It was a covert operation on behalf of the exiles living in the United States, the success of which was calculated to obtain massive benefits for America. Open participation on the part of the United States would, however, be tantamount to a declaration of war on Cuba and, as Kennedy had said, if America ever decided it should wage war on Cuba, it would not be as an afterthought on the coat tails of Cuban exiles.

Among the men who were mown down on the beaches at the Bay of Pigs were CIA agents. Those agents who survived, and those who mourned the loss of their colleagues, blamed John F. Kennedy for the carnage and suffering which the deadly fiasco brought. Theirs was a special hatred for the President. It was not a resentment so much as a deep-seated hatred they felt for the man they believed was responsible for the plan's failure. They did not know – or would not believe – that the CIA and the generals had accepted his stipulations before the scheme was embarked upon. Perhaps they were not aware of the faulty intelligence the CIA had provided for a faulty plan. They saw only that the President had turned his back on the Cuban exiles and his CIA men when the going got tough and they needed a little help. They hated Kennedy's guts.

The relationship between the CIA and the President was never to recover. Following the Bay of Pigs disaster Kennedy sacked the Agency's Director, Allen Dulles, his deputy, Charles Cabell, and the Deputy Director of Planning, Richard M. Bissell. Huge problems were detected in the Agency, which was observed to have become something it was never intended to be. It wielded enormous power, not just in the countries in which it was designated to be serving America, but within the borders of America itself. Its actions were reminiscent of that of an independent operator. It made decisions without consulting the government. It was, in fact, assuming the authority of a covert government all on its own. Retired President Harry S. Truman, who had formed the CIA, would say shortly after Kennedy's death:

> For some time I have been disturbed by the way the CIA has been diverted from its original assignment. It has become an operational arm and at times a policy-making arm of the government. I never had any thought . . . when I set up the CIA, that it would be injected into peacetime cloak and dagger operations. Some of the complications and embarrassment that I think we experienced are in part attributable to the fact that this quiet intelligence arm of the President has been so removed from its intended role.

David Wise and Thomas B. Ross, journalists for the *New York Herald Tribune* put a finger on it in an article they wrote:

> There are two governments in the United States today. One is visible. The other is invisible. The first is the government that citizens read about in their newspapers and children study in their civics books. The second is the interlocking, hidden machinery that carries out the policies of the United States in the Cold War. This second, invisible government gathers intelligence, conducts espionage, and plans and executes secret operations all over the globe . . . Major decisions involving war or peace are taking place out of public view. An informed citizen might come to suspect that the foreign policy of the United States often works publicly in one direction and secretly through the Invisible Government in just the opposite direction.

President Kennedy found he could not rely on the word of the Agency. An example may be taken from the case of the professor who taught history at Yale. The professor visited the Soviet Union and was arrested there for spying. When Kennedy heard about this he made enquiries of the Agency who told him the professor was not working for them. He was 'clean'. Consequent to this assurance, JFK made a personal plea to Khrushchev who, to please the President, released the professor. It was upon his return to the United States, at a meeting arranged for him at the White House, that Kennedy was told by the professor he had indeed been working for the Agency. The President must surely have wondered what was going through the mind of

Khrushchev, who appeared to have access to more reliable information about CIA activities than he did. In another instance, the CIA were instructed that a coup d'état planned by them for Vietnam must not involve the murder of leader Ngo Dinh Diem. Diem was killed and when news reached the President that the indications marked it out as a CIA killing, against his explicit orders, he was outraged.

There was ample evidence that the CIA were making their own decisions, regardless of the President. In the 'settlement' with Khrushchev which followed the Missiles Crisis, Kennedy had given his word that there would be no further attempts to invade Cuba or assassinate Castro. Unbelievably, he discovered that the CIA had secretly set up new camps to train Cuban exiles for a second invasion. Kennedy ordered them destroyed and FBI and police personnel were sent in to carry out his orders. It came to light, also, that the CIA had conspired with prominent figures from the ranks of organised crime to have Fidel Castro killed. From Chicago, Mafia mobsters Johnny Rosselli and Sam Giancana were recruited to murder the Cuban leader by CIA men who acted with the knowledge and approval of the then Deputy Director of Planning, Richard M. Bissell. Not only was the President kept in the dark, but such skulduggery flew directly in the face of Robert Kennedy's campaign against organised crime. While the Kennedys were slogging it out with the syndicates, the CIA, behind their backs, was secretly conducting negotiations with their members. Sam Giancana was, in fact, one of Bobby Kennedy's prime targets. Not only was the object of the exercise immoral, the whole episode served as another example of the Agency undermining the policy of the elected government.

It was only due to problems in Sam Giancana's love life that anyone ever found out about the CIA deal with the Mafia. Giancana suspected his mistress–said to be singer Phillis McGuire of the Maguire Sisters– was cheating on him with a well-known comedian, reputedly Dan Rowan. Giancana wanted to find out what was going on, and he asked Robert Maheu, an ex-FBI agent who was acting as liaison between the CIA and the mobsters, to plant a bug in Rowan's hotel room. After consultation with his masters, Maheu agreed, and engaged a private detective, Arthur J. Balletti, to do the job. A maid saw Balletti planting the device, however, and she told the manager. The manager called the police who, in turn, contacted the FBI. The whole mess soon landed on the CIA's doorstep, and knowledge of it could not be prevented from reaching the Attorney General. Robert Kennedy was furious.

Throughout his time in office, John F. Kennedy was at loggerheads with the CIA. He made his feelings clear to Senator Mike Mansfield when he told him his intentions were to tear the CIA 'into a thousand pieces and scatter it to the winds'. In fact, one of President Kennedy's last acts was to commission a review of US intelligence activities. The point had long since been reached when the President could no longer rely upon them to act in accordance with their purpose and mandate. Hence the time was reached when Kennedy chose not to tell the CIA of his plans. An example of this was seen in his decision to press for better relations with Cuba. He carried out his moves in secret without telling the CIA or the State Department. There is no doubt that the Central Intelligence Agency held no brief for John F. Kennedy. And if the CIA represented a faction, there was a faction within the faction which positively hated him.

The President gained steadily in popularity with the people during his term of office and it is a fair assumption that this was expected to happen by his enemies. They knew the electorate was warming to him. And what enemies John F. Kennedy had! They came from the ranks of all the groups already mentioned in this chapter: organised crime, the military, the leaders of the armaments industry, the oil men and the CIA, headed by the disenchanted group associated with the Bay of Pigs invasion. It is likely that President Kennedy was hardly installed in office before discussion began to take place between members of these mostly inter-related groups about what they saw as the castastrophe of a Kennedy-ridden White House and the likelihood that Kennedy's growing popularity would keep him there for a second term. There was even the dread prospect that after his second term he would be replaced by Robert Kennedy. The combination of Kennedy wealth and influence coupled to the power of the Presidency was awesome. There are strong indications that these discussions resulted in the formation of a secret fraternity which met for the purpose of examining the prospects of dislodging the grip of the Kennedys. The 'evidence' of the fraternity's existence may be dismissed by the unbeliever as speculation. At the very least, however, it is well-founded speculation and merits serious consideration. That it exists is writ large in blood on the recent history of the United States. As for its name, title or code, if it has one, it is unknown, as might be expected of such an organisation. Other researchers who have identified this fraternity in one shape or form* have, for convenience, given it a name. We shall call it the Consortium, for that, of sorts, is what it is.

As the Consortium saw it, the country was in deep trouble. The most powerful country in the world was retreating to a position in which it would not take up arms in its own interests. *The Bay of Pigs episode had been humiliating.* There is little doubt the Consortium's members were in possession of the details of what had happened in the White House and also of what had happened on the shores of Cuba in relation to this offensive, perhaps first-hand accounts. As they saw it Kennedy obviously had no regard for human life, not even American human life, as he had demonstrated. *Did he understand anything about running the country? Did he know anything about foreign affairs? Could he possibly know how to face up to communism? To the Soviets? He certainly had not faced up to the Cubans. Why, we could have taken that country back for Democracy: we could have thrown Castro and the commies out on their ears. The Bobby Kennedy appointment as Attorney General had been a scandal of a different kind. Here was pure, unvarnished nepotism. Look at the way he had had his knife into Jimmy Hoffa from the days when he served on the Senate Rackets Committee. Now he was using his new office to continue his vindictiveness. There was a touch of ruthlessness about this fresh-faced kid which made him not to be trusted. Is it true that the Kennedys are planning new legislation to help the blacks?*

The trouble with Jack Kennedy – perhaps a nice young guy in some ways, I mean, you could see why people voted for him – is that he has bad blood in his veins. Those Kennedys! Joe Kennedy was an old rogue. Some of us did business with him. A man not to be trusted further than you could throw him. And it's odds on he is really running the White House now. The Kennedy boy must simply be having to do as he's told. It's always been like that in the family, why should it change now? There is no doubt about it, gentlemen, the country has fallen into incompetent, untrustworthy hands. These are desperate, dangerous

* See Chapter 19

times. The question is, what can we do about it? It is quite clear that it is our patriotic duty to do everything in our power to protect the best interests of America and the American people. It's down to us.

One discussion would, no doubt, lead to another, with more 'facts' presented each time to underline the seriousness of the situation they saw. The Consortium by now was firmly entrenched in the belief that it perceived the true picture of what was happening in the United States, and that its members were the best kind of genuine patriots, who carried the responsibility for righting the wrongs they saw, a kind of unofficial government. *Kennedy has been in office more than a year now and things are going from bad to worse. Desperate times call for desperate measures. Since the Consortium began its discussions, the Berlin Wall has been erected, with nothing more than gutless squawks about it from America. Something really must be done as a matter of urgency. But how can Kennedy be 'reached'? There is no way of getting to him to exert the pressure which is needed to get the country right side up again. Perhaps the only way is to remove him from office altogether . . .*

It was probably early 1962 that members of the Consortium elected a small group of their number – we shall call them the Executive Group – who had the sole task of devising a means to remove John F. Kennedy from the White House. If it was successful in getting rid of John, Robert Kennedy would also go since his post was one of patronage. But how could it be achieved? Perhaps it was a CIA man who told the Group about the file Hoover had on the Kennedys. Not much went on without Hoover knowing about it. The FBI Director had files on everybody with something to hide, but he had his own uses for the information he gathered. Bobby Kennedy was not known for philandering, though his name was linked with that of Marilyn Monroe, and one affair was enough. The President's indiscretions with women were well known to Hoover, and he, also, had had an association with Marilyn Monroe. It would only take such information as this, with substantiation, to reach the press and it would lead to his impeachment. But there was not much chance of getting Hoover to expose the Kennedys. His files were his 'security of tenure'. While the files were safely in his possession, he was safe, impregnable.

But did the Executive Group next turn its energies to devising the means by which all this could be exposed?

CHAPTER FOUR

Beauty as the Pawn

Alice laughed . . . 'One can't believe impossible things.'
'I daresay you haven't had much practice,' said the Queen. 'When I was your age, I always did it for half-an-hour a day. Why, sometimes I've believed as many as six impossible things before breakfast.'
Lewis Carroll, *Through the Looking Glass*

IT WAS 1962 and Marilyn Monroe had been fired from the set of *Something's Got to Give* by Twentieth Century Fox. The ailing studio had had enough problems without Marilyn, who was costing them sums they could ill afford by her absences from work and her bickering about the script. It might be thought that Marilyn would not much care, but not so. The trouble was that, psychologically, she could not cope with being fired. The 36-year-old actress who had striven to achieve stardom and worldwide adulation was sick of mind and heart and, it was said, had it not been for the fact of who she was, she would have been institutionalised without the option. She survived with the help of those close to her and in spite of her booze and pills.

She had her housekeeper, Mrs Eunice Murray, who was prepared to stay over at night when necessary. She had her press secretary, Pat Newcomb, who irritated her no end when she stayed with her because she could sleep soundly and long, something which Marilyn longed to be able to do and of which she was quite incapable. And she had her doctors, Ralph Greenson, her psychiatrist, upon whom she leaned heavily, and Hyman Engelberg, her physician. Then she had a circle of friends whose company she enjoyed. There was Peter Lawford, the actor, who lived with his wife, Pat, sister of President Kennedy, in a beautiful beach house which had once belonged to film magnate Louis B. Mayer; baseball legend, Joe DiMaggio, who had been married to her, briefly, and who still loved her deeply; Ralph Roberts, her personal masseur, who was an old and trusted friend; and Lee and Paula Strasberg, her acting coaches, though recently their friendship had soured. Beyond these was another group she saw from time to time: Frank Sinatra and his mobster friends, Sam Giancana and Johnny Rosselli, Bob Slatzer, who claimed he had been married to Marilyn for a short time, and Allen Snyder, her make-up man. Periodically, she saw the man whose company she craved most, President John F. Kennedy, when he visited his sister and brother-in-law at their house.

It was believed that Robert Kennedy had sought to intervene in a liaison between Marilyn and his brother Jack which had the makings of a great scandal and, in meeting the glamorous star, a new relationship was formed which became just as threatening as the one he had succeeded in breaking up. Perhaps from foolish 'pillow-talk' she had come to believe – or had been led to believe – that Robert Kennedy intended to divorce his wife, Ethel, and marry her. To all those whom she told of this, the notion was at once utterly unbelievable, far fetched, but not to Marilyn, who was apparently quite convinced her future lay with the Attorney General. As for Robert Kennedy, the time inevitably came when he had to put an end to the relationship, whatever it had been, and this placed an intolerable burden on the unstable, unbelieving Monroe.

Shortly before the crisis with Robert Kennedy came, Marilyn accepted an invitation to spend the weekend, the last in July, with Frank Sinatra at the Cal-Neva Lodge, Sinatra's place at Lake Tahoe on the border between California and Nevada. His Mafia friend, Sam Giancana, who was a partner in the gambling establishment, was there with Johnny Rosselli, and Pat and Peter Lawford had been invited, too. Joe DiMaggio turned up with Marilyn's best interests at heart, since he knew the strain such company placed on her, but he only saw her from a distance and was unable to help. The trouble was that DiMaggio and Sinatra did not get along and Joe was there as a patron and not as one of the singer's guests. It was another tense, lost weekend for Marilyn, a hazy few days of sex, booze and pills, and DiMaggio resented Sinatra's invitation to her. The weekend over, it was Sinatra's six-million-dollar plane which took Pat Lawford to San Francisco, from where she flew to the East Coast, and Peter Lawford and Marilyn, both drunk, back to Los Angeles.

The following week proved a busy one for Marilyn. She was not short of new and exciting projects, and she spoke on the telephone to Jules Styne about a proposed musical version of *A Tree Grows in Brooklyn*, in which she would play opposite Frank Sinatra. She also spoke to Gene Kelly about another idea for a musical and made arrangements to meet Kelly and also Sidney Skolsky on the following Sunday, 5 August. She was discussing with Skolsky a proposal for a film dealing with the story of blonde bombshell, Jean Harlow. Later that Sunday she planned to go on for dinner with Frank Sinatra and night-club owner Mike Romanoff and his wife, Gloria. During that week Marilyn, reportedly recovering from an abortion carried out a few weeks previously in Mexico, made a dinner date with Dr Leon Krohn, a gynaecologist, who had treated her years before at the time of a miscarriage. She entertained make-up man Whitey Snyder and Marjorie Plecher, who worked in wardrobe, for drinks, and, a keen gardener, she made time to call at a nursery to buy some new plants on the Friday. The following week she planned to fly out to New York to see Jules Styne. Life was better now for Fox had reinstated her to *Something's Got to Give*, and she had bought a whole new wardrobe. It was certainly a busy week, and, in spite of her instability, it was not at all the kind of week which would be spent by someone contemplating suicide.

It was Robert Kennedy who worried her during those first few days of August but this was a time when she always seemed preoccupied with the Kennedys. Robert had 'cut her off cold', but since he was visiting California that weekend, prior to delivering an address to the American Bar Association followed by a holiday with Ethel and four of their children in Washington State, she would see him at the Lawfords' Saturday-night party and sort matters out then. There was much to be sorted out, for even her attempts to reach him on the East Coast by telephone had been fruitless. When Robert flew to San Francisco during the Friday, Marilyn's attempts to reach him were switched to the hotel he normally used on visits there. Her many messages were unanswered. Robert had, indeed, decided it was time to call it a day, but Marilyn had other ideas. She threatened to call a press conference on Monday to tell the world of their relationship if he refused to see her.

It seems that Marilyn had word on the Saturday that Robert Kennedy was not going to attend the gathering that evening at the Lawfords'. During the morning she received a package which contained a stuffed toy tiger, and afterwards became depressed. Did the tiger contain a message cancelling Kennedy's party attendance? Or was it receipt of the tiger itself which communicated an unwritten message from RFK, perhaps final severance of their relationship? Saturday was not a good day. She telephoned her psychiatrist, Dr Greenson, who called to see her during the afternoon. He saw her most days, and thought little of a visit on that day, though he hoped it would not extend too far into the evening, as he had arranged to take his wife out to dinner. She had tried more than once during the day to persuade her friend, Jeanne Carmen, to call round, asking her to bring 'a bag of pills' with her. Since it was Carmen's birthday, however, she had plans and declined, with misgivings over Marilyn's suggestion of pills. The final call was at about 10.00 pm, when Carmen pleaded she was too tired. As Dr Greenson recalled Marilyn saying earlier in the day, here she was, the most beautiful woman in the world, and she did not have a date for Saturday night.

It was just before 4.25 am the following morning that the police received a call from Dr Greenson to tell them Marilyn was dead. Sergeant Jack Clemmons, the Watch Commander at the West Los Angeles station, took the call and made his way to 12305 Fifth Helena Drive, where Marilyn lived. As Clemmons drove down Sunset Boulevard and on to Carmelina, he wondered whether this would turn out to be another of those sick calls the police had been receiving of late reporting the deaths of famous people. This time it was not to be so. He found Dr Greenson and Dr Engelberg at the house and was taken into Marilyn's bedroom where he found her outstretched, unclothed and face down across the bed, covered only with a sheet which Dr Greenson had pulled across her. Marilyn's hand gripped a telephone and she lay across the cord. On the night table were a variety of medicine bottles, some which could be bought over the

(Plate 1) John F. Kennedy celebrates his first election success with his parents and grandparents (*Courtesy John F. Kennedy Library*)

(Plate 2) The Kennedy family (*Courtesy John F. Kennedy Library*)

(Plate 3) Joe Jr, Kathleen and JFK in London, 1939 (*Courtesy John F. Kennedy Library*)

(Plate 4) The marriage of John F. Kennedy to Jacqueline Lee Bouvier on Saturday, 12 September 1953 (*Courtesy John F. Kennedy Library*)

(Plate 5) President Kennedy at the Berlin Wall (*Courtesy John F. Kennedy Library*)

(Plate 6) Executive Committee meeting of the National Security Council during the time of the Kennedy Administration (*Courtesy John F. Kennedy Library*)

(Plate 7) 'Happy birthday, Mr President' was sung by the inimitable Marilyn Monroe at a celebration held for JFK at Madison Square Garden on 19 May 1962 (*Courtesy John F. Kennedy Library*)

(Plate 8) Marilyn Monroe (*AP/Wide World Photos*)

(Plate 9) The bedside table in the bedroom in which Marilyn died. There are plenty of drug bottles in evidence, but why was there no trace of these drugs in her stomach? The small glass with water (extreme right edge of table) was not there when her body was discovered (*AP/Wide World Photos*)

(Plate 10) Dr Ralph Greenson. He saw Marilyn frequently and was called the night she was found dead

(Pate 11) Dr Hyman Engelberg, Marilyn's physician, called the police, but not until 4.35 a.m.

(Plate 12) Dr John Miner, Assistant DA, saw the autopsy performed on Marilyn Monroe. He talked to Matthew Smith of what he had seen

(Plate 13) The window to Marilyn's bedroom was broken. The housekeeper at first said it was broken to gain access because the door was bolted, but later confessed this was a lie. Who, then, broke it, and why? (*AP/Wide World Photos*)

(Plate 14) Peter Lawford's spacious beach house. It had once belonged to film mogul, Louis B. Mayer

(Plate 15)

pharmacy counter and others in which her prescribed drugs had been supplied. The bottle which had contained her Nembutal – 50 capsules – was empty. Eunice Murray, who had been asked to stay over that night, was keeping busy while Clemmons looked around, though his job was now done. He had come out primarily to establish that the call was genuine: it would be someone else's task to investigate the death. He noted that Dr Greenson had declared it suicide. The investigating officer would be along shortly.

At first glance it looked like an open-and-shut case of suicide. This was to be the finding of the 'suicide investigation team' appointed by the Coroner, Dr Theodore Curphey, to look into the matter. The official record softened this to 'probable suicide' which is a term used for suicide by accident. But then, with little probing, in every direction anomalies were seen to exist which screamed that there was nothing open and shut about the death of Marilyn Monroe. In the first place, by the time the police were called, Marilyn had been dead for some hours. The doctors present admitted to her having been dead for three hours, but the only – unlikely – reason given for the long delay in notifying the police was that they had to get clearance from the studio publicity department before releasing the news. To add to the time-delay problem, the undertaker, Guy Huckett, having to cope with a body advanced in rigor mortis, found it so stiff he had to 'bend' it to allow it to fit on the gurney for removal. In his opinion, Marilyn had been dead for six to eight hours. But researchers who questioned Miss Monroe's friends established that she had used the telephone as late as 10.30 pm on the Saturday night, and it was, therefore, strongly indicated that she had died soon after making that last call.

When Sergeant Clemmons asked who had discovered the body, Mrs Murray claimed that she had: 'At ten o'clock I went to bed, and the light was on under Marilyn's door. I just assumed Marilyn was sleeping or talking on the telephone with a friend so I went to bed. I woke up at midnight, and had to go to the bathroom. The light was still on underneath Marilyn's door.' Mrs Murray said she became concerned and knocked on the door to try and rouse Marilyn. When she failed to do so she called Dr Greenson who quickly came over. Greenson, who also failed to get an answer, went outside and looked through the window. Seeing her lying face down and motionless, he broke a pane of glass, opened the window and gained access that way. He ascertained she was dead and called Dr Engelberg, who came at once and pronounced Marilyn dead. But then came another huge anomaly. Dr Greenson said he had not been called until 3.30 am. Mrs Murray later explained this away by saying she had dozed off again after seeing the light under the door at midnight and she awoke again at about 3.30 am to find the light still on. It was then, she said, that she rang Dr Greenson. But then, Mrs Murray changed her story just about every time she told it. Clemmons observed that the room was inordinately – and uncharacteristically – neat for a bedroom in which a suicide had taken place. Eight pill bottles were by the bed but there was no glass. There was no cup, tumbler or glass of any kind which could have been used for water to assist in the taking of the pills to be found anywhere in the room, and Marilyn's friends said she did not find it easy to take pills without water. Clemmons found the absence of a glass very odd. He must have found it even odder when he viewed the police photos taken later on for they showed a receptacle half full of water in clear view. (See plate 9)

Detective Sergeant R. E. Byron relieved Sergeant Clemmons at the Monroe house and carried out an investigation. He appeared to be content with the doctors' word that Marilyn had committed suicide and treated the investigation as such. His was not an impressive investigation. The body was despatched first to the undertakers, but they were then instructed to transfer it to the morgue for autopsy.

The pathologist given the job of examining the body was the doctor destined to become known as the Coroner of the Stars, Doctor Thomas Noguchi, who, by reputation, was brilliant at his work. Of the 47 Nembutal capsules Marilyn was believed to have swallowed, there was no trace whatsoever in her stomach. More important still, there were no traces of the contents of the capsules. There were no barbiturates present in her stomach at all, and no trace of the yellow dye often found on the path taken by Nembutals, though the colouring by itself was not necessarily significant. Noguchi's toxicologist, Ralph Abernathy, on the other hand, found enough barbiturates and chloral hydrate in her blood to have killed several people. A total of four-and-a-half milligrams per cent of barbiturates and eight milligrams per cent of chloral hydrate were found. Abernathy also found 13 milligrams per cent of barbiturates in her liver. The autopsy, however, was not a full one. The intestines were not examined and when Noguchi decided he should carry out further checks it was found that the organ specimens had been destroyed. Not only this but slides made from the specimens and the medical photographs later disappeared.

The implications of the autopsy were that had Marilyn Monroe swallowed the capsules all together, clear evidence should have been in her stomach. The only alternative was for her to have swallowed them in slow succession over a period of hours, which was unrealistic. The drugs could have been introduced by injection, of course, and that would have been consistent with them not being found in the stomach. Dr Noguchi, with the assistance of John Miner, the Deputy DA, there to represent the District Attorney at the autopsy, examined every part of Marilyn's skin with magnifying glasses seeking tell-tale needle marks. There were none present. The astute John Miner had forensic experience and was a specialist in medical and psychiatric law. Had the marks been there they would have found them. There were two other means of introducing drugs into the system which were also considered. One way was by suppository, but this was likely to leave behind indications which were not present on the corpse. The other way was by enema. The official decision reached by the Coroner was that Marilyn swallowed the capsules, though Noguchi reportedly expressed misgivings about this, saying he felt 'uncomfortable'.

Rumours surrounded the death of Marilyn Monroe from the very beginning. Accounts given by those involved with the actress changed from interview to interview, and some of those nearest to her simply took off. Peter Lawford left at once for an unknown destination, which turned out to be the Kennedy compound at Hyannis Port. Mrs Murray left for Europe and Pat Newcomb, also, went overseas for a holiday. Pat Newcomb has made very little comment on Marilyn's death, and steadfastly refuses to discuss it. Stories circulated that Robert Kennedy visited Marilyn's house on the Saturday night and this kindled speculation that he was in some way involved with her demise. The suicide verdict was quickly challenged by people who knew Marilyn and, though evidence was sadly lacking, the cry of murder was raised in some quarters, based largely on hunch and mistrust of the official verdict. Private investigations on the part of a number of interested parties found no difficulty in undermining the case put forward by the police and by the press who took their line, but real evidence of murder remained elusive for many years. The evidence winkled out over the years since the tragedy in a succession of investigations has now reversed things. It is now hard to see Marilyn Monroe's death as a suicide. More and more evidence points to murder.

The inquiries conducted by the Los Angeles Police Department for instance, alerted some critics from the outset that there was something not quite right. They felt they did not have to be closely observant to notice gaps in the so-called investigation. Sergeant Byron encountered clues all over the place which he did not appear to see. Clemmons, there to make but a superficial appraisal of the situation, seemed to see a great deal more than his colleague, whose job it was to make a detailed investigation. Byron listened to Mrs Murray contradict what she had said to Sergeant Clemmons, yet there is no record of him taking her to task for it. Why did Byron not delve into the obvious irregularity of the body having been discovered at least four hours before the police were notified? Was Byron less observant than Clemmons? Was he not aware that there was no drinking glass in the bedroom, the bathroom adjacent to which had no running water at all because it was having alterations made to it? Did Byron not question the sudden appearance of a receptacle for the police photographs? Did he investigate why Mrs Murray was engaged in doing washing in the middle of the night with her employer lying dead? The officer was certainly aware that Mrs Murray was not co-operating with him as she ought to have been, for his report notes:

> It is this officer's opinion that Mrs Murray was vague and possibly evasive in answering questions pertaining to the activities of Miss Monroe during this time. It is not known whether this is or is not intentional. During the interrogation of Joe DiMaggio Jr,* he indicated he had made three phone calls to the Monroe home, only one of which Mrs Murray mentioned.

---

* Joe DiMaggio Jr, son of Marilyn Monroe's ex-husband by a previous marriage, kept in touch with her.

The housekeeper kept repeating that she saw a light from beneath Marilyn's bedroom door, yet a cursory look at the newly laid, high-pile carpet would have told Byron that when the door was closed it was impossible to see light beneath it. Had he pressed her he may have obtained the information she gave to a BBC interviewer for a programme made in 1985. She then admitted she had been lying. She saw no light beneath the locked door. The door was standing ajar. There was, therefore, no need to break a window for entry. Had that been done to support her first story, or was there more to tell about the window? In turn this would have generated other questions like, who put her up to telling the lies she had told? When did she really find out Marilyn was dead? How long was Dr Greenson really there? This author tried on two occasions to interview the now-retired Detective Sergeant Byron, who complains he really cannot remember a thing about the investigation, and gives the impression he hardly even remembers the name Monroe. His amnesia must be of a rare variety, since, in his entire career, he was not likely to be assigned to another case involving a celebrity of the standing of Marilyn Monroe. But there is possibly a reason for his silence.

Dr Greenson was interviewed by Deputy District Attorney John Miner on the Wednesday following the death of Marilyn Monroe. The outcome of a lengthy, off-the-record discussion which Miner agreed should not be made public because it would violate doctor-patient confidentiality, was that Greenson had changed his mind about the cause of death, even at that early stage. He now believed Miss Monroe had been murdered.* But if Mrs Murray 'came clean' with the BBC, Dr Greenson played a bigger part in what happened at the house that night than he ever admitted. If the door was ajar Dr Greenson would have no need to knock on it to try to rouse Marilyn as he said he did. He would not have found it necessary to go outside and look in the bedroom window as he said he did. And he would not have found it necessary to break a pane of glass to gain entry through the window as he said he did. If Mrs Murray was finally telling the truth—and what she said made sense and cleared up a few things—then Dr Greenson

---

* Greenson was interviewed by Anthony Summers for *Goddess: The Secret Lives of Marilyn Monroe*, Gollancz, London, 1985, and Robert F. Slatzer for *The Marilyn Files*, SPI Books, New York, 1992. John Miner was interviewed by this author

was in cahoots with her, the window was broken for another reason or by someone else, and the Doctor knew more than he admitted. It also raises the question of whether Dr Engelberg was part of a deception.

Another very important piece of evidence which has surfaced is that an ambulance was called to Marilyn Monroe's house at about 1.00 am that Sunday morning. Walter Schaefer, who ran the ambulance service involved, for years denied he had supplied a vehicle to the Monroe residence.* He now admits it,† names the driver and his associate in attendance, and confirms that Miss Monroe was taken to Santa Monica Hospital 'suffering from an overdose'. Said to have been accompanied by Peter Lawford, by all accounts she was dead on arrival. But what would explain the decision to return the body to her home for 'discovery' later on? Peter Lawford could have explained a great deal about the mystery of what happened that night but he would not even admit to being at her house. Deborah Gould, Lawford's third wife, much later confirmed, 'He went there and tidied up the place, and did what he could, before the police and the press arrived.' It appears he went there with Fred Otash, a Hollywood private detective, and they went through the place, removing anything which would link Marilyn to Robert Kennedy. Deborah Gould also spoke of a note which Peter Lawford found which he destroyed. These, of course, were criminal actions, but Lawford was not interviewed by the police until 1975, 13 years after Marilyn's death.

Peter Lawford was the link between Robert Kennedy and Marilyn Monroe. The Attorney General was frequently entertained by his brother-in-law at his impressive beach house and there is no doubt that Kennedy conducted his liaison with Marilyn by means of the Lawford connection. When RFK became infatuated with the actress he relied upon Lawford to provide the occasions for his clandestine meetings with her right up until the time he decided to call a halt to it all. It was clear that Marilyn received some kind of 'end-to-it-all' communication—perhaps the stuffed toy tiger—from RFK‡, and was

* Neighbours saw an ambulance at Marilyn's door
† Schaefer was interviewed by Robert F. Slatzer for *The Marilyn Files*, SPI Books, New York, 1992
‡ Perhaps a note, which may have been the one Peter Lawford destroyed

furious about being dumped. She tried every way she knew to contact him and failed. According to Deborah Gould, she phoned Lawford complaining she couldn't take any more and that it would be best for everybody if she died, and she was going to kill herself. 'Nonsense, Marilyn, pull yourself together but . . . whatever you do don't leave any notes behind,' had been Lawford's response, according to Gould. Robert Kennedy's movements that weekend in relation to Lawford's actions and various remarks have given rise to serious allegations and further confusion over the matter.

When Robert Kennedy arrived in San Francisco with Ethel and the children they were due to go on to their friends, the Bates' ranch, 60 miles south of the city, where they had accepted an invitation to stay. According to Bates, Kennedy was with him all day until 10.00 pm, and since he attended 9.30 am mass next morning, the implication was that there was no way he could have been in Los Angeles that Saturday. On the other hand there was overwhelming eye-witness testimony to the fact that Kennedy was in Los Angeles, and that he called at Marilyn Monroe's house that evening, flying back to San Francisco in the small hours of Sunday morning. Even Mrs Murray, in her 1985 testimony, says he did, though she said the visit took place in the afternoon. Other eye-witnesses say he called at about 7.45 pm, and this author prefers their testimony to that of the unreliable Mrs Murray. To some people that clinched it: Robert Kennedy was involved in the murder of Marilyn Monroe. Perhaps he even murdered her himself. Such people were entirely wrong, but before the events of the Saturday evening and night may be understood, a totally new dimension must be added to what has been told. This dimension extends into the 'other world' of surveillance, bugs and sound recordings.

In his book, *The Marilyn Conspiracy*, Milo Speriglio says of Marilyn's house:

> Everything that took place within the confines of her walls was tapped, taped, bugged and recorded. Every word she or anyone with her uttered would find itself transposed on to tapes. They even listened in her

bathroom. Some of the most advanced bugging apparatus of its time—such as the voice-activated recorder–was operating in her home.*

Those behind the operation were not interested in Marilyn for herself. They were interested in Robert Kennedy. Who were they? There were three quite separate and distinct groups at work. First there was the Mafia who, in the person of Jimmy Hoffa, had the place bugged by one of the greatest experts in the field of electronic surveillance, Bernard Spindel. Hoffa had but one motive for his surveillance of the Attorney General: blackmail. The FBI were another group who listened in, and no doubt transcripts from their recordings found their way into Director Hoover's secret files, and finally, the CIA, whose interest appears to have been inspired by the security risk they considered Robert Kennedy constituted, also had the house bugged. If Speriglio's statement did not make it clear, the tapping operation referred to Marilyn's telephones. There is reason to believe that Peter Lawford's telephone was tapped, also. So all the interested parties monitored the philanderings of the Attorney General who, incredibly, allowed himself to become a pawn in their game. Since it is also known that Sam Giancana had a bug planted in Robert Kennedy's Washington office, and that Robert Kennedy acquired–it is not clear when–an anti-bug device he carried in a brief-case, the situation had assumed ludicrous proportions. And it is not unlikely that each group knew what the others were doing and they all knew about Kennedy's anti-bug device.

When it is said that the house was tapped, bugged and taped, it should not be thought that those listening were bound to know exactly what was happening and exactly what was being said. Bugs, in those days, for instance, were notorious for transmitting poor-quality sound, complete with 'buzz' and 'mush'. Recordings made from such transmissions often, therefore, require interpretation before they are of any value and, as must be obvious, such interpretation is open to bias on the part of the interpreter. Additionally, tape recording is vulnerable to all manner of tampering which, for instance, makes tapes unpopular in courtrooms. In the hands of an expert, a tape can be made to say just about anything desired and the manipulation can

* Milo Speriglio, *The Marilyn Conspiracy*, Corgi, London, 1986

be extremely difficult, in fact, almost impossible, to detect. Another problem is that, in the normal way, a tape does not register any evidence of the time a recording is made on it, nor, for that matter, any evidence of the place in which the recording is made. For all of these reasons, while a tape recording made from a concealed transmitting device may be an efficient means of collecting information, its value as a means of extortion has limits. The implication of this is that recordings made from bugs placed in Marilyn Monroe's home would be more useful to the CIA and the FBI, for their dubious purposes, rather than Jimmy Hoffa and the Mafia for blackmail.

A number of people claim to have heard snippits from the Bernard Spindel tapes. This, by itself, does not mean a great deal, for none of them is able to guarantee the authenticity of what they listened to. The purpose in allowing certain individuals to hear extracts from the tapes was no doubt to have them vouch for what they heard, but how could they? They could only say what they *apparently* heard and what they were *told* they were hearing. From the few extracts of the tapes' contents which have been published, the following will serve to demonstrate the problems which arise. A printed extract appears in Milo Speriglio's book, *Marilyn Monroe, Murder Cover Up*,* where a man who claimed he listened to one of the tapes is quoted:

> 'What do we do with her body now?'–words to that effect. I remembers there was some concern over where to put her body or something like that. It is all on the tape.

Words to what effect? Were these the words used or is this an interpretation–subject to bias–of what was on the tape on somebody's part? If the exact words were audible why did they require summation? In the same author's book, *The Marilyn Conspiracy*,† presumably the same informant is quoted rendering the same extract, which has become:

> What are we going to do with her *dead* body?

This gives rise to many questions. Assuming it was the same informant, was he asked to quote the tape extract on two separate

* Milo Speriglio, *Marilyn Monroe, Murder Cover Up*, Seville Publishing Co., Van Nuys, California, 1982, p.123
† Milo Speriglio, *The Marilyn Conspiracy*, Corgi, London, 1986, p.66. Emphasis added

occasions? Allowing this to be the case, who added the word 'dead'? Was it the informant? Or was it the person to whom he rendered the quotation? Clearly the impression, inevitably, is that the first rendering was not sufficiently explicit and the word 'dead' has been added for emphasis. In his first book, Speriglio quotes further from his informant:

> You could actually hear her being slapped, even hear her body fall to the floor. You could hear it hit the deck, and all the sounds that took place in her house that night . . .

But how was this possible? Author Robert Slatzer, in his book, *The Marilyn Files*,* states that he was in her house only a few days after her death and confirmed what was visible in police photographs. The pile on the new carpet Marilyn had had fitted only a few weeks beforehand

> . . . was so deep, the legs of Marilyn's bed disappear into the nap; the mattress appears to be lying on the floor.

How, then, was the sound of a body falling into this deep pile ever going to register on tape via a bug? In an even more questionable example, the tapes are said to contain the sounds of thumping and:

> . . . of something being lowered on to a bed.

The reader is invited to conduct a small experiment of his/her own, attempting such a recording and then asking a friend to listen to it and describe what is happening.

This author finds no difficulty in believing that Spindel bugged Marilyn's house and that tape recordings were made of the sounds therefrom. And though they were confiscated in a raid on Spindel's premises by the Los Angeles Police Department in 1964 and destroyed by them, the continued existence of the recordings by means of copies is not doubted. Professional sound recordists normally make duplicate copies of their tapes soon after making them for security purposes, to insure against accidental erasure, fire or

---

* Robert F. Slatzer, *The Marilyn Files*, SPI Books, New York, 1992, p. 126

theft.* There is little doubt that Spindel carried out such a procedure. In any case he probably despatched a copy to Jimmy Hoffa with all haste. The LAPD was wasting its time raiding Bernard Spindel's premises. This author's problem is not in believing the tapes exist; it is in believing what the tapes are purported to contain.

A final consideration of the Spindel tapes must involve the question, why did the mob not use them? A case against Sam Giancana was dismissed on a technicality, and this has been quoted as a sign that Robert Kennedy was blackmailed. But this was hardly the outcome which might have been expected from such 'weighty' evidence. Robert Kennedy kept up the pressure on the Mafia until he left office in 1964, suggesting Hoffa did not use the tapes for blackmail. Or perhaps—and more likely—it indicated that Hoffa *could not* use them for blackmail. The fuzzy, indeterminate noises which they were likely to contain, though useful, as we shall see, in indicating what was happening were more than likely to be no use whatever for extortion.

What really happened to Marilyn Monroe, and how did Robert Kennedy come into it? The Attorney General was involved in an illicit and ill-advised liaison with the star. Over a period he saw her from time to time and the FBI, the CIA, Jimmy Hoffa and, probably, his wife knew all about it. It was likely that Ethel put her foot down and demanded he put an end to the relationship. It has been suggested that Ethel threatened to divorce him, and he had no option but to comply, for divorce would certainly have ruined him politically, would have led to the downfall of his brother John, and finished up bringing shame and dishonour on the whole family. But Marilyn was not going to be shaken off easily. She had her own ideas about a future with the Attorney General and as part of one of America's wealthiest and most influential families. It would have represented to her something akin to marrying into royalty. Marilyn dug in her heels and refused to accept Robert's 'sorry but it's over'. This crisis scenario was likely to transmit alarm signals to the CIA and FBI, listening in to

* This author has personal experience of such security arrangements pertaining to recordings difficult or expensive to replace

developments at her home. It would also be of very special interest to Jimmy Hoffa, monitoring the affair through Spindel's tapes.

The Executive Group, speculation of whose existence was developed in Chapter Three, would have a greater interest than any of the other interested parties. They would probably have been kept informed of developments by both the CIA members and those who represented the Mafia who, after consultations with the Consortium, had been invited to participate in the work in hand. For them it was time to act: it was now or never. The idea of exposing Kennedy through the press was probably the first hard proposal put forward and, after much discussion, abandoned, for the same reason as Jimmy Hoffa had abandoned it. There were two prime reasons for this. First, the tape 'evidence' was not copper-bottomed, and it was not likely to 'stand up' by itself. Secondly, the enormous influence of the White House combined with the clout carried by the Kennedy family would more than likely persuade the media not to run with the stories. They would be buried, as they had been before when reporters had come up with such stories. The situation called for a crisis decision. The worrying part came when they discovered that Marilyn Monroe was threatening to go to the press. If the high-powered Executive Group felt they could not handle it, and Jimmy Hoffa felt unequal to it, what chance did Marilyn have in making it to the nation's front pages? The problem was that if she tried and failed, any value which might lie in Bernard Spindel's tapes would go completely down the tubes. Hoffa would be back to square one, and the Executive Group would have lost its chance. But, then, to the Group's way of thinking, all was not lost.

Robert Kennedy was due to arrive at San Francisco on Friday and it was likely that he would seek the opportunity to see Marilyn to put a final word to their relationship. And with Marilyn threatening to go public and Robert, desperate to ditch her—since Ethel was on his back—what if Marilyn was murdered at this critical point? There was no way the press would bury a story in which Robert Kennedy was in some way involved in *murder*. The consequences would certainly lead to impeachment for the President when *his* liaison with Marilyn was exposed—and it would be—and Robert would be lucky to stay out of jail. Here was a plan which accommodated all of the Group's needs.

Not only did such a plan provide for the needs of the Executive Group but it more than satisfied the desires of the Mafia in general and Jimmy Hoffa in particular. It requires no stretch of the imagination to believe that the mob volunteered to provide all that was necessary to carry out the plan, but they would have to act quickly. All attention was concentrated on the Monroe house, though by all accounts a tap had also been placed on Peter Lawford's phone, and little could transpire without them knowing. There is no doubt the listeners felt crisis in the wind when they heard Marilyn Monroe being kept awake on Friday night until 5.30 in the morning by an anonymous caller telling her to 'Leave Bobby alone . . .' and calling her a tramp. Was this Ethel Kennedy?

Marilyn clearly expected to meet Robert Kennedy at the Lawford place on Saturday night, but this arrangement was probably made before Robert made his decision to wind the affair up, for it was cancelled. Marilyn was rather more than piqued: she was angry. She had tried to reach RFK several times by telephone in Washington before he set out for California without success, and she had had no more luck in contacting him at the hotel where he usually stayed in San Francisco. Her many calls had attracted no reply. It was at this point that she threatened to call a press conference on the coming Monday at which she would expose her relationship with the Attorney General and, no doubt hearing of it via Peter Lawford, it seems it was this which persuaded Kennedy to pay her a visit. He arrived at her house at dusk, at about 7.45 pm, and was, apparently, just as furious with Marilyn as she was with him. Meanwhile the power-factions of the Mafia, the CIA and the FBI hovered like vultures listening to what was taking place. Kennedy was livid that Marilyn would not hand over her red diary in which she had made notes about what he had told her on previous occasions when they had met. RFK knew of its existence and was reluctant to leave it in her possession now that he was terminating the affair. It is believed he offered her compensation, and no doubt would have been generous, but to no avail. Marilyn had well and truly hidden it and was defiant. He left without it: it would be someone else's job to negotiate its purchase. It is likely that Robert Kennedy went back to Peter Lawford's beach house for a while to relax and discuss the situation before flying back to San Francisco. Marilyn spent her time making and receiving telephone calls.

By all indications Marilyn's murderers arrived shortly after 10.30 pm, when she was last known to speak on the telephone. Their means of entry was probably through her bedroom window, which was later found to have been broken. She may even have known at least one of their number, for she knew a number of mobsters, some quite well, including Sam Giancana and Johnny Rosselli. But whoever they were, this was no friendly call. Judging by bruises which were left on Marilyn's body, she was manhandled, and probably quickly rendered unconscious. This may not have taken much doing, since calls she made after RFK had left indicated she was already drowsy and speaking in a slurred voice. One of the calls had been to Peter Lawford, when she talked of taking her life. Lawford did not respond to this cry for attention, for, no doubt, this is what it was. Although he had seen Marilyn rushed to hospital with an overdose before, in the light of what he had seen earlier at her house with RFK, it seems he judged the call a ploy and decided this time it was not genuine. Indeed, as he would recollect, all the indications in Marilyn's activities and demeanour prior to this time revealed no trace of an intention to take her own life.

Mrs Murray was likely in her own room at this time. Perhaps her very first statement was true and she had retired at 10.00 pm. It seems she either heard nothing or was terrified out of her wits, and stayed where she was. One of the men appeared to have a medical background, for all the evidence points to him having produced the equipment to administer by enema the lethal cocktail of barbiturates and chloral hydrate which killed her. It proved the only way the large volume of drugs—enough to kill several people—could have entered her body. They would lose no time in leaving. Marilyn was then sleeping what remained of her life away.

It is extremely unlikely that Mrs Murray would have survived if she had known what was happening. Exactly when she became aware that Marilyn was desperately ill is not certain, but it would seem she first rang Peter Lawford. He probably thought at first that he had been wrong and that Marilyn *had* taken an overdose. The indications and time scale would suggest that Robert Kennedy was still at Lawford's home when he heard something was wrong* and, fearing the Attorney General would become involved in Marilyn's suicide bid, had him bundled off to San Francisco without delay, while he went off to Marilyn's rescue. Mrs Murray also called Dr Greenson.

Peter Lawford's first act was to call an ambulance which, as it happened, was in the vicinity and was directed to the house quickly by radio. By now it was after 1.00 am and though Marilyn was promptly rushed off to Santa Monica Hospital, she never regained consciousness. She was probably dead by the time they reached the hospital or died soon after arrival and Peter Lawford was faced with the nightmare scenario which the Executive Group had planned. It was probably the tell-tale bruises on Marilyn's body which made him suspect foul play, and he knew that if he left her at the hospital everything would come to light concerning the Attorney General, his affair with Marilyn and his wish to end it, his visit to her house that night and their blazing row, and it was on the cards he would be suspected of being involved in her murder. At this point the Group had achieved all they had set out to achieve.

It was the fast-thinking Lawford who changed the course of history, though it is doubtful he had the slightest hint of what he was getting into. He did what was probably the only thing he could think of doing at that moment. He ordered the body to be returned to Marilyn's home, so that he would have more time to think and have a semblance of control over events. Greenson was, no doubt, bewildered at Lawford's instructions, since Marilyn's condition had displayed all the symptoms of a straightforward drugs overdose and they had been too late. He was unlikely at that moment to know anything more than this, but it is hard to believe that Lawford did not enlighten the doctor as to his fears on the return journey. In the meantime, a vigilant FBI listener to all that had been happening at the house would seem to have made contact with a high-ranking police officer who quickly grasped the implications of the events and took control over what was to become a massive cover-up exercise, not to protect the guilty parties, but to protect the innocent Robert Kennedy, and through him, the President. This would explain the

---

* It is claimed that on the Spindel tapes the Attorney General, presumably telephoning from San Francisco after his return and anxious about Marilyn, was heard to ask 'Is she dead?' There have been attempts to interpret this in an incriminating light.

presence of the police car, seen by the neighbours, which accompanied the ambulance.

Before the police were officially called—at 4.25 am—Mrs Murray had no doubt been made aware of what was happening. The body had been stripped of nightclothes, which had been soiled during the administration of the enema and these, with the soiled bedlinen, were taken away to be washed. When Sergeant Clemmons arrived shortly after 4.30 am he was surprised that the washer and drier were in operation. That should also have alerted Sergeant Byron, but then, Byron had probably been briefed by a senior police officer before he arrived. The same senior police officer would probably have contacted Santa Monica Hospital to tell them to forget that Marilyn Monroe had ever been brought to them. It was many years before Walter Schaefer, the owner of the ambulance company, would admit to having answered the call to Marilyn's home. One of the two men said to have been in attendance, Murray Leibowitz, who still denied he was there, was reported by someone who knew him to have come into a large sum of money.* Conveniently, Mrs Murray and Pat Newcomb had the means to take overseas holidays away from enquirers. Pat Newcomb still refuses to talk. Mrs Murray, though purporting to 'come clean' in 1985, changed her story so many times it is hard to know when she was telling the truth. John Miner, the ex-Deputy District Attorney, told this author he believed Mrs Murray had not told all she knew.

John Miner who was, it will be recalled, present at the autopsy, also talked to this author of noting the discolouration of the colon. Had a full autopsy been carried out, there would have been no doubt from the beginning that Marilyn Monroe was murdered. Miner told me he later consulted surgeons well qualified to render an opinion on what he described to them and they confirmed that, had the autopsy extended that far, the intestine was likely to have been found to contain the drugs. The implication of this is that the lethal dose had been administered by way of an enema. The answer to the puzzle was there to be found all the time.

---

* Leibowitz is reported as saying, 'After her funeral, I came into a very large sum of what you would call hush money, and I bought these [six] car washes. I own them. And the only reason that I'm still working at Schaefer's is to keep up appearances.'

The expert cover-up provided by the Los Angeles Police Department clearly defeated the objectives of the Executive Group. With the co-operation of the FBI they quickly salted away the telephone records relating to Marilyn Monroe's calls so that the times she called—and attempted to call—Robert Kennedy remained a secret for many years. They went through the motions of an investigation into her death and, generously, brought in a verdict of 'Probable Suicide', which effectively means death by accident, which allowed her studio, Twentieth Century Fox, to draw on a million-dollar insurance they held on her. And the mystery surrounding Marilyn's death was allowed to ferment. When the news broke, the Executive Group would no doubt be livid that their plans had been thwarted. They would now have to find some other way to get rid of John F. Kennedy and his brother.

CHAPTER FIVE

Other, More Desperate Means

'. . . a small oligarchy of landowners, bankers, speculators, merchants, artisans, adventurers, and tattermalions, avid for pleasure, excitement and sudden gain, proud, turbulent, corrupted by life in the city, and placing their own interests ahead of even the most salutary reform . . .'

Guglielmo Ferrero, writing of Rome

THE NEWS WHICH circulated on Sunday, 5 August 1962, concerning Marilyn Monroe must have been very disturbing to the members of the Executive Group. It was all about suicide, pills and what people were saying. But there was no mention of Robert Kennedy. By Monday the newspapers had the story and all the leading dailies were scoured for the expected bombshell but, again, mention of Robert F. Kennedy was conspicuous by its absence. Not a word about the Attorney General's affair with the star, let alone suspicion that he was mixed up in her murder. But there was no talk of murder, either. How could that be? The police were still talking of apparent suicide. Perhaps it would take a little longer to come out, but at the end of the day, the police could not fail to recognise a murder, could they?

The members of the Executive Group were frustrated and puzzled. From their viewpoint everything had gone exceedingly well and this setback was something they had not expected. When anxiety was expressed by the Consortium, they could only explain that nothing had gone wrong. They had skilfully baited the trap by murdering Marilyn and it should only be a question of time before the police got round to exposing Robert Kennedy's affair with the murdered woman and, subsequently, complicity in the crime. They might even decide he had killed her, but the scandal of involvement – in any way – would be sufficient to draw attention to John F. Kennedy and his liaison with Marilyn and that would be the end of the Kennedys. John would be impeached and Robert would be completely discredited, even if a charge did not stick. When the verdict of 'Probable Suicide' was announced it was totally inexplicable to the Executive Group.

By the end of 1962 the Consortium was frustrated beyond measure with President John F. Kennedy and his administration, and its members were more dedicated than ever to getting rid of him. If the events of the spring had not been enough, the President's summer madness combined with the disasters of the fall of that year left no semblance of doubt that the country was in the hands of a dangerous incompetent who did not understand the first thing about American enterprise and the pride every American took in standing on his own feet. It had been in the September of 1961 that, as an anti-inflationary measure, Kennedy had written to the leaders of the steel industry pointing out that profit expectations were such that price increases were not warranted. On 6 April 1962 it had been the turn of the Steelworkers Union to be approached by the Federal Government, which asked them to limit wage demands to a modest 10c-an-hour increase for the period to begin 1 July. They agreed, but hardly had the agreement been reached when, on 10 April, the greedy steelmen hiked the price of steel by six dollars per ton. The President was embarrassed, the Union inflamed and the consumers flabbergasted. The day after the increase was announced the President, in his press conference, lambasted the steel industry leaders in a way which opened mouths and caused jaws to sag.

> . . . the American people will find it hard, as I do, to accept a situation in which a tiny handful of steel executives whose pursuit of private power and profit exceeds their sense of public responsibility can show such utter contempt for the interests of 185 million Americans.

The President had the measure of the Titans and his denunciation was quoted in newspapers across the world. There followed an exchange in which the leaders of the steel industry tried to justify their increase, but public opinion had been mobilised and precious government contracts were in jeopardy. They climbed down and restored the price to what it had been. The ferocity of the President's attack sent tremors through the corridors of business power in the United States. Was this shades of a price and wages control policy?

On 28 May Wall Street suffered its worst day since the 1929 crash. Steel fell to 50 per cent of its 1960 level. Though it was only a massive 'blip' and the stockmarket was to recover well, it presented a nasty shock and the unions began to show their nerves. Kennedy held his ground and lectured the nation on being behind the times, clinging to a 'thirties' mentality and the business community drew little comfort from the attitude he revealed. He was out in the open with his vision of a welfare-state America which provided for the poor, the disadvantaged, the sick and the elderly. The businessmen had no illusions about where the money would come from for such benevolence. This was socialist talk and, as one leading businessman wrote, 'Socialism [is] often a forerunner of communism.' And all this was fuel to the fire for the members of the Consortium. As James Hepburn observed in his book, *Farewell America*:

> Big business grew more and more concerned about the tendencies of the Kennedy administration, and industrialists aren't the type of people to sit around and chew their fingernails.*

The oil men were particularly tetchy. It would only be a matter of time before Kennedy put the axe to their favoured tax position and then the good times would be gone forever. Reports that some of the Texas oil men were especially inflamed by the attention the President was giving to the tax benefits—the depletion allowances—which had been enshrined in the country's tax law for a generation, came as no surprise. They saw interfering moves on the part of the President as 'criminal offenses' against 'the American system'.†

John F. Kennedy was hacking at the roots of the American way of life as it was seen by those Consortium members who hailed from the business community. They saw lights flashing and heard alarm bells ringing. Never had they felt so justified in belonging to a Consortium dedicated to the downfall of this misguided man who was setting

---

* James Hepburn, *Farewell America*, Frontiers Publishing, Liechtenstein, 1968
† Attributed to Dallas oil billionaire, H. L. Hunt

course for the country's ruin. If the Group had failed with their Marilyn Monroe scheme, another way must be found. As they saw it, the mere idea of this man being allowed a second term in office–and it was clear that he was gathering the people behind him–was unthinkable. It represented more than folly, it represented sheer disaster for all Americans in their right minds.

With these sentiments the CIA members of the Consortium could not agree more. Everything they observed persuaded them that the Kennedys had opened the door to notions which had no place in this country. Since the time of the Bay of Pigs invasion the President had run a foreign policy, not only in respect of Cuba but many other countries besides, which cut across the policies established by the Agency. Had he not the sense to leave the experts in control of looking after America's best interests? He had dismissed Dulles, the CIA's Director, along with others over the Bay of Pigs débâcle where, in fact, it was his and his brother's fault the invasion had so miserably failed with such huge cost in human life, not to mention the humiliation attracted to the United States in general and the CIA in particular. After the CIA had worked so successfully for the country's welfare for 15 years, Kennedy had tried his hand at establishing his control over the Agency through the Special Group 54/12.* Happily, like his predecessor, he had failed.

Reports reaching the Consortium from Mafia contacts made it clear that they were just as frustrated as the Executive Group that the Marilyn Monroe plan had not succeeded and they wanted it to be known that they would be happy to continue the relationship, lending their assistance to any plan the Group came up with which would achieve mutual objectives. The organised-crime contacts complained they had had, perhaps, the roughest time of all from the Kennedys during the year. The war being waged by Robert Kennedy was having a 'knock-on' effect, and law enforcement officers across the country were being inspired to try their hands at prosecutions which, at one time, they would not have even considered. Kennedy had even coerced J. Edgar Hoover into joining the fray and they had not had anything to fear from Hoover for a very long time. Things

* Special Group 54/12 had been set up in Eisenhower's time for the purpose of establishing greater control over the CIA. The CIA managed to dodge the group's control

were changing rapidly and the contacts wanted to make it clear the Executive Group had the full support of the Mafia if it meant getting rid of the Kennedys. It was a matter of the greatest urgency for them. Their sincerity could be measured by the fact that no one had greater need than the Mafia for the government to be rid of the brothers.

It was this last point which rankled with the Consortium. They really did not like working with the Mob, but circumstances had dictated they could not be stand-offish when it had come to needing Marilyn Monroe disposed of and they realised there could be other tasks yet to be carried out to which they were particularly suited. There might be distinct advantages attached to having the expertise of mobsters available to them, so they bit their tongues and made appropriate responses.

As far as the military members of the Consortium were concerned it was they who were suffering most. Over the past year things had gone from bad to worse as far as the Pentagon was concerned. President Kennedy had frozen funds for the Nike-Zeus anti-missile programme and the B-70 bomber, both of which the Pentagon wanted. When Republic Aviation announced the future of their Long Island plant was endangered, Kennedy made $1.3 billion available instead of the $10 billion which had been requested. Had it not been that some 20,000 jobs were at stake they might have got nothing. Robert McNamara, Kennedy's new Defence Secretary, was wreaking havoc from his office at the Pentagon. There was a bloody war being raged in its corridors. *He had no respect for the superior knowledge of the country's top military men, and it was demeaning to be answerable to such a man.*

Those saner members of Pentagon top brass who had been attempting to warn the nation of the President's folly had even had their wings clipped by an order restricting their public expression of political opinions. It was outrageous. General White, who was Chairman of the Air Force Chiefs of Staff, had spoken for a lot of them when he said:

I am profoundly apprehensive of the pipe-smoking, tree-full-of-owls type of so-called professional defence intellectuals who have been brought into this nation's capital. I don't believe a lot of these over-confident, sometimes arrogant young professors, mathematicians and other theorists have sufficient worldliness or motivation to stand up to the kind of enemy we face.

And you had to hand it to Walker – General Edwin Walker – with his blood and thunder speech,

> We must throw out the traitors, and if that is not possible, we must organise armed resistance to defeat the designs of the usurpers and contribute to the return of a constitutional government.

In October the Russians exploded a 50-megaton test bomb. Is there nobody at the White House that understands what is happening? The President doesn't seem to understand the mind of the communist at all. His high-minded principles would never win a war, that's for sure. If you ever wanted an example of muddle-headed reasoning just look at how he handled the Missiles Crisis. Did you ever see such a mess? It was more by good luck than good management we came out of it as we did. And it wasn't for the lack of sound advice, either. There were those of us who advised him to send the bombers and blast those missiles out of Cuba. What a chance we lost to show the Russians who was boss.

The only change in the attitude of the military Consortium members was that they wanted action now, without any further delay, to deal with Kennedy. They saw it as a matter of the highest national priority.

To the Executive Group the Marilyn Monroe plan had been particularly attractive, for apart from a certain subtlety and a distinct touch of irony, it had the outstanding feature of never being traceable to its perpetrators. Now the Consortium were pressing for another action, one which, this time, would not fail. Meeting after meeting had brought them into 1963 and an additional sense of urgency was generated by the knowledge that Kennedy would soon begin campaigning for the 1964 election, for he always worked well ahead of everyone else. The Executive Group was told that this time no finesse would be necessary. If there was no other way, plans should be made to kill Kennedy. Some Consortium members, at first, shrank from this alternative. Some had wanted out but realised there really was no way to resign from such a fraternity. The killing of Marilyn Monroe had not rested comfortably with these members but they had accepted it as a necessity. But to kill the President. That was something else. To resolve the problem they were reminded that the true patriotism expressed in the Consortium was their safeguard; that the taking of life in this context should not be thought of as murder but rather judicial execution. 'Think of it as war,' they had been enjoined. And they did.

The Executive Group now met with an agenda of only one item: how to execute the President of the United States, and this time they had invited a Mafia representative to be present at their meeting. A general consideration of the various aspects of their task soon raised the additional question of how to achieve their objective without being identified as the perpetrators and that depended, they realised, on *how* the President was to be 'disposed of'. However it was done it was going to cost money, big money, but that was no problem. Money was available in abundance.

In such a discussion it is logical to suppose that the first thoughts to exercise the imagination would involve ideas for some sort of an 'accident' to befall the President, and a whole procession of such notions tumbled out from Executive Group members. The main problem with these proposals was that they always left too much room for failure; too much chance for another accident to occur which caused the arranged 'accident' to misfire. For much the same reason a suggestion for the planting of a bomb was quickly disposed of.

It was soon apparent that the cleanest, easiest and surest way of killing John F. Kennedy would be by shooting him. It carried the bonus that they would know at once that they had been successful. The rest of the meeting dealt with *where* rather than *how*, and, allowing that it would take some months to set up a meticulous plan, it was details of the President's engagements in the fall which occupied the attentions of the members of the Executive Group.

Logic told them they would profit enormously by specifying a city and state in which the President was least popular and least respected. Here there would be less of a sense of outrage and the drive to investigate would be tempered with lack of zeal. With this as a stated objective the attention of the Group was soon focused on reports that the President was to put a tour of Texas in his diary for the fall. This was agreed by all to be their best choice of location, but since the cities to be visited had not been announced, they now proceeded with those aspects of the plan which would apply whichever city they chose.

From the time it had been decided that a shooting should be arranged, certain Executive Group members had seen a prospect for building into the plan more than merely the avoidance of detection. If the blame for the killing could be placed on Castro there would be no detailed investigation into the crime at all, for it would be regarded as a political assassination. For some members of the Consortium it would be a huge plus to the plan if the consequence of their actions was a war with Cuba. The Mafia representative said he could arrange for a team of marksmen when it was known how many they would need, provided the Executive Group found the cash to pay the substantial bill for services rendered. He pointed out, however, that for such an operation there was no possibility he could enlist the most expert shooters unless there was, built into the plan, a means by which they could escape. It would be necessary to set someone up as a patsy so that attention was focused elsewhere if the plan was to work. It was the CIA representative who agreed to find the patsy.

When the itinerary for the President's Texas tour was made known, the Executive Group quickly decided that the operation should be carried out in Dallas. The city's pride in its gleaming new Trade Mart was such that it was not difficult to guess in advance where the reception would be held, and, therefore, what the route would be assuming the President would travel in motorcade. Thus advance plans were laid subject to any changes that became necessary. It was the Group's military member who produced a street map and identified the most likely place for the shooting. An ambush was planned in strict military fashion in the Dealey Plaza.*

At this point it was considered circumspect for the members of the Executive Group to totally disengage from the planning. A completely reliable man had been found to act as Operations Chief and a very large sum of money had been placed at his disposal. It now befell the Operations Chief to liaise with the leader of the team of marksmen and the CIA agent responsible for the patsy. Though the Operations Chief would be in overall control, it was agreed that the plan should

---

* Remarkably, the official route was changed to include Elm Street, which was not in the original planning

be carried out in two completely separate strands of activity: one leading to Elm Street and the ambush, and the other involving the running of the patsy, a young CIA agent with exactly the right background. To run two strands of activity separately added considerably to the security of the overall plan.

Additional security for the Executive Group's plan was to be obtained from 'ghosting' an assassination plot in Chicago and another in Miami. The Chicago plot would be leaked prior to the President's visit to that city on 2 November. A group of four men would be found to have high-powered rifles and ammunition in their possession.*

Details of a Miami 'plot' would be provided by right-wing extremist Joseph Milteer shortly before the President's trip to Miami on 18 November.† These ghost plots would hopefully cause a degree of confusion and give the impression that plots to kill the President were popping up everywhere. The date set for the President's visit to Dallas was 22 November.

The CIA agent responsible for the patsy had found a young agent who had recently returned from a mission in Russia. He had assumed the cover of being a communist and a defector and continued to develop his leftist background on his return to the United States. In preparation for using him as the patsy a fake mission had been invented for him. On this supposed mission the agent in question believed he was to go to Cuba to establish firmer credentials for himself before going on to Moscow. In all respects except for one feature, it was a completely authentic mission design, in preparation for which the chosen agent would be required first to go to New Orleans to be 'sheepdipped'.‡

This would provide new background for him, establishing him as strongly pro-Castro, ideal for the role he was destined to play in the assassination of the President. The one exception to the complete authenticity of his mission preparations was that when he visited Mexico to obtain a visa with which to enter Cuba, the CIA handler

---

* Only two of the four men were captured. The President's visit was cancelled, the cancellation being made so late that people were already gathering to see him.
† Joseph Milteer was secretly recorded telling of a plot to kill Kennedy. On the day of the President's visit the motorcade was cancelled. He was flown in and out of Miami by helicopter.
‡ 'Sheepdipping' was a term used in the intelligence agencies referring to the acquisition of social or other character needed by an agent to create the desired image.

and his colleagues must make sure he did not succeed. This introduced to his mission design the necessity for him to fly out of Dallas by light aircraft. He would depart the Dealey Plaza for Red Bird Airfield at the point when the President was killed. It dovetailed exactly. The patsy's name? A totally expendable, keen young agent called Lee Harvey Oswald.

CHAPTER SIX

The Hit

*'A shocking crime was committed
on the unscrupulous initiative of a few individuals,
with the blessing of more, and amid the passive
acquiescence of all.'*

Tacitus

JOHN F. KENNEDY only just scraped past the winning post ahead of Richard Nixon in the election of 1960 and he was conscious of the need to improve on this in 1964. The man in office–the sitting tenant–carries both advantages and disadvantages into a bid for a second term. By the time re-election comes around he is totally exposed. His track record goes before him and while the achievement of his first term is known, similarly, his lack of achievement is also known. There is no way he can pull the wool over the electorate's eyes.

It was creditworthy that, though John F. Kennedy was aware of his narrow victory all during his Presidency, he could not be seen running away from unpopular issues, nor could he be seen buttering up those who would be influential in the next election. The Bay of Pigs fiasco had given him a bad start, and this had not inspired confidence. His handling of racial issues including segregation and discrimination had given him a growing popularity among the Negro voters who recognised his sincerity, but this had to be weighed against the votes he lost for his efforts in this direction. In many of the decisions he made he was as likely to offend as to please but, overall, his record in domestic affairs earned him a welcome degree of popularity. In international affairs he had, with the vast majority, scored heavily in his handling of the Missiles Crisis and his negotiation of the nuclear test-ban treaty. It was with confidence that he approached the 1964 election, though he was by no means over-confident. And he was a brilliant electioneer, and there was a great deal he could achieve before election day, particularly in the South.

The state of Texas represented a challenge for JFK at any time, but never so much as in 1963, when rival factions among the Democrats threatened to hand the election to the Republicans. There were 25 electoral seats at stake and Kennedy was unhappy that his Vice-President, Lyndon Johnson, a Texan himself, was making no impression on sorting out the feuding in the Party in his home state. It was for this reason, therefore, that the President decided he and Jackie would tour Texas in the fall, in the company of LBJ, so that he might pour oil on troubled waters and be seen in the company of both Governor John B. Connally Jr and Senator Ralph Yarborough, who represented the warring factions.

The tour began well. Visits to San Antonio and Houston had been great successes, and by the time the Presidential party arrived at Fort Worth's Texas Hotel spirits were high. It was 21 November and the next day, after two speeches in Fort Worth, one outside and one inside the hotel, at breakfast time, JFK would fly to Dallas. As far as politics was concerned, there was no place in the world like Dallas— the 'south-west hate capital of Dixie'. To put it briefly, Dallas was oil and armaments. Dallas lived and breathed oil and armaments. They were the foundation on which the city stood. Big 'D' was a violent place. More murders took place inside its borders per month than in all England. In 1963 the toll before 22 November stood at 110.

To say that Dallas was right wing was quite inadequate to describe its politics. It was at least ultra-right wing. It was John Birch Society and Minuteman territory. To be left wing was to be totally unacceptable: to be communist was anathema, and anything that even smacked of communism was lumped in with their hatred of that creed. This, then, was the President's next stop, the President who had just broken a chink in the Iron Curtain by signing a nuclear test-ban treaty with the communists and who had agreed to the sale of surplus American grain to the Soviet bloc: the President who had sweated out a peaceful solution to the Missiles Crisis to the chagrin of advisers who advocated the use of force, had struck a blow to the hearts of the armaments industry by keeping US forces out of Cuba, and, to boot, was now involved in the withdrawal of US personnel from Vietnam. He was the man in the White House who had declared an intention to re-examine the special tax benefits—the oil depletion allowances—which had made millionaires of the oil barons. He had committed every sin in the Dallas book: a full set. In the 1960 Presidential elections, even before his sinning, of the 73 counties which made up north-east Texas, 72 had seen Kennedy and Nixon scrapping it out, neck and neck. Not so the 73rd. It was Dallas, and Kennedy was totally rejected here. No, the President was not popular in Dallas by any stretch of the imagination.

It was raining on the morning of the 22nd and JFK half expected his outdoor speech would be a flop, for his audience would be made up of people who had stopped off on their way to work. He was surprised and delighted at the huge turn out. Declining a raincoat, he climbed up on to the back of a wagon to address the crowd and the speech went well. The breakfast address to 2,000 in the hotel's Grand Ballroom also went well. His speech, laced with pleasant quips and delivered in his easy manner, beguiled his audience and, altogether, his day had started extremely well. A blight was put upon things by the arrival of the *Dallas Morning News*, however. The Connally–Yarborough feud was featured with the unwelcome headlines, STORM OF POLITICAL CONTROVERSY SWIRLS AROUND KENNEDY ON VISIT, and PRESIDENT'S VISIT SEEN WIDENING STATE DEMOCRATIC SPLIT. Connally and Yarborough were doing nothing to support the President's efforts. To Yarborough, Vice-President Johnson was a Connally man and he refused to sit next to him in the car which would take them to the airport. An exasperated President put his foot down at this and sent an aide to give him no alternative but to take his seat. Ungraciously, Yarbcrough complied.

It wasn't just Yarborough who was causing headaches for the President, either. Connally was up to his tricks, also. In spite of Yarborough having sold over $11,000 worth of tickets for the dinner scheduled that night for Austin, the Governor had seen to it that he was to be demeaned at the event, playing a minor role. At a reception Connally planned for afterwards at the Governor's mansion, Yarborough was not even invited. Kennedy decided it was time the nonsense was stopped and he sent for Connally and proceeded to take him to task. The Governor agreed for the sake of peace and for the occasion to place Senator Yarborough at the top table at the dinner, which pleased the President immensely. He might not have been so pleased if he had known that Connally had planned a two-tier top table, and he had not specified at which tier the Senator would be seated.

Of the 12-man committee lined up to receive the President at Dallas's Love Airfield, nine were Republicans and two were known as Dixiecrats–there was but one liberal in the line-up–and Connally broke protocol and approached them ahead of the President. The formalities over, Jack and Jackie spent a little time with the people who had gathered to welcome them and it was not long before the motorcade set off for the luncheon reception scheduled for 12.30 pm in the brilliant new Trade Mart building. The sun was now shining and the President had declined a protective bubble for the Lincoln. It looked as though people had turned out in large numbers for him.

The Dallas liberal minority had certainly excelled themselves in the number of their members who were lining the streets and the warmth of their greeting for the President. But some cast nervous glances over their shoulders, conscious that many of those standing behind did not cheer. They merely looked. The brave HOORAY FOR JFK and similar placards were augmented by such as HELP KENNEDY STAMP OUT DEMOCRACY, YOUR A TRAITER (sic), and YANKEE GO HOME. In response to a placard held by a group of children at Lemmon and Alto Drive which said, MR PRESIDENT PLEASE STOP AND SHAKE OUR HANDS, Kennedy called for the motorcade to halt and he came close to being mobbed. He was to stop the car once more, to speak to a group of nuns he spotted in the crowd. Turtle Creek Boulevard ran down to Cedar Springs Road and on to Harwood Street. Main Street was a sharp right from Harwood and as the motorcade, a long snake of cars with noisy motorcycle escorts and complete with unstately VIP bus, streamed around the corner, it was in line with the Dealey Plaza.

The Dealey Plaza had been named after one of Dallas's most honoured citizens, George B. Dealey, the father of Ted Dealey who ran the *Dallas Morning News*. The *News* was something of an institution in Dallas, having been founded in 1842, before Texas joined the Union. E. M. 'Ted' Dealey was no friend to John F. Kennedy, as he had demonstrated at their last meeting. It was at a White House luncheon for Texas publishers that Dealey subjected the President to a tirade in which he lambasted him, advocated the use of strong-arm tactics against Russia and criticised the Kennedy administration. He said that what was needed was 'a man on horseback to lead this nation, and many people in Texas and the South-west think that you are riding Caroline's tricycle.' Kennedy was greatly embarrassed, not so much for the offensiveness itself but more by the reference to his three-year-old daughter. It was an icy Kennedy who replied, 'Wars are easier to talk about than they are to fight. I'm just as tough as you are, and I didn't get elected President by arriving at soft judgments.' Ted Dealey had disgraced himself that day, and he was to disgrace himself again today. He had accepted a full page 'advertisement' for the 22 November edition of the *News* from the so-called 'American Fact-Finding Committee', which ran under a hollow WELCOME MR KENNEDY headline.* Inside a solid black border, answers were demanded NOW to 12 questions (see page 98). The text contained accusations of the President being responsible for the imprisonment, starvation and persecution of thousands of Cubans and of having sold food to the communists who were killing Americans in Vietnam. There was also innuendo that the President had reached a secret agreement with the US Communist Party. 'Why have you ordered or permitted your brother Bobby, the Attorney General, to go soft on communists, fellow travelers, and ultra-leftists in America, while permitting him to persecute loyal Americans who criticise you, your administration, and your leadership?' ran another question.

The advertisement shocked the President and a great many other people that day, and reports of it later shocked the world. But it was not the only offensive print in circulation on the day of the Dallas

---

* The 'American Fact-Finding Committee' included a local John Birch Society official and millionaire oilman H. L. Hunt's son, Nelson Bunker Hunt

WELCOME MR. KENNEDY

TO DALLAS...

...A CITY so disgraced by a recent Liberal smear attempt that its citizens have just elected two more Conservative Americans to public office.

...A CITY that is an economic "boom town," not because of Federal handouts, but through conservative economic and business practices.

...A CITY that will continue to grow and prosper despite efforts by you and your administration to penalize it for its non-conformity to "New Frontierism."

...A CITY that rejected your philosophy and policies in 1960 and will do so again in 1964—even more emphatically than before.

MR. KENNEDY, despite contentions on the part of your administration, the State Department, the Mayor of Dallas, the Dallas City Council, and members of your party, we free-thinking and America-thinking citizens of Dallas still have, through a Constitution largely ignored by you, the right to address our grievances, to question you, to dis-agree with you, and to criticize you.

In asserting this constitutional right, we wish to ask you publicly the following questions—indeed, questions of paramount importance and interest to all free peoples everywhere—which we trust you will answer...in public, without sophistry. These questions are:

WHY is Latin America turning either anti-American or Communistic, or both, despite increased U. S. foreign aid, State Department policy, and your own Ivy-Tower pronouncements?

WHY do you say we have built a "wall of freedom" around Cuba when there is no freedom in Cuba today? Because of your policy, thousands of Cubans have been imprisoned, are starving and being persecuted—with thousands already murdered and thousands more awaiting execution and, in addition, the entire population of almost 7,000,000 Cubans are living in slavery.

WHY have you approved the sale of wheat and corn to our enemies when you know the Communist soldiers "travel on their stomachs" just as ours do? Communist soldiers are daily wounding and/or killing American soldiers in South Viet Nam.

WHY did you host, salute and entertain Tito — Moscow's Trojan Horse — just a short time after our sworn enemy, Khrushchev, embraced the Yugoslav dictator as a great hero and leader of Communism?

WHY have you urged greater aid, comfort, recognition, and understanding for Yugoslavia, Poland, Hungary, and other Communist countries, while turning your back on the pleas of Hungarian, East German, Cuban and other anti-Communist freedom fighters?

WHY did Cambodia kick the U.S. out of its country after we poured nearly 400 Million Dollars of aid into its ultra-leftist government?

WHY has Gus Hall, head of the U.S. Communist Party praised almost every one of your policies and announced that the party will endorse and support your re-election in 1964?

WHY have you banned the showing at U.S. military bases of the film "Operation Abolition"—the movie by the House Committee on Un-American Activities exposing Communism in America?

WHY have you ordered or permitted your brother Bobby, the Attorney General, to go soft on Communists, fellow-travelers, and ultra-leftists in America, while permitting him to persecute loyal Americans who criticize you, your administration, and your leadership?

WHY are you in favor of the U.S. continuing to give economic aid to Argentina, in spite of that fact that Argentina has just seized almost 400 Million Dollars of American private property?

WHY has the Foreign Policy of the United States degenerated to the point that the C.I.A. is arranging coups and hav-ing staunch Anti-Communist Allies of the U.S. bloodily exterminated.

WHY have you scrapped the Monroe Doctrine in favor of the "Spirit of Moscow"?

MR. KENNEDY, as citizens of these United States of America, we DEMAND answers to these questions, and we want them NOW.

THE AMERICAN FACT-FINDING COMMITTEE

"An unaffiliated and non-partisan group of citizens who wish truth"

BERNARD WEISSMAN,
Chairman

P.O. Box 1792 — Dallas 21, Texas

The Dallas Morning News *carried this full-page 'advertisement' on the day of President Kennedy's visit to Dallas.* (Courtesy National Archives) visit. Cheap handbills had been printed in the style of a police 'wanted' poster showing front and profile pictures of the President, and bearing the legend WANTED FOR TREASON. 'This man is wanted for treasonous activities against the United States,' it read, listing 'examples' of his treachery (see plate 16). A pamphlet also appeared showing an illustration of a hangman's noose and saying, 'Impeach the traitor John F. Kennedy for giving aid and comfort to the enemies of the USA.' Earlier in the day a man watching the President embark on his plane for Dallas had made no bones about it. 'That's the hell-hole of the world,' he said.

Three parallel streets, Commerce, Main and Elm, were gathered together in the Dealey Plaza to pass, side by side, below a railway overpass for access to the Stemmons Freeway, Commerce veering to the right and Elm to the left with Main Street taking a straight route between them. The intention had been for the motorcade to proceed in a straight line down Main Street, but an alteration to this had been introduced, ostensibly to facilitate smoother access to Stemmons. When the motorcade reached the top of the Plaza, it took a sharp right turn to Houston Street and joined Elm with an acute dog's-leg left turn, which necessitated the cars slowing down, almost to a walking pace, to take the bend. (See sketch on page 100.) The President's Lincoln had just passed the Texas School Book Depository when shots rang out.

It was a classic ambush situation from which there was no escape. As the shots echoed round the Plaza there was panic. People threw themselves to the ground and parents shielded their children. The President had sustained a number of wounds and within moments the Lincoln sped off to the Stemmons Freeway and thence to the nearest hospital. It took only minutes to reach Parkland Hospital, where every effort was made to save him. But John F. Kennedy was effectively killed on Elm Street. At 1.00 pm the President was pronounced dead. As the news of the assassination was transmitted the world stood still, paralysed, numbed with shock.

When the shooting was finished a swarm of people ran up a grassy knoll located on the north side of Elm Street. People said shots came from the rear of the motorcade and from the front right, from the knoll, and the notion of catching the shooter was uppermost in the minds of those who dashed up the grassy slope. As they passed

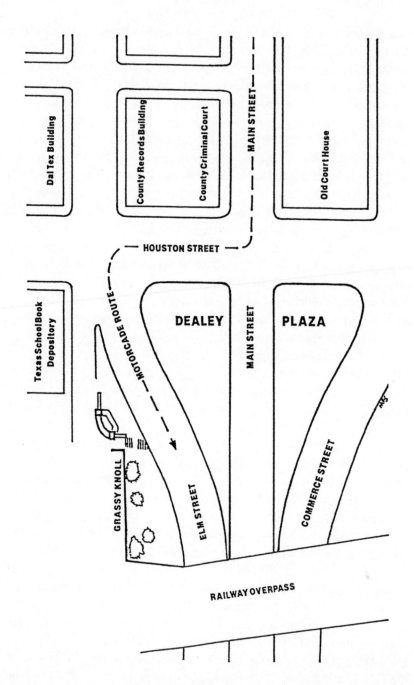

The diagram shows the Dealey Plaza where Kennedy was ambushed on Elm Street.

beyond the picket fence which marked the boundary to a car park at the top of the rising, however, they were stopped by a man displaying Secret Service credentials who sent them away. To their frustration, it was later discovered his credentials were false. The Secret Service confirmed that at no time did they have an agent stationed on the knoll.

A great many questions began to be asked about the apparent lax security which had surrounded the President's visit to Dallas. Why was the grassy knoll not covered by security men? Why had the tall buildings not been scrupulously checked out? Why had so many of Kennedy's security men been out partying till the early hours that same morning , calculated to make their reactions at Dallas sluggish? Why, also, was the–usual–military security detail cancelled for that day? For an assassination of the President to be attempted in downtown Dallas in broad daylight and in front of throngs of people was daring, if not foolhardy. For it to succeed was incredible, but such an operation would surely carry the penalty that the assassins would quickly be caught and brought to justice. Everybody had seen it and knew what had happened. Didn't they?

That was the remarkable thing about the assassination. Eye-witness accounts varied and, at times, conflicted. Many were not sure exactly where the shots came from–or even how many shots there were. The local press reflected the confusion by contradicting their first-edition account in their second, and then contradicting their second edition account in their third. The police appeared to know no more than those who were watching the parade. Apparently convinced that shots had come from the Texas School Book Depository, they made their way there. Within minutes of beginning their inquiries they put out an APB on a member of the Depository staff on the strength of him having left the building. The young man was Lee Harvey Oswald, who was arrested, according to the official version, after shooting and killing a police officer.

The new President, Lyndon B. Johnson, was sworn in without delay, for there was considerable tension building up on the part of those who feared the assassination was the preamble to a nuclear attack and the country was at its most vulnerable without a President. The idea that the Soviets were behind the assassination was commonly held at the time, though just as common was the belief that the Cubans had sent the assassins. The popular theory was that the communists were behind it one way or another, and this was strengthened by the news that the man they had arrested was a known communist who had defected to Russia for two years.

The notion that John F. Kennedy had been struck down by one of his own was, at that time, a vile, unthinkable thought, unworthy of an American. It was, therefore, an entirely acceptable conclusion which was reached by the Warren Commission, established by Lyndon Johnson to investigate the assassination, that though the killer was an American, he was a communist and besides this, he was deranged. Well, if he was an American, he would have to be a nutcase to kill the President, wouldn't he? And since he was shot and killed while being transferred from Police Headquarters to the County Jail but 48 hours after the President's death, that was good riddance to bad rubbish.

The Warren Commission took ten months to publish their report, 26 volumes in all, including details of the hearings and exhibits, which ran to ten million words. The Commission declared that Lee Harvey Oswald had alone and unaided, shot and killed the President and that he also murdered Police Officer J. D. Tippit while attempting to escape. There was no communist conspiracy or conspiracy of any kind. Though Oswald was a communist, a defector, and had links with a pro-Cuban organisation, he was a 'lone nut' and had acted entirely on his own. He possessed a rifle and that rifle was the one which had been used to kill the President. It had been found on the sixth floor of the Texas School Book Depository, from which the shots had been fired. A night-club owner, Jack Ruby, also acting only for himself, had shot and killed Oswald, and that was an end to the matter.

During the months which the Warren Commission took to reach its conclusions, the American people had followed the investigation via newspapers and television, and this was the expected outcome, for most people at any rate. There were some, however, who, from the beginning, had lingering doubts. There was something not quite right about the ease with which Lee Harvey Oswald had shot the President with an outmoded Italian carbine. He must have been an incredible marksman. And it was strange that Oswald, himself, had been shot and killed before he had ever reached a courtroom. It was not long before the flames of doubt were kindled. To the relief of those who were dissatisfied, critics of the Warren Report appeared, raising all kinds of questions about its conclusions and how they were reached.

At first the critics found it difficult to make their voices heard, for the media at large sought to discredit them, castigating them for being unpatriotic. But in spite of the opposition, in spite of being spurned by the press and television, they persisted with their challenge and they found their audience. They wrote books which went into circulation and slowly began the task of combating the might of government – and the re-education of the nation. They showed how evidence had been ignored by the Warren Commission, how witnesses had been passed over or stifled in making their statements while others, whose testimony would have been regarded as dubious and unreliable in a court of law, were honoured because they were, apparently, saying what the Commission wanted to hear. They found overwhelming reasons why the Report should not be believed, in the light of arrows pointing in every direction towards conspiracy.

When the confusion among the eye-witnesses was sorted out, there was strong evidence that bullets had been fired from behind the President, from the School Book Depository and, perhaps, another building. There was also evidence of shots having been fired from in front of the motorcade, from the grassy knoll. Photographic evidence played a greater part in the investigation of this crime than any other in history. Of the film shot that day, that of Abraham Zapruder, a dressmaker using a home-movie camera, was to provide a continuous record of the ambush, from start to finish, and compelling evidence of shots from the front as well as behind. Still cameras, also, recorded much that had escaped the eye, such as the shadowy figure on the knoll in one of the slides taken by Major Phillip Willis at the moment the President was hit by a bullet. Another Willis slide showed that the figure disappeared within seconds of the shots being fired. Mary Moorman (now Mary Krahmer), with her Polaroid camera, also took a picture of the grassy knoll, which experts have painstakingly enhanced to show the figure which has become known as the 'badgeman'.

No photographic record ever emerged showing Lee Harvey Oswald at the sixth-floor window of the School Book Depository, from which he was accused of firing the fatal shots. The only person to claim he saw Oswald there was Howard L. Brennan, who dithered so much, changing his statements periodically, that his evidence would have been demolished in a court of law. The first police officer to enter the Depository was a motorcycle officer named Marrion Baker. Without delay, he drove his cycle up to the entrance, dismounted and was inside within about one minute of the shooting. With the Building Superintendent, Roy S. Truly, he quickly made his way to the second floor (first floor in British terms), where he saw a young man standing outside the lunch-room drinking a Coke. 'This boy work here?' demanded Baker. 'Yes,' replied Truly and they dashed up the stairs to the next floor, unable to use the elevator because someone had left the gates open on a higher floor. The young man was Lee Harvey Oswald. Had Oswald lived to appear in court, Marrion Baker would undoubtedly have become his star defence witness. How could he have descended from the sixth floor to the second – without the help of the elevator – have found coins, obtained his Coke, taken off its cap and, without showing any sign of breathlessness, been standing there drinking it in the time it took Baker to reach him? How, then, could he have shot a rifle from the sixth-floor window? In fact, a photograph taken by press photographer, James Altgens, caused great argument because it appeared to show Oswald standing in the front doorway of the Depository watching the parade, and it would have been feasible for him to have covered the distance between the front door and the lunch-room, where he was found.

Many other facts emerged. A cloud hung over the 'discovery' of a 6.5 mm Italian Mannlicher-Carcano rifle on the sixth floor, claimed to be Oswald's. First reports of the discovery of a weapon referred to a 7.65 mm German Mauser, and three police officers present when it was found confirmed that it was a Mauser. Two of them later changed their minds and said it was a Mannlicher-Carcano, but the third resolutely refused to do so. That two experienced police officers both made the same error in identification was curious, to say the least. They were well used to the identification of weapons: Dallas was a violent city.

While the Mauser and the Mannlicher-Carcano bore a superficial resemblance to one another (see plate 24), there could not be any doubt which was which. The German gun had MAUSER stamped on the barrel, while the Italian carbine bore the legend MADE IN ITALY on the butt! Could these officers not read? There was no mistake that it was originally identified as a Mauser. This description reached the District Attorney, Henry Wade, who announced it on television, and consequently it was widely reported in the press. The third officer present when the Mauser was found refused to change his identification. This was Roger Craig, who was dismissed from his post for disobeying an order not to speak to the press. He was shot at, suffered injuries which left him in lifelong pain after having his car run off the road, and was eventually found dead. A suicide, they said.

But there was not the slightest doubt about the weapon Lieutenant Carl Day found on the sixth floor of the School Book Depository when he went to collect the find. It was an Italian 6.5 mm Mannlicher-Carcano which was lying there and which he took back to Headquarters. Asked recently by this author if he had any doubts about the circumstances, he said he had none. It was the only weapon there, and it was well photographed as he took it away. A fingerprint examination revealed that there were no prints on the weapon from Lee Harvey Oswald. A palm print which was not discovered until much later is regarded as extremely dubious evidence, and receives little credence from researchers. It was suggested that it could have been 'lifted' from Oswald's body and placed there. Whether, in fact, Oswald owned this rifle became open to dispute as the investigation proceeded. It was established that it had been bought in the name of A. J. Hidell by mail order from Klein's Sporting Goods Company in Chicago, and delivered to Lee Harvey Oswald's post-office box in Dallas. It was also established that Oswald used this alias, and an identity card bearing the name and Oswald's picture was conveniently claimed to be found on his person, though it was never mentioned until the day after he was arrested. But here is where the plot thickens.

On the day of the assassination, Lieutenant Colonel Robert Jones, Operations Officer for the 112th Military Intelligence Group, contacted men under his command who were in Dallas, asking for information about the assassination. They reported to him that 'A. J.

Hidell' had been arrested. But from where did they get this name, since it did not receive mention until the following day? Years later it was revealed that Military Intelligence had a file on Lee Harvey Oswald under the name of A. J. Hidell, but by the time they were asked to hand it over (by the House Assassinations Committee who re-investigated the assassination in the mid-seventies), they said it had been 'routinely' destroyed. This was one of many indications which emerged that Lee Harvey Oswald was neither a defector nor a communist, but an intelligence agent working for the United States government.

In this author's book, *JFK: The Second Plot*, a new and careful study of Oswald's background from the time he joined the Marines revealed he was recruited into the CIA while on service in Japan and was sent on a mission to Russia in the guise of a defector.* When he returned home he continued to work for the CIA, was engaged by the FBI, and had connections, we know, with Military Intelligence and probably Naval Intelligence, also. It was not uncommon for agents to double up. Oswald spent months in New Orleans during 1963 preparing for a new mission which, it appeared, was to take him first to Cuba and then back to Russia. But he had no way of knowing that he had, by then, fallen into the hands of a group of renegade agents who were involved in a conspiracy to kill the President. The 'mission' for which he had been prepared, and which he came back to Dallas to set in motion, was not known to CIA Headquarters in Langley.

Oswald visited Red Bird, a small commercial airfield on the outskirts of Dallas on the Wednesday before the assassination in the company of two other agents, a man and a woman. The man and woman did the talking, seeking to hire a small aircraft for a trip starting on the afternoon of Friday 22 November. This author was given a full, detailed account of the visit by Wayne January, who operated a business at Red Bird and had small aircraft which he rented out. He feared they had ideas different from those they mentioned to him. The trip to Yucatán they tried to negotiate sounded like a cover for a trip to Cuba, he felt, and he backed off. When they left he took a look at the third person, a man, sitting waiting in the car. Two days later he saw that face again on television

---

* Matthew Smith, *JFK: The Second Plot*, Mainstream, Edinburgh, 1992

and in the newspapers. It was Lee Harvey Oswald. Events later indicated they had more success with another operator.

The 'mission', it appears, involved Oswald making his way to Cuba in a small aircraft. It seemed likely the plane would put down in Houston where, for the rest of the journey, it would be piloted by an agent with much experience as a pilot and of making trips into Cuba, David Ferrie. Oswald's purpose, he believed, was to ingratiate himself by handing over secret information of value to Castro, in order to obtain backing for his second 'defection' to Russia. The date he was given for his departure was 22 November, and his trips with agents he knew to Red Bird seeking to hire a plane seemed entirely in line with preparations for the mission on which he believed he was setting out. His instructions were to leave the School Book Depository after the motorcade had passed so that his departure would pass unnoticed amid the excitement generated by the President's visit. Arrangements had been made for a police officer to provide him with transport to Red Bird so that there would be no traffic problems. They would meet at a point near to his lodgings, at which he could call to pick up his revolver and anything else he needed to take with him.

As has already been said, there was no such mission. It was an elaborate device to get Oswald to undertake a journey to Cuba, a journey designed by his masters to implicate him in the conspiracy to kill the President. Once he had departed for Cuba—it didn't matter too much about arriving—he would not only be seen as the killer, he would clearly be recognised as having carried out the deed for Castro. There would then have been no investigation since the murder would have been recognised, not only by America but the world, as a political assassination. With this scenario, it would be hard to believe that the likelihood of war with Cuba—with the possibility of escalation to a nuclear war—could have escaped the considerations of the conspirators. But their plans came to grief with Officer Tippit, who became suspicious of the young CIA man he was due to transport to Red Bird Airfield. He was shot dead by the agent monitoring the pick-up when it was seen he was backing out of the arrangement. He knew too much. Lee Harvey Oswald escaped to the Texas Theater where he waited for his handler to contact him—it was the practice of agents in trouble to make for the nearest theatre to await instructions—but he was arrested by the police. The conspirators' most anxious time was when Lee Harvey Oswald was in jail. The plan to involve Cuba had failed, but the President was dead, and if they were to escape detection it was imperative that Lee Harvey Oswald be disposed of. If he succeeded in establishing his innocence the game was up. The conspiracy would soon be exposed. Curiously, Lee Harvey Oswald was killed, not to keep secret what he knew, but to keep secret what he didn't know.

Jack Ruby was the man sent to kill Oswald. He was probably given no option, and may have been promised his eventual freedom, with rewards beyond his wildest dreams. Ruby was the Mafia connection in Dallas, a small-time hoodlum with big ideas, and connections in gambling, prostitution and drugs. Well known to members of the Dallas Police Department, he was generous in their direction with drinks and hospitality at the Carousel nightclub which he ran, and they treated him with favour. Many have wondered whether Jack Ruby was responsible for a 6.5 mm bullet being found on a stretcher at Parkland Hospital. The bullet rolled off an unused stretcher at the hospital when it was moved. Darrell C. Tomlinson, a senior technician at Parkland, was asked about it and declared he could not see that Governor Connally had ever occupied the stretcher in question, which raised obvious doubts about how it got there. In pristine condition, it was claimed to be the famous 'magic bullet', and named so because of the amazing flight attributed to it and all the injuries it was said to have caused.

Jack Ruby was certainly at Parkland Hospital within an hour of the President being taken there. He was seen by Seth Kantor, a member of the White House Press Corps, who told the Warren Commission all about the meeting. The Commissioners who, apparently, did not want to establish Ruby's presence there, declared he must be mistaken, and let the matter go. But Seth Kantor knew Ruby was there. He had met him before. They had shaken hands and had had a conversation in which Ruby asked advice about closing his club as a mark of respect. Was Ruby acting as errand boy for someone he knew who was involved in the conspiracy? Ruby was connected in some way, but probably only superficially. He was hardly the man to trust with secrets.

The wounds sustained by the President were expected to shed a great deal of light on what had happened on Elm Street but, instead, they proved only to be a source of further confusion and argument. When the President lay in Parkland Hospital gasping for breath, the doctors in attendance there decided to perform a tracheotomy so that he would be able to breathe more easily. Since there was a small, neat bullet wound in his throat, they decided to extend this to allow the tube to be inserted. They saw no reason to introduce another opening. Small, neat wounds of this kind indicate the point at which a bullet has entered the body, and the Parkland doctors identified the wound as such.

The wound which primarily concerned them, however, was located at the right rear of the head, for this was gaping and extremely serious. A bullet had struck with the effect of exploding the skull and the hole made was big enough for the doctors to see the President's brain. No amount of effort on the team's part could reverse this extensive damage. To all intents and purposes the President was dead when he arrived at Parkland Hospital.

The body was flown to Washington, to the Bethesda Naval Hospital, for an official post-mortem examination to be carried out. The team of doctors there, led by Commander James J. Humes, failed to recognise that the tracheotomy opening was not one specially made for that purpose. When the Parkland doctors told them what had happened, they examined the now enlarged wound and identified it as an exit wound. By doing so they resolved an enormous problem for the Warren Commission, to whom details of the autopsy were sent. The Commission were dedicated to proving that there had been no conspiracy to kill the President and, therefore, that all the bullets fired had come from the rear of the motorcade, from the rifle of Lee Harvey Oswald. The throat wound was crucial, therefore, to its case. Had it been identified as an entrance wound, it would have indicated a shot from the front and that there had been two shooters. Two marksmen taking part would have constituted a conspiracy. Because the Parkland doctors had already described the wound as one of entrance at a press conference, the Commissioners approached them on the subject and they agreed to change their statement, saying the press had omitted the word 'possible' from their reference to the wound being one of entry, and the gloss rescued the Commission's case. A wound high in the President's back was declared the point of entry for the bullet which had exited the throat, and the rear head wound was attributed to a shot from the rear, also.

On examination of the Zapruder film it was deduced that Oswald could have fired no more than three shots in the period of the shooting activity. Since one shot fired was known to have missed, the Commission still had a huge problem on their hands. From two shots fired, how could they account for JFK being hit twice and Governor Connally, seated in front of the President, being wounded – though not fatally – three times? The Commission's answer became known as the single-bullet theory. They said that the bullet which passed through the President's neck, exiting the throat, hit Governor Connally in the back, went through his chest and, exiting again, passed through his wrist and made a final wound in his thigh. It was astounding that Warren was ever able to persuade the American people to accept this solution and it was not surprising that the critics gave the Commission a thoroughly hard time because of it, declaring it both highly imaginative and unrealistic. Some went further and declared it quite impossible. The bullet which supposedly caused all this mayhem was, understandably, nicknamed the 'magic bullet'. And it was the 'magic bullet', listed in evidence as CE 399, the Commission decided, which had obligingly rolled off a stretcher at Parkland Hospital. A satisfactory explanation for its pristine condition was never given. In a strong argument against the single-bullet theory, it was said that the combined weight of the fragments dug out of Governor Connally added to the weight of CE 399 made it heavier than that type of ammunition was when manufactured.

The wound in the President's back was, in fact, lower than the Commission led the public to believe, which made it hard to accept that a bullet fired in a downward direction could exit JFK's throat. This added even more to the 'magic bullet's' propensity for changing direction. Further, the Bethesda doctors had noted a back entry wound for which neither the bullet which had caused it nor an exit for it was found which added a new mystery. When the Commission identified the bullet found at Parkland Hospital as the 'magic bullet', they were actually in competition with the autopsy team who had already suggested it may have been the bullet which caused the back wound then disappeared.

It has been calculated that if the single-bullet theory was correct, the bullet path would have been something like this. Small wonder it was nicknamed 'the magic bullet'.

David Lifton, a researcher who spent 15 years collating and studying evidence and information relating to the President's wounds, created a considerable stir when his book, *Best Evidence*, appeared in 1980. He argued that the President's wounds had been tampered with after leaving Parkland Hospital and before arriving at Bethesda. Comparing measurements taken at both places, he claimed the wound to the right rear of the head had been enlarged. It was because of this, he said, that the doctors at Bethesda identified it as having been made by a shot from behind, where in fact it was made by a shot from the front, as the Zapruder film had shown. He supported his thesis with a further claim, that the body arrived at Bethesda in a different coffin from the one in which it had been despatched at Parkland Hospital. Quoting an eye-witness present when the coffin was opened at Bethesda, he added that the President's remains were wrapped in a body bag of the kind used for the bodies of those killed in battle.* Since the Parkland staff could confirm that this was not the manner in which they had despatched the body, it must have been tampered with en route, he asserts. Though Lifton's work is well respected and his argument compelling, while some researchers have accepted it, there is uncertainty and unease among others when it comes to accepting his theories outright.

* Paul O'Connor, Lifton's witness, repeated his claim in this author's presence while this book was in preparation

BA 89-30
FXO/JWS:df1
3

transportation of the President's body back to the White House.
AMC CHESTER H. BOYERS, U. S. Navy, visited the autopsy room
during the final stages of such to type receipts given by FBI
and Secret Service for items obtained.

At the termination of the autopsy, the following personnel
from Gawler's Funeral Home entered the autopsy room to
prepare the President's body for burial:

JOHN VAN HAESEN
EDWIN STROBLE
THOMAS ROBINSON
Mr. HAGEN

Brigidier General GODFREY McHUGH, Air Force Military Aide
to the President, was also present, as was Dr. GEORGE BAKEMAN,
U. S. Navy.

Arrangements were made for the performance of the autopsy
by . the U. S. Navy and Secret Service.

The President's body was removed from the casket in which it
had been transported and was placed on the autopsy table, at
which time the complete body was wrapped in a sheet and the
head area contained an additional wrapping which was saturated
with blood. Following the removal of the wrapping, it was
ascertained that the President's clothing had been removed
and it was also apparent that a tracheotomy had been performed,
as well as surgery of the head area, namely, in the top of
the skull. All personnel with the exception of medical
officers needed in the taking of photographs and X-Rays were
requested to leave the autopsy room and remain in an adjacent
room.

Upon completion of X-Rays and photographs, the first incision
was made at 8:15 p.m. X-Rays of the brain area which were
developed and returned to the autopsy room disclosed a path
of a missile which appeared to enter the back of the skull
and the path of the disintegrated fragments could be observed
along the right side of the skull. The largest section of
this missile as portrayed by X-Ray appeared to be behind the
right frontal sinus. The next largest fragment appeared to
be at the rear of the skull at the juncture of the skull bone.

The Chief Pathologist advised approximately 40 particles of
disintegrated bullet and smudges indicated that the projectile
had fragmentized while passing through the skull region.

*In this FBI report, agents Sibert and O'Neill state that, on arrival at Bethesda Naval
Hospital for the autopsy, the President's body showed signs of surgery having been
carried out to the top of the skull. No such surgery was carried out at Dallas's
Parkland Hospital.*

Lifton appears to get support from the two FBI agents present at the
autopsy, whose report adds fuel to the fire. Agents Sibert and O'Neill
are on record for witnessing the arrival of the body and noting that
surgery appeared to have been carried out to the President's head (see
above). No surgery had been carried out to the head at Parkland
Hospital, however, and the appearance they described was inconsistent with that recalled by the Parkland staff. The same two agents

had signed a receipt for a 'missile' removed from the President's body and handed over to them by Commander Humes. It was argued that the agents were, in fact, referring to 'fragments' of metal, but in another report they specifically refer to 'fragments', and it therefore does not make sense for them to use the term 'missile' in the receipt if they really meant 'fragment' (see below). Experienced agents knew the importance of accuracy in their reports, and confusion and inconsistency in the terms they used would have rendered them quite unreliable. The question arises, however, what happened to the 'missile'? But then, what happened to the President's brain which, prepared for preservation, also disappeared? In photographs presented to the medical panel of the House Assassinations Committee, which re-investigated the assassination in the mid-seventies, the very wound to the rear of the President's head which Lifton argued had been enlarged also disappeared. The pictures showed a right front wound and a neat hole drilled in the cowlick area, but no gaping right-rear wound.

22 November 1963

From: Francis X. O'NEILL, Jr., Agent FBI
James X. SIBERT, Agent FBI

To: Captain J. H. STOVER, Jr., Commanding Officer, U. S. Naval Medical School, National Naval Medical Center, Bethesda, Maryland

1. We hereby acknowledge receipt of a missile removed by Commander James J. HUMES, MC, USN on this date.

Francis X. O'NEILL, Jr.

James X. SIBERT

FBI agents Sibert and O'Neill signed this receipt for a missile removed from the President's body during the autopsy. It has been argued they meant fragments of metal, but in other documents the same agents use the term 'fragments' when they are referring to such. It would be reasonable to assume that in this case they were talking about a bullet. If so, where has this piece of important evidence gone?

What had been presented to the American people in 1964* as an open-and-shut case was declared a sham by the critics, and as the months turned into years, more and more evidence of this was placed before them. It would be ten years before they were shown the Zapruder film on television, and when they saw it they were shocked.

They were not just shocked by the sight of their President's head exploding, they were shocked at the sight of their President's head exploding in response to a shot from the front, when their government had told them all the shots came from the rear, from the rifle of a deranged loner. They were not impressed with a futile argument which came much later, that when the President's head was seen thrown violently backwards it was due to a muscular spasm caused by a shot from behind. The people had seen for themselves and believed the evidence of their own eyes.

During the next few years the grip of the Warren Report was finally broken. It had held sway for 15 years because the people trusted the government, but the people now believed their government had deceived them. The House Assassinations Committee, which reported in 1979, tried hard to re-establish the central findings of the Warren Report, though it did not succeed. Acoustics evidence obtained from police dictabelts and accepted with reluctance by the Committee, supported that at least one shot had come from the front, which totally demolished the Warren 'lone assassin' case, and the existence of a conspiracy to kill the President was established at last, though, in their Report, the Committee still hedged, rating it no more than a 'high probability'.

Looking back over the time since the assassination, the people of America view a period in their history in which, too often, scandals have beset their government. Watergate and Irangate, which have rocked the country, are seen as symptoms of serious shortcomings in the leadership of the country. This stocktaking has been accompanied by a growing realisation that it was at the time of the JFK assassination that things started going wrong, and a belief that

* The Warren Report was published in October 1964, almost a year after the assassination

114

confidence in government can never be restored until the truth about the assassination of President John F. Kennedy has been established. This, in part, has been expressed in popular clamour for the release of the documents sealed away by, first, the Warren Commission, not to be opened until 2039, and then the House Assassinations Committee, not to be opened until 2029. Expectations vary on what the documents will reveal. Some believe that all the essential answers to the greatest mystery of the century will be exposed, but since the Warren Commission, for instance, at no time investigated the possibility of a conspiracy to kill President Kennedy, it is unlikely its documents will be earth shattering.

It is this author's opinion the Warren Commission documents may reveal the reasons Earl Warren, a man of enormous integrity, acted in the manner in which he did, seeking to place the blame for the assassination on Lee Harvey Oswald. From what we already know, Warren was in a 'catch-22' situation. Since there was a deep suspicion that either the Russians or the Cubans were behind the assassination, had a conspiracy of any kind been identified the people would have construed it to be the work of communists and the risks of a nuclear war would have been overwhelming. It would seem he placed the lives of forty million Americans and possibly countless millions from other countries before the truth and his personal integrity. The documents may even reveal that Warren was ordered to establish the guilt of Lee Harvey Oswald by President Lyndon Johnson. When it comes to the documents from the House Assassinations Committee, however, they may prove to be another matter entirely. They could be most illuminating.

Whatever was the case in 1964, when the Warren documents were locked away, or in 1979, when the House Assassinations Committee concluded its work, it is hard to see a legitimate argument for preventing the truth to be made known now. The American people long for the day when they can, as they did before, enjoy complete confidence in their government. It is unlikely to come before the secrets of the assassination have been unlocked. In the meantime, a great deal of satisfaction would be obtained from examining the contents of the files the CIA have locked away. They do not occupy cabinets; they fill warehouses.

CHAPTER SEVEN

New Evidence

'I'm going to tell it like it is.'
Favourite expression of Robert Kennedy

ABOUT TWO DAYS before Christmas, 1992, while I was taking a break from research for this book, I was called home to wait for a telephone call from Phoenix, Arizona. Though the line from my home to America is kept pretty busy, I wasn't expecting a call, and a call from Phoenix ranked as unusual. A member of the family had taken the brief call earlier from someone who wanted to speak to Matthew Smith. Since I was not at home, the caller had said he would call back later. Sensing something important, the family made an offer to bring me home within an hour to wait for the call, which was accepted. The first call had been made at about 3.00 pm, which was 8.00 am in Phoenix, so it was clear this was not a reader with a comment or a question.

It was about an hour-and-a-half later that the caller rang again and asked if he was speaking to the author of the book, *JFK: The Second Plot*. After being assured that he was, he then said he had read about the work, featured in the book, concerning Red Bird Airfield, and he had something very important to tell me. He had kept it a secret for almost 30 years but felt it about time it was made known. The reason he had not told anyone was that he had felt his life – and the lives of his family – would be endangered if he told what he knew. He said he would not say what he had to tell on the telephone because he still felt threatened, but he agreed to write it out and send it by public fax.

There was no way it would be acceptable to repeat information given in this way without making enquiries about the informant, or in some way obtaining satisfaction as to his bona fides. In this case nothing would be better than meeting him and talking to him. We met at a small town – little more than a village – just outside Phoenix and talked for a long time. He proved to be a man of considerable integrity who told me that when he had sent that fax it was like having an enormous burden lifted from his shoulders. He had somehow learned to live with it but it had always been there, nagging away. Now that he had revealed what he knew he felt light and refreshed. But even though nearly 30 years had passed since President Kennedy was killed, he asked that his name should not be used when the account of what he said was written up for publication. Many conversations – and further faxes – followed his first contact. In place of his real name, I have used the name Hank Gordon and made other minor changes to preserve his real identity. Otherwise what follows is a reliable translation of the notes he transmitted.

Woburn Incorporated was a relatively small company which operated out of Red Bird Airfield. It ran a small fleet of Douglas DC-3 aircraft to satisfy the demands of a contract it held in 1962, but disposed of them when the contract came to an end in 1963. The last of the DC-3s was sold in a deal struck by phone in early November, and the new owner arrived on 18 November to collect the plane. He was a well-dressed man who brought his pilot with him. As part of the deal, Woburn would provide the owner's pilot with assistance, completely checking the aircraft out and making it ready for flight. For this work the company needed the services of an aircraft mechanic conversant with the Douglas and they had engaged Hank Gordon from Phoenix. They knew Gordon to be reliable and well-experienced with the DC-3. Gordon was already in Dallas when the new owner arrived and, before lunch, he was introduced to the pilot who would share the work with him. Thus Hank Gordon came to spend several days working closely with the man who was to pilot the last of the fleet of Douglas planes from Red Bird Airfield. The departure date would be 22 November.

Working at close quarters with the pilot, Gordon observed him and began to get to know him. In his late thirties, he was well built and not short of muscle. A man of medium weight and height, he dressed well and wore his brown hair neat and short. An intelligent man, he conversed on a number of subjects during the days they worked together. Speaking with no trace of accent, he told Gordon he had been born in Cuba. As Monday gave way to Tuesday and Tuesday to Wednesday they exchanged stories about the danger and excitement they had experienced in their flying careers, and conceded they were both lucky to be alive. Gordon asked about his boss, was he a pilot? 'Oh yes,' was his reply. 'He is an Air Force colonel who deals with planes of this category.'

The conversation drifted around for a while and came back to flying. Noting how well his workmate knew the DC-3, Gordon asked where he had obtained his experience of this particular type of aircraft. Their relationship having been cemented during the few days of intensive close co-operation, the man was by now becoming more forthcoming in his answers. He told Gordon he had served with the Cuban Air Force, rising to a considerable rank, which he did not specify. This caught Gordon just a little off balance but he tried not to show it. Come to think of it, in view of what he had observed during their long conversations he was not surprised to learn he had held high rank: it fitted the man. They chatted on about other things.

On Thursday 21 November, they took stock of what remained for them to do and found they were behind in their schedule. A few things had begun to bother Hank Gordon by then. The Air Force colonel was never seen on the airfield. It seemed a bit peculiar that he did not show up now and then to check on progress. Gordon knew that no contact of any kind – business or social – was being made with the mysterious colonel. Where did he spend his time? The pilot, also, had developed some peculiarities. He resisted invitations to join Hank at the airport restaurant saying he did not want to leave the job since time was short. When Hank bought sandwiches at the restaurant and brought them back to the aircraft, however, he then had no problems about stopping for lunch breaks. And he was not a bum. He would have paid for everything Hank bought if he had been allowed to.

That Thursday they sat, leaning against the wheels of the plane eating, when a lull came in their conversation. It was between 12.30 and 1.00 pm. The pilot looked up at Gordon and said, 'Hank, they are going to kill your President.' The mood had changed from pleasant chit-chat. The pilot was sombre. The atmosphere was suddenly chill. 'What do you mean?' Hank asked. The pilot solemnly repeated himself. 'They are going to kill your President.' Gordon did not know how to take this. It was certainly no sick joke. The man was serious and Hank felt somewhat embarrassed. He looked at his workmate. 'You mean President Kennedy?' The pilot nodded. 'But what makes you say that? Why would anybody want to do a thing like that?' asked the incredulous Hank. Perhaps it was that this man felt he owed it to the burly mechanic from Phoenix who had befriended him, looked after his welfare and made life so pleasant these last few days, to confide in him. A gesture of goodwill. He called him again by his first name. 'Hank, I'll tell you. I was a mercenary pilot, hired by the CIA. I was involved in the Bay of Pigs planning strategy which was operated by the CIA. I was there involved with many of my friends when they died, when Robert Kennedy talked John Kennedy out of sending in the air cover which he'd agreed to send. He cancelled the air support after the invasion was launched. Many, many died, far more than was told. I don't know all that was going on but I do know that there was an indescribable amount of hurt, anger and embarrassment on the part of those who were involved in the operation.'

Gordon asked, 'Is that why you think they will kill the President?' The pilot, having finished his sandwich, screwed up the cellophane pack it had come in and dropped it in their rubbish box. He looked up at Hank. 'They are not only going to kill the President, they are going to kill Robert Kennedy and any other Kennedy who gets into that position.' Gordon was now acutely embarrassed. He didn't want to put an abrupt end to their friendship by telling him he was nuts, and the circumstances did not allow for him timidly to ask whether he might be mistaken. He simply didn't know how to handle the situation. Feeling his way, Hank said, 'To be honest with you – and myself – I have to take what you have just told me with a grain of salt, not meaning to insult you, or hurt you in any way.' Hank wriggled a little. 'It's just too far fetched for me to believe. If I went and told anybody what you have just told me my reputation as a man of business would be up the creek: they would laugh at me and, more important than that, they would say I was a nut and never let me fly a plane again. You can't have crazy people flying airplanes, you know.' The pilot turned to him. 'You will see,' he murmured, in a very matter of fact manner. Hank opened his mouth but nothing came out. He had no answer to such a statement.

They were both working by now, conscious that there was so much remaining to be done. The conversation changed to other more pleasant topics but, inevitably, drifted back to the topic which now stood between them. 'They want Robert Kennedy real bad,' the pilot volunteered, pensively, without stopping his work. 'But what for?' quizzed a rattled Hank. 'Never mind,' replied the pilot, snapping out of it. 'You don't need to know. Let's get this job done, time is running out. My boss wants to return to Florida and I thought we'd be through today. I told him we'd be through tomorrow, by early afternoon.' For the time being nothing more was said. Gordon worked late that night to oblige. The next day was 22 November.

On Friday morning nothing seemed unusual. There were 'finishing-off' jobs to be done like buttoning up inspection plates and latching the engine cowling. By lunch-time the only important thing left to do was to fuel the aircraft and it was ready for take-off. It was then that Hank heard a commotion going on in the terminal area. He spotted a Texas Ranger captain he knew making off in his car at speed. Curious, he made his way across in the direction of the terminal building, but before he got there a man he recognised, driving past in his car, slowed down, put his head out of the window and bellowed, 'Have you heard?' 'Heard what?' replied Hank. 'The President has been shot!'

Hank was dazed. He wandered over to the terminal building and found a radio by which he sat until the news of the President's death was announced. He knew the pilot had not been involved because he had never left the airfield, but he had a curious wish to find out what the man's reaction would be. He walked to where the DC-3 was located and noted that the plane was now fuelled up. The pilot was loading baggage and needed a hand with a few cases of oil. Hank asked him if he had heard what had happened and, without stopping, the pilot said the man on the fuel truck had told him. There was a long, uncomfortable pause, a sadness hanging on the air near to Hank. The pilot said, 'It's all going to happen just like I told you.' Hank was sickened. He did not want to work any more that day. He shook the pilot's hand to signal his departure, asking if they were leaving that day. 'Whenever the boss is ready,' replied the pilot. Hank went to find a television set, a deep fear beginning to dominate his mind and his heart. It was early afternoon.

Good researchers are cynics and they always seek innocent scenarios to explain otherwise explosive statements. This, however, is a difficult story to explain away. It would require imagination to find an innocent scenario to accommodate the facts of it. Hank Gordon's credentials check out well and his integrity is such it would never allow him to be misleading over a matter such as this. He would not give a name for the pilot, for instance, because he genuinely could not remember it and would not guess. There certainly were DC-3s used for a contract by the company concerned at Red Bird Airfield, and the number of the final DC-3 sold, recalled by Hank, checks out with the Aircraft Owners' and Pilots' Association. Everything checkable checks.

Hank Gordon's statement raises many questions and answers some. The reason he did not dash off as soon as the pilot confided in him to report what he had heard, was clearly given in his statement, though it appears he thought of it. Keeping it secret afterwards, however, fearing for his life and the lives of his loved ones—a completely understandable human reaction—proved an enormous burden. Who was the shadowy Air Force colonel, whose Cuban pilot was, no doubt still, a CIA man? Where did the colonel go those four-and-a-half days? Presumably he had friends in Dallas. Who were they? Could it be a coincidence that he was picking up a DC-3 from Dallas's Red Bird Airfield on 22 November? The Douglas DC-3 is a 24-seater aircraft which could have been used for many things on 22 November. One of them was transportation of the team of assassins who had killed the President. We know they were there in the Dealey Plaza and they had to get out of town somehow. Were they being given safe conduct by an Air Force colonel and a CIA man?

Another interesting question concerns why the departure of this aircraft was unknown at the time of the assassination. Why did it not come under the scrutiny of the FBI? Where are the police reports of its departure showing the names of the shadowy owner and his CIA pilot? Since the pilot knew of the conspiracy to kill the President, and the same conspirators were already plotting to kill Robert Kennedy and 'any other Kennedy who gets into that position', does this imply that his boss was party to the assassination of the President and Robert Kennedy? A colonel in the Air Force? Was the colonel a military member of the Executive Group? And was the pilot a CIA renegade member?

Efforts were made to trace this Douglas DC-3 through the appropriate authority with the aircraft number given by Hank Gordon. The help of Wayne January was sought in this task. January at one time worked at Red Bird Airfield and had supplied information to this author relating to Oswald's visit to the airfield seeking to hire a small aircraft two days before the day of the assassination*. Being knowledgeable of aircraft matters, he was asked to assist by taking up correspondence with the appropriate authorities on this author's behalf, regarding the aircraft number and data supplied by Hank Gordon. The AOPA replied saying that no such plane existed. They said the number *had* been issued to an aircraft, but not a DC-3: it was a plane of totally different description. This sparked off a series of telephone calls between January and the AOPA.† Sheer persistence eventually obtained an answer to the effect that the number quoted had, in fact, been issued to a DC-3, but the number had, *after the date of the DC-3's purchase from Woburn Incorporated, been transferred to another plane.* The author discussed this with Colonel L. Fletcher Prouty (USAF retired), who said that the identification numbers of aircraft were *never* changed. There were no innocent circumstances in which he had known this happen.

The next step was to try to identify who had purchased the plane. The search was difficult because records held by the aviation authority had long since been packaged and deposited in accommodation devoted to old and unused files. There were more surprises in store when the appropriate document was recovered and details sent, as requested, to Wayne January. The transfer of the aircraft was not registered at the time of purchase. This taken by itself was not surprising, for transfers are frequently not registered at once by those

---

* See Chapter 6, page 106
† Interestingly, while January was conducting his negotiations with the aircraft authority, he also authenticated that he owned the small Cessna which was sought for hire by Oswald's renegade handlers

buying and selling aircraft. It seems that because tax becomes payable on the transaction at that point, the evil day on which the demands of the Revenue Department must be met is often put off until registration becomes necessary, often when the aircraft is being sold once again. Woburn, for instance, is shown as acquiring the DC-3 on 16 September 1963. They had owned the plane for some time but it became necessary to register ownership when they decided to sell. The records showed that the DC-3 was acquired by Houston Air Center, and though, apparently for the reasons described above, the registration date was shown as 27 October 1965, the actual sale date, according to Woburn Inc., was in 1963, only a few weeks before the assassination.

The Houston Air Center turned out to be an extremely interesting organisation. It was formed during 1962 and occupied premises on the well-to-do Airport Boulevard. The nearby airport, this author was assured, was the airfield used by the CIA, and on the authority of a highly reliable investigator, Houston Air Center is known to have been a front for the Agency. The company was wound up in 1969. This takes us full circle. The DC-3 was bought by an Air Force colonel who brought with him a Cuban-born, CIA-connected pilot. The pilot knew about the vendetta against the Kennedys. He not only knew about plans to kill the President but also plans to kill Robert Kennedy and any other Kennedy who approached the Presidency, which would account for the Chappaquiddick tragedy and its disastrous effect on Edward Kennedy's presidential ambitions. It has been established through the AOPA that the number of the aircraft bought from the company at Red Bird Airfield was changed after purchase, something which is quite unknown except, as Colonel Fletcher Prouty says, when it is done by the CIA. The aircraft was prepared for acquisition by the new owners during the few days before the assassination of JFK and was made ready for take off by lunch time on Friday 22 November. The records show that the plane was purchased by the Houston Air Center, a company which fronted for the CIA. There can now be no doubt that CIA personnel were involved in the conspiracy to kill President John F. Kennedy, the conspiracy to kill Senator Robert Kennedy and the Chappaquiddick conspiracy against Senator Edward Kennedy. The author cautions, however, that there is no evidence that the CIA *per se* were involved in any way. The evidence shows that renegade agents plotted against the Kennedys and used all the facilities and the cover of the Agency to achieve their objectives. Taken with other evidence and indications, it is also strong evidence that they were aligned to others in what we have called the Consortium.

This new evidence from Red Bird Airfield undoubtedly represents an enormous crack in the JFK conspiracy. While it comes as no surprise to many of us, who have been convinced of the involvement of CIA agents for a long time, this is the first tangible evidence to appear in 30 years. It could be argued that, if Hank Gordon had gone to the authorities with his information on the day he received it, the lives of President Kennedy and Robert Kennedy might have been saved, but would anyone have listened? Had he even come forward during the time the Warren Commission were trying to persuade America and the world that Lee Harvey Oswald, on his own and without any assistance, killed the President, his statement would have been pure dynamite to those prepared to listen. But who was prepared to listen? We might have had a chance to identify the colonel and the CIA pilot within days of the assassination; or we might have added the name of Hank Gordon to the grizzly roll of those who met with nasty accidents or unexplained deaths. In the circumstances his reluctance to come forward earlier is completely understood. Surely there are others who could make similar contributions to our understanding of the deaths of John and Robert Kennedy who have still not told what they know.

Author's note:
Hank Gordon's stipulation that he should remain anonymous causes some problems which this author has sought to resolve. Gordon was asked if he would consent to an interview with another researcher, on condition that that person would also be bound by the rules of total confidentiality. He agreed and that distinguished researcher, Mary Ferrell, was asked to meet him. Gordon made the trip to Dallas, where he presented Mrs Ferrell with all the information sent to this author. After the interview, in respect of the detailed investigation of Gordon's data and having thoroughly checked his 'credentials', she agreed the information supplied could be completely relied upon.

CHAPTER EIGHT

Two Hundred Billion Dollars

'May they bear in mind that it is neither gold nor
even a multitude of arms that sustains a state, but its
morals.'

Diderot, 1782

IT IS LIKELY that on the night of 22 November there were a number of
furtive, guarded telephone calls made. The members of the Consortium would have been agitated and anxious. They had not been
provided with the details of the plan to kill the President: that had
been an agreed part of the arrangements. But they had been told what
would happen in outline. They knew enough to know that everything
had not gone according to plan. Of all things the patsy had been
picked up in Dallas straight after the shooting. Wasn't he supposed to
be in Cuba, or arrested trying to get there? What had gone so wrong?
Was there a danger the whole thing would backfire and lead back to
the Executive Group and through it to the Consortium?

The murder of Lee Harvey Oswald in Dallas Police Headquarters
on Sunday 24 November came as no surprise to them and certainly
brought a measure of relief. Their remaining worry concerned how
much damage had been done while he was in custody. Had he
managed to convince the authorities he was a patsy, and was there a
secret hunt in progress for the members of the Executive Group? But
their anxiety was to continue until there was a full Consortium

meeting. Yes, the plan had gone wrong. Oswald had been picked up before reaching the airport as a consequence of the police officer who had been given the job of driving him there getting windy. He had backed off and had had to be disposed of. Perhaps it had been a rash act to kill the officer on the spot, or perhaps a mistake had been made earlier on in putting the police on to Oswald as early in the proceedings as they had. Oswald had scattered and it was him they picked up for shooting the police officer. This had necessitated bringing in Ruby to kill Oswald at the first possible time and, by all accounts, he had not succeeded in persuading them he was the patsy, so no damage had been done to security. They were safe. What was now required was a careful sealing off of loose ends created by the hiatus, and this had been put in hand. It was going to cost a lot more money than had been expected.

The last thing Consortium members were concerned about at this time was expense. A discussion followed in which they examined the situation in detail, and they became less unhappy the more they took stock of things. Their main objective had been achieved: the President was dead. Oswald was dead and the police officer who could have blown everything was dead. The Executive Group's people had quickly got everything under control. They could breathe again. There was still a chance that Oswald would be linked with Cuba or even Russia and, therefore, there must be prospects of a war. Even if that did not materialise, Kennedy's Vietnam withdrawal had been nipped in the bud, attitudes could now change towards the Pentagon and a generally more sensible and suitable administration would create a new atmosphere in politics. Things had worked out quite satisfactorily.

On the afternoon of 22 November Lyndon Baines Johnson had returned to Washington as President of the United States of America. He had always wanted to become President, and now his ambition was achieved. His becoming Vice-President had been a glorious non-event. The Vice-Presidency was a vacuum role. It attracted jibes, like the comment someone had once passed, 'Being Vice-President isn't exactly a crime, but it's a kind of disgrace, like writing anonymous letters.' It was true, Johnson had to admit: Kennedy had attempted to make more of the post than any of his predecessors, but it had still not amounted to anything. It was Sam Houston Johnson, LBJ's brother, who had complained on his behalf:

> . . . they made his stay in the Vice-Presidency the most miserable three years of his life. He wasn't the number-two man in the administration; he was the lowest man on the totem pole . . . I know him well enough to know he felt humiliated time and time again, that he was openly snubbed by second-echelon White House staffers who snickered at him behind his back and called him 'Uncle Cornpone'.

The Vice-President's role was little more than one in which the incumbent hung around—like a vulture—waiting for misfortune to overtake the President, when he would step into his shoes. Now it had happened.

When John F. Kennedy had gone to the polls in the race for the Presidency, he had had to decide upon a 'running mate', who would become Vice-President if the bid was successful. Those near to Kennedy could not see him choosing Johnson to run with him, and Johnson had said categorically that he would not accept the nomination anyway. The two were poles apart. They were different varieties of political animal. Kennedy was an intellectual, polished, well spoken and accomplished; Johnson was larger than life, criticised for his lack of culture and for his unashamed vulgarity.

That Kennedy needed Johnson, whether he knew it or not, was evidenced in the fact that had he not had the votes pulled in by Johnson in the South and West he would not have been elected President. But Kennedy offered the nomination to Johnson un-accountably and against all predictions. According to research on J. Edgar Hoover conducted by Anthony Summers, Kennedy was blackmailed into taking Johnson on the ticket by Hoover. Johnson and Hoover were known to be friends, and it was known that Hoover kept dossiers on all politicians who had skeletons in their cupboards.*

There is a story told that the President made up his mind to get rid of the crusty Director of the FBI and had information compiled which would 'persuade' him it was time he retired. Kennedy invited Hoover

---

* Anthony Summers, *The Secret Life of J. Edgar Hoover*, Victor Gollancz, London, 1993

to lunch at the White House with himself and Bobby, and they sat down to start the meal. During the main course JFK took out of his inside pocket an envelope and placed it on the table. Hoover responded, continuing the meal, by taking out of *his* inside pocket a somewhat larger envelope which he laid on the table. The President picked up the large envelope and he and Bobby examined the contents. The President ate no more of the meal and Bobby raced for the bathroom to vomit. Hoover persevered, reached the dessert course and ate it, the only one left at the table. Whether this is true or merely apocryphal is unknown. There is little doubt, however, that Hoover survived in power for a long time on the strength of his files, and anyone trying to beat him at his own game would have to be a master. It is entirely believable that the Director's clout was such he could, if he wished, have his friend Lyndon Johnson placed on the Kennedy ticket. It was also another way of reminding the young man contending for the Presidency, if he didn't already know it, who held the trump cards.

Johnson wanted to place the investigation of the assassination of President Kennedy in the hands of J. Edgar Hoover, but when he heard noises to the effect that other bodies—notably Congress—were contemplating investigations he realised he was likely to lose control. By establishing a Presidential Commission—which superseded all others—to look into the killing, he effectively spiked their guns. Through Earl Warren, whom he coerced into accepting the chairmanship of the commission, he retained all control over the investigation and its findings.

The line taken by the Warren Commission—as it became known—was closely monitored by the Executive Group who saw it defusing the tense and volatile situation which existed immediately after the assassination. People were at first fearful that the murder of the President was the preamble to an attack by Russia, perhaps some kind of retaliation for the Cuban Missiles episode. Others thought, as the Consortium had calculated they would think, that Fidel Castro was behind the assassination, getting even for the repeated CIA attempts on his own life. But in the ten months before the Warren Report was published, tensions had eased and passions were spent.

The Consortium had to accept that any hopes they had had for hostilities with Cuba were not to be realised. Still, the Warren Commission could not have been more effective in protecting its best interests as it pursued the idea of Lee Harvey Oswald as the lone assassin. This put their members well in the clear. The trail being followed by Warren would never lead back to the Executive Group, and the Consortium was being distanced from the coup d'état—for that is truly what it was—as one day followed another. And long before the Warren Commission had completed its work the replacement of Kennedy by Johnson had brought benefits in other directions.

In accordance with the wishes of President Kennedy, Robert McNamara had announced on 2 October 1963 that 1,000 of the US personnel serving in Vietnam would be repatriated before the end of the year. On 31 October, JFK himself had reiterated this, adding:

> I think the first unit or first contingent would be 250 men who are not involved in what might be called front-line operations.*

Two hundred and twenty men were, in fact, withdrawn on 3 December. On 14 November eight days before he was killed, the President was also to say:

> We are going to bring back several hundred before the end of the year. But I think on the question of the exact number, I thought we would wait until the meeting of 20 November.†

On 20 November, the Wednesday before the assassination, a conference was held at Honolulu where Dean Rusk, Robert McNamara and McGeorge Bundy met with Admiral Felt, General Harkins and Henry Cabot Lodge, the US Ambassador to South Vietnam. This conference discussed the implementation of the decision which had first been announced by Robert McNamara on 2 October repatriating 1,000 personnel. Agreement was reached and an announcement was made, the number being withdrawn having been increased to 1,300.‡ On John F. Kennedy's death his plans were reversed with unseemly haste.

---

* Public Papers, p.828
† *New York Times* 15 November 1963
‡ Pentagon Papers, II, 170; V, 224

On 24 November, just two days after Kennedy died, and before his funeral, President Johnson, at an unofficial emergency meeting held in Washington, met quietly with most of those who had attended the Honolulu meeting—an additional member in attendance being CIA Director John McCone—and cancelled JFK's plans. It took but two days to reverse John F. Kennedy's policy of repatriation and withdrawal from Vietnam, part of an overall plan to pull out altogether by the end of 1965. The openings which existed for a political settlement in Vietnam were being ignored. Foundations were being laid for the development of the war. Peter Dale Scott,* writing in 1976, revealed:

> With the publication of the Pentagon Papers, we have learnt that the results of the emergency meeting on 24 November were embodied in National Security Action Memorandum 273 of 26 November 1963† . . . NSAM 273 . . . tends to minimise the novelty of its provisions; but this appearance of continuity with the policies of the deceased President Kennedy is misleading.
>
> Where Kennedy had already, on 5 October 1963, ordered initial troop withdrawals as part of an overall United States withdrawal programme (approved and even accelerated at Honolulu on 20 November), Johnson's NSAM 273 'stressed that all military and economic programmes were to be kept at the levels maintained during the Diem regime'. Where Kennedy, as late as October 1963, had refused to *commit* America to the 'overriding objective' (in language proposed by McNamara) of 'denying' Vietnam 'to communism', Johnson's NSAM 273 (following a new proposal from McNamara) contained just this commitment; it made 'the central objective' of winning 'the test of all US decisions and actions in this area'. And where Kennedy had initiated troop withdrawals as the first step in a gradual US disengagement from the area, NSAM 273 'authorized planning for specific covert operations, graduated in intensity, against the DRV' (North Vietnam).
>
> . . . It was 'in keeping with guidance in NSAM 273' that the Joint Chiefs of Staff, on 22 January 1964, proposed an escalation of intelligence

---

* Peter Dale Scott, born in Montreal, was at one time a Canadian diplomat and later became a lecturer in English at the University of California. He is well known as a writer and a JFK assassination researcher. He also researched the origins of the Vietnam war

† Scott was writing in 1976. When NSAM 273 was eventually released in 1991, it was found that, while it was *issued* on 26 November, it was actually dated 21 November, the day *before* Kennedy was killed

operations, an abandonment of 'self-imposed restrictions', and preparations 'for whatever level of activity may be required'.

. . . What could have forced the new President to reach a 'crisis' decision on Vietnam 48 hours after being sworn in? The answer, I think, was fear of a negotiated political settlement in Vietnam.*

A negotiated settlement was exactly what the Consortium did not want and covert escalation and expansion of the war in Vietnam was exactly what they did want.

Detectable in the extract above was that Lyndon Johnson tried to give the appearance that he was stepping into Kennedy's shoes and picking up the threads of the Kennedy administration. He retained many of Kennedy's people, telling them that he needed them more than Kennedy had. In his first address as President to Congress, he said:

> . . . No memorial oration or eulogy could more eloquently honour President Kennedy's memory than the earliest possible passage of the Civil Rights Bill for which he fought . . .
>
> And, second, no act of ours could more fittingly continue the work of President Kennedy than the earliest passage of the Tax Bill for which he fought . . .

Indeed, it must be said, greatly to Johnson's credit, that in domestic matters he bravely forged the vision of his 'Great Society', the broad thrust of which was much in line with the direction Kennedy took. At home he met with considerable success except, notably, in one particular direction: that of the fight against organised crime. Robert Kennedy stayed on in the Justice Department and continued his work for the better part of a year, when the war against the mobsters came to an abrupt end. The Consortium had served the Mafia well. The Mafia had been well recompensed for their participation in the Executive Group's plot to kill Kennedy.

In November 1964 LBJ was swept into power in his own right. His 61 per cent of the votes was a record breaker in the history of Presidential elections, and he settled down to enjoy the power he had yearned for. Strangely, his pleasure was short lived. In his fourth year,

---

* Peter Dale Scott, 'The Death of Kennedy, Vietnam, and Cuba', in *Assassinations*, Random House, New York, 1976

when he should have been looking forward to automatic re-election and a second term,

> Johnson looked and sounded tired, a broken man. At the end of March in concluding a television address about Vietnam he announced to a stunned nation that he did not intend to seek a further term as President the following November.*

Could it have been that during his time in office, where he might have expected to feel the reassuring presence of an American Eagle over his shoulder, there was, instead, the menacing shadow of a circling vulture? No other President in history was as conscious of the existence of the Consortium as Lyndon Baines Johnson. More recent accounts of Johnson's Presidency record that his mental health appeared to deteriorate before he stood down.

Lyndon Baines Johnson must hardly have been able to believe his incredible luck when, at that particular moment in time, he became President. This had nothing to do with gain: rather more political survival. There was a storm about to burst over his head regarding his close association with Bobby Baker, who had been charged with influence peddling and was also suspected of irregular financial manipulation. Bobby Baker had started his career as a Senate page and became 'a sort of valet to some of the most powerful men in America'. He was Johnson's protégé and, as the years progressed, they became very close friends. Baker was eventually appointed Secretary for the Senate Democratic Caucus, and he and Johnson controlled the funds for the organisation.

When Baker was charged he resigned his post, but this did not end the matter. He was being pursued in the courts and, because of his strong links with Johnson, the press were soon devoting a lot of space to the subject. It had all the makings of a first-class scandal and it would only be a matter of a very short time before Johnson would know how closely he would be tied into it and whether he

---

* Daniel Snowman, *American Since 1920*, Heinemann Educational Books, London, 1978. First published as *USA: The Twenties to Vietnam*, Batsford, London, 1968

would survive politically. The Baker affair steadily grew in the importance attached to it by the press and had reached national-daily headline proportions during the period before the President's Texas tour. *Time-Life* ran a cover story featuring a picture of Johnson with Baker in their edition of 8 November under the heading, THE BOBBY BAKER BOMBSHELL and trailed LBJ to his Texas ranch where he purported to be preparing to receive the President on his tour. His flight to Texas was interpreted as little more than ducking out of sight of the press and, turning up at his door, the ardent journalists, not surprisingly, drew nothing more than 'No comment'.

This did not stop *Time-Life* running a second cover story on the subject, SCANDAL GROWS AND GROWS IN WASHINGTON, which hit the news-stands the day the President reached Dallas, 22 November. On that same day the *Dallas Times Herald* carried three stories on the Bobby Baker scandal. It would be difficult to think that the affair was not uppermost in the Vice-President's mind while he was participating in the visit. It is not unlikely that it was in the mind of John F. Kennedy, also, for if taint of scandal attached to the Vice-President, it was a matter of grave concern for him, also, lest it tarnish his administration. It was small wonder that stories circulated that he planned to drop LBJ from the 1964 ticket.

This was not the first time scandal had touched the Vice-President. His neighbour and long-time friend Billy Sol Estes had been in deep trouble since 1961 concerning his contracts for the storage of government grain and his Federal cotton allotments. Agricultural Agent Henry Marshall was sent to investigate malpractices and, soon after his report was submitted, he was found dead in a Texas ditch with five bullets in his body. Without an autopsy being held, he was declared a suicide. Five bullets made this hard to swallow. An incompetent suicide might achieve two shots before losing consciousness, but five? It is not surprising that the body was exhumed, when it was discovered Marshall had suffered a blow to the head and had been subjected to carbon-monoxide poisoning in addition to being shot. The new verdict was murder, but the exhumation and autopsy did not take place until some years after the event. Three other deaths giving rise to questions were also linked to the Billy Sol Estes affair. Living next door to Johnson in a home which boasted a portrait of LBJ in a prominent position, Billy Sol Estes was not the kind of friend for the Vice-President of the United States to have.

There is no doubt that Lyndon Johnson derived considerable benefits from the timing of the assassins' bullets and the fact that the murder of the President wiped out of the headlines all other stories, stories which were getting too close to home. It has to be wondered whether, in fact, it was not this which accounted for Johnson's insistence on being sworn in as President at once on board the Presidential aircraft, Air Force One, at Love Airfield, with the body of the dead President lying in a coffin in another compartment of the plane. Johnson claimed this was because of national security but, since the Vice-President automatically became President on the death of Kennedy, many were shocked at the decision to hold up the departure of the Presidential plane and have an ad hoc ceremony in Dallas, attended by the dead President's widow, still wearing garments stained with his blood.

It is true that there was tremendous world tension following the assassination of John F. Kennedy, and the swearing-in of Johnson advertised to the world that a new President was in office and in charge. It is also true that the swearing-in advertised to those writing stories about his strong links with Baker that he was no longer Vice-President but President. It is even possible that he feared the scandal might erupt and that he might never be sworn in. This is not to say he was completely out of the woods. The Baker affair cast a shadow over his Presidency. Baker was indicted on seven counts of income-tax evasion, larceny and conspiracy in 1966 and came to trial in 1967.

With a swift reversal of JFK's Vietnam policy, Consortium members, as has been said, quickly felt the benefit of Johnson's accession to the Presidency. When news of the secret meeting leaked to their sources they were likely to be informed without delay. No doubt with their warped sense of patriotism, they believed they had acquitted themselves well in ridding their country of John F. Kennedy and restoring, as they saw it, balanced, sensible government. There would soon be a progressive momentum in the war in Vietnam which would generate business estimated as in excess of 200 billion dollars to those involved in the provision of arms, armaments and oil.

The cost to the American nation was calculated in human lives: 50,000 killed in the conflict. To the people of Vietnam this was small. Their dead were numbered in millions.

CHAPTER NINE

The New Threat

*'Violence breeds violence, repression brings
retaliation, and only a cleaning of our whole society
can remove this sickness from our soul.'*
Robert F. Kennedy, Cleveland, Ohio, 1968

ON THE WHOLE, the Johnson administration must have been very satisfactory to the members of the Consortium. Johnson pursued the broad domestic issues which John F. Kennedy had embraced which included civil rights and poverty at large, and though some members of the Consortium, doubtless, had misgivings about progress made in the direction of civil rights, they had little cause to worry for, as his term progressed, the programme ran out of steam. The war in Vietnam opened up during the Johnson term and the ratio of 'hawks' to 'doves' in the White House was satisfactorily maintained. When a crisis occurred in Vietnam the answer was more troops and an escalation of engagement, which appalled and worried the people, but which allowed those feeding off the war by providing the means of warfare to get fatter.

The concern over the war, in which America was seen to be getting more and more involved, made depressing daily news headlines. It became a standard topic of conversation and the question of why the United States had ever allowed itself to get so deeply into what was proving to be a quagmire began to be asked at all levels. The politicians' answers became less and less acceptable. The United States had originally gone in to support the South Vietnamese in their quest for self-determination but it had turned out they had no liking for their own government in Saigon and the future it offered. The reason given for continued American participation in the war had then changed to one which added up to national security. 'Better fight the communists in South Vietnam than in the United States' became, broadly, the argument. Across the years of Johnson's time in office, though there were hawks and doves in society at large, the man in the street became generally less convinced of the argument and more and more disenchanted with the idea of America's involvement in the war. The death toll was rising, the cost to the nation enormous and the benefits – if any – were elusive. There was also a growing conscious-ness of the suffering inflicted on the Vietnamese people. The horrendous reports of death and destruction steadily began to demoralise many Americans.

Voices began to be raised in protest and, when that was of no avail, demonstrations were organised to allow the people the right to make their views known to the government. When these went unheeded violence was given a natural opening as a means of expression, since those who favour violence thrive on frustration. It was during Lyndon Johnson's term of office that the doves in high places began making their voices heard loudly and more clearly. Among these the passionate voice of Robert F. Kennedy was identified, marking him out as a leading opponent of the war in Vietnam.

Robert Kennedy's appointment as Attorney General had been one of patronage and when President Kennedy was killed, therefore, it was automatically terminated, though President Johnson asked him to carry on for the remainder of what had been JFK's term of office. Nonetheless, overnight he had found himself in a political wilderness which would only worsen when he left the Attorney General's office. It was during 1964, therefore, the year in which Lyndon Johnson successfully campaigned for the Presidency in his own right, that Robert Kennedy decided to run for the Senate. He was no stranger to the campaign trail, with which he had become familiar when his brother had bid for the Senate and for the Presidency. He launched himself into a bitter fight for the New York seat and, on 4 January 1965, found himself Junior Senator for New York State. There is no doubt that the fact of his entering the Senate was observed by the members of the Consortium. Robert Kennedy was seen as no threat to them while he remained outside the Presidential orbit, and when he ended his appointment as Attorney General the Mafia had heaved a huge sigh of relief, for the intensive drive against organised crime came to a grinding halt. He was, at that point, a nonentity as far as the Consortium and its allies were concerned. Whatever his thoughts or words, he had no powers which would allow him to affect them.

But now it was unbelievably different. The talk of Jack Kennedy occupying the White House for two terms then handing on to Robert for a further two terms of Kennedy rule—with Edward coming in to the reckoning then—were not forgotten. It was this prospect which had spurred the Consortium to desperate measures to get rid of John F. Kennedy and break the hold of the Kennedys on the White House. Now there was an expectancy that Robert would pick up the threads and run for President in 1972. The Consortium would keep him under close observation. Though some of their number had had him firmly on their hit list from the time they had murdered Marilyn Monroe, most Consortium members were likely to have favoured leaving him alone had he remained in the law business. They did not see their vendetta extending to a Kennedy out of harm's way. Now it had all changed.

In 1967 Robert Kennedy was in a dilemma. The war was steadily escalating. Where there had been 23,000 troops in Vietnam in 1964, there were more than 20 times that number in 1967. Johnson had sacked Robert McNamara, who had kept alive the hope of a negotiated settlement, from his post as Secretary of Defence and replaced him with a known hawk, Clark Clifford. Arthur M. Schlesinger Jr, in his fine biography of Robert Kennedy, recalls Henry Kissinger coming away from Washington 'with a conviction that LBJ's resistance to negotiation verges on a sort of madness'.*

With the benefit of hindsight we can see that if LBJ was oppressively conscious of being under constant observation by the Consortium his deep fear may have been reflected in his opposition to negotiations. RFK had come to believe that another four years of Johnson would be an outright disaster for the United States, yet he

---

* Arthur M. Schlesinger Jr, *Robert Kennedy and His Times*, Andre Deutsch, London, 1978

was acutely aware of the Presidential incumbent's inalienable right to run for a second term. He said:

> Now we're saying we're going to fight there so that we don't have to fight in Thailand, so that we don't have to fight on the west coast of the United States, so that they won't move across the Rockies . . . Maybe [the people of South Vietnam] don't want it, but we want it, so we're going in there and we're killing South Vietnamese, we're killing children, we're killing women, we're killing innocent people . . . because [the Communists are] 12,000 miles away and they might get to be 11,000 miles away.
>
> Do we have a right here in the United States to say that we're going to kill tens of thousands, make millions of people, as we have . . . refugees, kill women and children? . . . I very seriously question whether we have that right . . . Those of us who stay here in the United States, we must feel it when we use napalm, when a village is destroyed and civilians are killed. This is also our responsibility . . .
>
> We love our country for what it can be and for the justice it stands for and what we're going to mean to the next generation. It is not just the land, it is not just the mountains, it is what this country stands for. And that is what I think is being seriously undermined in Vietnam.*

There were others who shared Robert Kennedy's misgivings about the dangers of LBJ serving a second term. They suggested Kennedy should run against him for the Democratic nomination for the Presidency but, at first, he considered this unthinkable. He had his eye on the nomination for the 1972 election and had not thought of running as early as 1968. He did not think he could oust Johnson and did not relish splitting the party in the attempt. The fact that there was no love lost between him and Johnson only served to make the idea less acceptable. He feared being seen as opposing Johnson out of spite. His fears about Johnson gaining a second term did not diminish, however, hence his great dilemma.

It was Senator Eugene McCarthy of Minnesota who first took up the cudgels against Johnson. He had reasoned as Kennedy had reasoned and had decided to take action, and soon had a healthy following, notably among young intellectuals. Robert Kennedy felt he could not go with McCarthy. To support him in an attempt to oust Johnson would imply a willingness to support him all the way to the

---

* *Face the Nation*, 26 November 1967

White House, and he did not see McCarthy as Presidential material. And there were other aspects to his dilemma. If he didn't run against Johnson for the nomination himself, he would be expected to campaign for LBJ in his second-term bid. He found this idea repugnant. Campaigning for a man he believed would bring ruin to the United States would have made him dishonest.

'Your plunging in might be an act of conscience to some people. But it would likely also be political suicide for you,' a valued adviser wrote to Robert Kennedy. Wise words but they did not solve or even improve the dilemma. Another totally different dimension to his problem was that he could announce his candidature, win all the primaries and still not receive the party's nomination to run for the Presidency. Eugene McCarthy, meanwhile, was gaining the support of those who would have been his own people while he carefully weighed the pros and cons. Not only this, but Kennedy was being castigated by those who thought he should have been first in the fight against Johnson as a peace candidate.

Jack Newfield, a friend of Kennedy's, writing in the *Village Voice*, was one who helped him to make up his mind:

> If Kennedy does not run in 1968, the best side of his character will die. He will kill it every time he butchers his conscience and makes a speech for Johnson next autumn. It will die every time a kid asks him, if he is so much against the Vietnam war, how come he is putting party above principle? It will die every time a stranger quotes his own words back to him on the value of courage.*

Robert Kennedy's feelings were summed up for him in a quotation by Jules Feiffer:

> *Good Bobby*: We're going in there and we're killing South Vietnamese, we're killing children, we're killing women . . . we're killing innocent people because we don't want the war fought on American soil . . .
> *Bad Bobby*: I will back the Democratic candidate in 1968. I expect that will be President Johnson.
> *Good Bobby*: I think we're going to have a difficult time explaining this to ourselves.†

---

* The *Village Voice*, 28 December 1967
† Halberstam: 'Unfinished Odyssey'

His problems may not have been understood by the people, but his indecision was observed. Brooklyn College students displayed a placard for him to see: BOBBY KENNEDY. HAWK, DOVE OR CHICKEN? His strong support was turning against him. McCarthy was settling in to his campaign, though it was not doing well. RFK must now, finally, make up his mind about whether he would run or not.

It was the Tet offensive which pushed Robert Kennedy into announcing his intention to run for the Democratic nomination. The North Vietnamese had launched a fierce attack on South Vietnam, devastating 30 cities and fighting their way into the US embassy in Saigon, and the Pentagon's reaction was to ask for more than 200,000 additional troops. He felt he no longer had a choice. He threw himself into his campaign in the essentially three-cornered contest between President Johnson, Eugene McCarthy and himself. By now he was too late for the New Hampshire primary, which McCarthy–whom Kennedy saw as a formidable opponent–took with flying colours. But now sure of his decision, Robert Kennedy–single-minded, determined, his qualms gone–squared himself for the fight. Slightly misquoting *The American Scholar*, he wrote a note to a friend:

> They did not yet see, and thousands of young men as hopeful, now crowding to the barriers of their careers, did not yet see if a single man plant himself on his convictions and then abide, the huge world will come round to him.

Jacqueline Kennedy made a curious observation when she heard her brother-in-law had announced his intention to run for the nomination. 'Do you know what I think will happen to Bobby? . . . The same thing that happened to Jack . . .'

Robert Kennedy was at first strongly criticised for joining the fray late in the day, opposing McCarthy and generally rocking the boat. He explained he felt that had he been first in, he would have attracted criticism for joining in a personality struggle between himself and President Johnson. He pointed out that McCarthy's success had highlighted the split which existed in the ranks of the Democrats. He had not created it. But there was now no time for rancour. There was a great deal to do and, as his critics reminded him, he was a late starter.

Kennedy's campaign proved to be an experience none of those who worked with him would ever forget. Not just for its dynamism, its enthusiasm, its exuberance or its momentum, but for the warm compassion and concern expressed by their leader everywhere he went. It was during this campaign that Robert Kennedy might be said finally to have stepped out of the shadow of his brother. The message he presented was warm, sincere and compelling, and the people rallied to him in an extraordinary fashion. The need to seek a negotiated settlement in Vietnam coupled with American withdrawal was his platform for peace. It was vital, not just to those with the lives of sons, husbands, brothers and friends at stake, but to the millions who were depressed by what they saw as a never-ending war. But he was much more than a peace candidate.

His speeches revealed a deep concern for the plight of the poor, the blacks, the Indians, Puerto Ricans, Mexican Americans, white Appalachians, and all those who had fallen victim to the 'system'. 'I have to win through the people, otherwise I am not going to win,'* he said. By March he had spoken in 16 states.

> Our brave young men are dying in the swamps of South-East Asia. Which of them might have written a poem? Which of them might have cured cancer? Which of them might have played in a World Series or given us the gift of laughter from the stage or helped build a bridge or a university? Which of them would have taught a child to read? It is our responsibility to let these men live . . . It is indecent if they die because of the empty vanity of their country.†

This was his message when he reached California. The people went wild. They crowded him, pulling his hair and touching his face. It took the police 30 minutes to get him out of the venue. 'I'm beginning to feel the mood of the country and what they want,' he said. By the end of the day his hands bled, his cuff-links were missing and his face bore scratch marks. He talked a language they understood, the language of the common man, the honest American citizen. They loved him. He loved them.

* The *New York Post*, 5 June 1968
† The *New York Times*, 25 March 1968

On 31 March, Lyndon Baines Johnson dropped the bombshell that he would not be running for a second term. He confided to Hubert Humphrey, his Vice-President, that he '. . . could not function on these great issues if he were subjected every day to attacks from Nixon [pursuing the Republican nomination], McCarthy and Robert Kennedy.' Johnson was a man who dreaded defeat and, it seemed, he preferred to retire than run the risk of being booted out. Johnson was also in the unhappy position of knowing that he was in the White House by courtesy of the Consortium. He had known this from the very beginning, and he must have been acutely aware that the Consortium had expectations to which he had to measure up. In retiring from office he side-stepped the Consortium and he side-stepped the possibility of ignominious defeat in the nominations. It was a politician's answer to a politician's problem, a political manoeuvre. It preserved his public image. In an interview with Doris Kearns, who wrote a book on Johnson, he would confess to the experience of a recurring nightmare, in which:

> . . . I was being forced over the edge by rioting blacks, demonstrating students, marching welfare mothers, squawking professors, and hysterical reporters. And then the final straw. The thing I feared from the first day of my Presidency was actually coming true. Robert Kennedy had openly announced his intention to reclaim the throne in the memory of his brother. And the American people, swayed by the magic of the name, were dancing in the streets.*

The impact of Johnson's decision not to run for a second term had, obviously, a profound effect on the battle for the Democratic nomination. Hubert Humphrey, now free to enter the contest, did so, but whatever chance he might have had was sharply diminished by the lateness of his announcing. It was McCarthy and Kennedy who found themselves slugging it out, a curious situation since they belonged to the same peace camp. But then, at the time of his withdrawal, Johnson had somewhat blunted the impact of the peace contestants' campaigns by leaning towards a changed policy on Vietnam in which major escalation was rejected and negotiation was now mooted. Hitherto, Kennedy and McCarthy had both devoted

* Doris Kearns, *Lyndon Johnson and the American Dream*, New York, 1976

their energies to scoring points off Johnson. Now they found themselves scoring points off one another. The essential difference between the two was that McCarthy appealed to the middle classes, the well-to-do, whereas Kennedy addressed himself and his campaign to the plight of the poor, the disadvantaged and the downtrodden:

> We are more divided now than perhaps we have been in a hundred years. [We need] to heal the deep divisions that exist between races, between age groups and on the war . . .
>
> I want to work for those who are not represented. I want to be their President.

After Martin Luther King came out in opposition to the Vietnam war in the early part of 1967, his path and Kennedy's began to veer towards each other. Collaboration soon began to take place in their quest for economic and racial justice. The idea for what became known as the 'Poor People's Campaign' originated with Kennedy, though it found its hands and feet with King. The campaign involved an invasion of Washington by large numbers of the poor who demanded action from Congress.

In Indiana, Kennedy's determination to take his message to the black community saw him speaking in the 'worst' area of the ghetto. It was just before he boarded his plane for Indianapolis that he received the news that Martin Luther King had been shot in Memphis, and when he arrived in Indianapolis he heard that he was dead. It would seem that when King sent the poor in large, perhaps frightening, numbers to Washington, he had signed his own death warrant. He had worried the Establishment by this move. No doubt he had also worried the 'other government' – the Consortium – and it was probably the Consortium members who decided he must be removed. The night Martin Luther King died, it was Robert Kennedy who took the sad tidings to the black ghetto in Indianapolis.

The police warned Kennedy not to go to the ghetto, refusing to accept responsibility for his safety. His police escort was withdrawn when he refused to abandon his meeting. He climbed to the back of a truck to address the crowd:

I have bad news for you, for all of our fellow citizens, and people who love peace all over the world, and that is that Martin Luther King was shot and killed tonight.

There was a gasp from the crowd as they struggled to take the message in:

Martin Luther King dedicated his life to love and to justice for his fellow human beings, and he died because of that effort.

In this difficult day, in this difficult time for the United States, it is perhaps well to ask what kind of a nation we are and what direction we want to move in. For those of you who are black–considering the evidence there evidently is that there were white people responsible–you can be filled with bitterness, with hatred, and a desire for revenge. We can move in that direction as a country, in great polarization–black people among black, white people amongst white, filled with hatred toward one another.

Or we can make an effort, as Martin Luther King did, to understand and to comprehend, and to replace that violence, that stain of bloodshed that has spread across our land, with an effort to understand with compassion and love.

For those of you who are black and are tempted to be filled with hatred and distrust at the injustice of such an act, against all white people, I can only say that I feel in my own heart the same kind of feeling. I had a member of my family killed, but he was killed by a white man. But we have to make an effort in the United States, we have to make an effort to understand, to go beyond these difficult times.

My favourite poet was Aeschylus. He wrote: 'In our sleep pain which cannot forget falls drop by drop upon our heart until, in our own despair, against our will, comes wisdom through the awful grace of God.'

What we need in the United States is not division; what we need in the United States is not hatred; what we need in the United States is not violence or lawlessness, but love and wisdom, and compassion towards one another, and a feeling of justice towards those who still suffer within our country, whether they be white or they be black . . .

We've had difficult times in the past. We will have difficult times in the future. It is not the end of violence; it is not the end of lawlessness; it is not the end of disorder.

But the vast majority of white people and the vast majority of black people in this country want to live together, want to improve the quality of our life, and want justice for all human beings who abide in our land.

Let us dedicate ourselves to what the Greeks wrote so many years ago: to tame the savageness and to make gentle the life of this world.

Let is dedicate ourselves to that, and say a prayer for our country and for our people.

The Kennedy camp was quite convinced that Martin Luther King, had he lived, would have declared for Kennedy. There was no doubt that the cause of the blacks was firmly established as his cause, as was the cause of the Indians and those other minorities which were kept at a distance by white society. His was the cause of the poor, and the people were rallying behind him. RFK was due to meet a group of black militants after the Indianapolis rally. He was very late and when he arrived the group were angry. 'Our leader is dead tonight, and when we need you we can't find you.' Looking back at the reply Kennedy gave, it could easily have been believed he was starkly aware of the existence of the Consortium and its intentions. He said:

Yes, you lost a friend, I lost a brother, I know how you feel . . . You talk about the Establishment. I have to laugh. *Big business is trying to defeat me because they think I am a friend of the Negro.* [Author's emphasis added]

Unlike large parts of his speeches which were written by his speech-writers, these were entirely Kennedy's own words. At the end of their talk, those in the group promised their support for his campaign. Afterwards, Arthur Schlesinger recorded: '. . . Kennedy seemed over-whelmed, despondent, fatalistic. Thinking of Dallas, perhaps . . .'*

Riots in over 100 cities followed King's death. Thirty-nine people were killed and 25,000 injured. National Guardsmen and Federal troops were called out. Washington was placed under curfew. This, however, did not stop the many white notables who turned out for King's funeral in Atlanta. Richard Nixon, Nelson Rockefeller, Hubert Humphrey and Eugene McCarthy were there. Britain's Roy Jenkins took particular note of the popularity of Robert Kennedy, who marched the five miles from the church in his shirt-sleeves.† Jenkins asked where Lyndon Johnson was. Johnson was not present, though that might have reflected wisdom rather than the cowardice he was accused of.

* Arthur M. Schlesinger Jr, *Robert Kennedy and His Times*, Andre Deutsch, London, 1978
† Roy Jenkins, *Nine Men of Power*, London, 1974

Robert Kennedy was not renowned for pulling his punches. He did not reserve a patronising attitude for those who were untouched by his message and what he stood for. Speaking on health care at the Indiana University Medical School he condemned the national health system as having 'failed to meet the most urgent medical needs of millions of Americans'. He was met with polite applause. When asked where the money was to come from for his proposed health programme he cried:

> From you. Let me say something about the tone of these questions. I look around this room and I don't see many black faces who will become doctors. You can talk about where the money will come from . . . Part of civilised society is to let people go to medical school who come from ghettos. You don't see many people coming out of the ghettos or off the Indian reservations to medical school. You are the privileged ones . . . It's our society, not just our government, that spends twice as much on pets as on the poverty programme. It's the poor that carry the major burden in Vietnam. You sit here as white medical students, while black people carry the burden of the fighting in Vietnam.*

It was John Bartlow Martin who wrote:

> He plodded ahead stubbornly, making them listen, maybe even making some of them care, by the sheer power of his own caring. Indiana people are not generous nor sympathetic; they are hard . . . but he must have touched something in them, pushed a button somewhere.†

Indeed he must. When it came to the vote, his Indiana victory was decisive in a three-cornered contest. McCarthy, unsuccessful there, took Oregon and Orange County, but Kennedy took Nebraska and beat Hubert Humphrey in the District of Columbia, and would go on to take South Dakota, also.

There was no doubt the members of the Consortium were following Robert Kennedy's progress with growing concern. They had not

---

* Jules Witcover. *85 Days: The Last Campaign of Robert Kennedy*, New York, 1969
† John Bartlow Martin, *RFK Notes*

expected to see a following for him until 1972 and here he was rallying incredible support and riding on a tide of popularity. The time for urgent action had arrived. Their plans must all be brought forward. It was imperative that he didn't reach the White House. Having found it necessary to kill the President to rid the country of the combination of Kennedy power and presidential might, it was unthinkable that their actions could be negated by Robert Kennedy bringing the Kennedy influence to the White House again. They stood at the same crossroads again, but their advantage this time was that it was easier to kill a senator than a president. The Executive Group would again ask the CIA members, who had a vested interest, for a significant contribution to what they had to do.

For Robert Kennedy it was now on to California, with speeches in Los Angeles, San Francisco, Sacramento, Oakland and San Diego. There was a wonderful zest present in the campaign in which Kennedy revelled. It became a 'huge, joyous adventure'.* California was the last and biggest of the primaries, and Robert Kennedy's popular acclaim was at its height. During the campaign he had emerged as a charismatic leader, a man of compassion who, having captivated the poor and the disadvantaged, seemed capable of drawing all sides of the nation together.

But, not long before this time, a group of newspaper reporters had sat discussing Kennedy. One of their number had asked whether he had the stuff to go all the way. It was John J. Lindsay of *Newsweek* who spoke up in reply: 'Of course he has the stuff to go all the way, but he's not going to go all the way . . . Somebody is going to shoot him . . . He's out there now waiting for him.'†

---

* Charles Quinn in a recorded interview by Jean Stein, 19 October 1968 (Stein Papers).
† Jack Newfield, *Robert Kennedy*, New York, 1969

CHAPTER TEN

The Murder of Robert Kennedy

'Violence goes on and on . . . Why? What has violence ever accomplished? What has it ever created? No martyr's cause has ever been stilled by his assassin's bullet.'
Robert Kennedy, Cleveland, Ohio, 1968

HERE IS [CALIFORNIA] the most urban state of any of the states of our Union, South Dakota the most rural of any of the states of our Union. We were able to win them both. I think we can end the divisions within the United States . . .

. . . What I think is quite clear, is that we can work together in the last analysis, and that what has been going on within the United States over a period of the last three years–the division, the violence, the disenchantment with our society; the divisions, whether it's between blacks and whites, between the poor and the more affluent, or between age groups or on the war in Vietnam–is that we can start to work together. We are a great country, an unselfish country, and a compassionate country. I intend to make that my basis for running.

The crowd went wild. Robert Kennedy, who had delivered what had perhaps been the best speech of the campaign, smiled his boyish smile and gave the victory sign to his audience. 'My thanks to all of you and now it's on to Chicago and let's win there,' he said. To the 1,800 supporters packed into Los Angeles's Ambassador Hotel ballroom there could be no doubt they were looking at the next President of the United States of America. They cheered and cheered.

Robert Kennedy was out on his feet. The California primary had been critical to his campaign. He had won, and that enormous sense of well being was his at this, his moment of triumph. But it was after midnight and, doubtless, all he wanted now was to be allowed to go to his hotel room, unwind for a while with those closest to him, and turn in for whatever sleep would be his that night. There was one more thing he must do, however, before he could retire. He had arranged to speak to press reporters, and so it was he was shepherded away, straight after his speech, by the shortest possible route to the room in which the ladies and gentlemen of the press were waiting. The shortest route led through the kitchen pantry.

Ardent photographer, 15-year-old Scott Enyart, who owned and used a professional camera, had taken pictures of RFK making his speech, and now joined the throng making its way through the pantry, taking pictures as he went. And some throng it was. The pantry resembled a kind of spacious corridor or passageway in which items of equipment and various tables were placed, and it was packed with people. To obtain a vantage point, Scott jumped up on a table to continue his photographic record of the Senator's progress. Tired though he was, Robert Kennedy, led by Karl Uecker, the hotel maître d', stopped to shake hands with members of the kitchen staff, which was typical of the man. Thane Cesar, an agency guard employed by the hotel, had appeared behind Uecker and gripped the Senator's arm. There was another pause while Kennedy turned to his left to shake the hand of another member of the staff, then it was as he turned to face the front again that it happened.

A young man of Palestinian stock leapt forward towards him, a gun in his hand, crying 'Kennedy, you son of a bitch.' The gun belched over and over again. Karl Uecker threw himself at the man, gripping his head in a lock beneath his arm and wrestling his wrist down to an adjacent steam table to make him drop the gun. With demoniac strength the gunman held on to his weapon and it continued to fire again and again until the chamber was empty. Pandemonium had broken loose. People screamed while others cursed. Robert Kennedy lay on his back in a pool of blood. 'Come on Mr Kennedy. You can make it,' encouraged Juan Romero, a member of the hotel staff, who

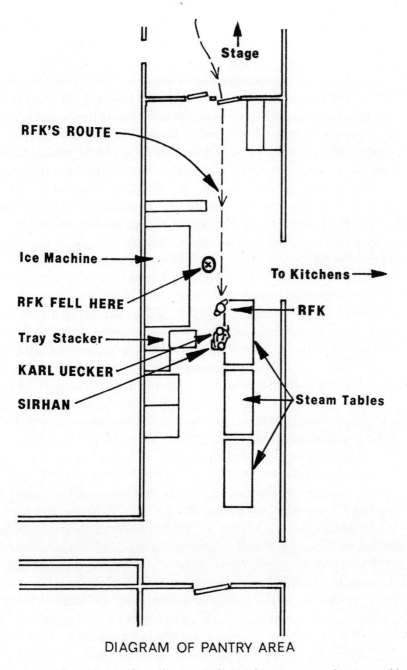

Stage

RFK'S ROUTE

Ice Machine

To Kitchens

RFK FELL HERE

RFK

Tray Stacker

KARL UECKER

SIRHAN

Steam Tables

DIAGRAM OF PANTRY AREA

Note that Karl Uecker was always between Sirhan and Senator Kennedy. How could
Sirhan have fired into Kennedy's back?

gently cradled his head. 'Is everybody all right?' the Senator managed to ask. A young man in the crowd of over 70 people jammed into the pantry area handed his rosary beads to Romero for him. A doctor, Stanley Abo, was quickly found among the guests and he gave what little assistance was possible. Ethel Kennedy, the Senator's wife, who had been following at a distance, cut off by the throng, had lost no time in pushing through to kneel by his side to give what comfort she could. 'Oh, Ethel, Ethel, am I all right?' he asked, in a voice barely audible. Robert Kennedy had been shot three times and five others had been wounded. Within minutes the police arrived to take charge of the crime scene and begin their investigation into what had happened. It was 17 minutes after the shooting that an ambulance arrived and the injured were taken to hospital. They were taken first to the Central Receiving Hospital before being sent on to the Good Samaritan Hospital. It was 1.00 am before they arrived there, three-quarters of an hour after the shooting, and Robert Kennedy was rushed to the operating theatre to begin what would be a three-hour operation.

The gunman was Sirhan Bishara Sirhan, a 25-year-old who had been born in Jerusalem and brought to the United States after his family had survived the ordeal of becoming refugees in Israeli-occupied territory. In their investigation, the Los Angeles Police Department discovered a notebook at Sirhan's home in which he appeared to make threats against Robert Kennedy, with whom he was angry for supporting Israel in general and, more specifically, for approving the sale of 50 Phantom jets to that country. He was said to have connections with communism, and it was established that he had spent several hours earlier on the day of the meeting at the Ambassador, practising rapid fire at the San Gabriel Valley Gun Club with a weapon of the same calibre to that fired at the Senator.

It was not by accident that there was no police presence at the Ambassador Hotel when Robert Kennedy was shot. The Senator had expressly forbidden it. Apart from one or two of his friends who kept an eye out for him and Bill Barry, who had once worked for the FBI and who had taken leave from his job as a bank vice-president to accompany him on his campaign, acting as his personal bodyguard, there was only the hotel's security service. They provided ten plainclothes personnel and eight armed guards under a contract they held with the Ace Guard Service, a local company. RFK did not want to be seen surrounded by policemen. At one point on the campaign, Bill Barry had hired off-duty policemen to hang around the lobby of the hotel they were in, but when Kennedy had learnt of it he cancelled the arrangement. 'He only accepted as much protection as he got because he liked me . . .' said Barry. 'He wouldn't have had anybody if really left to his own choice.'

During the night hours, the police began taking statements from the many guests and from members of the hotel staff. They also explored the pantry area for marks made by the bullets and for bullet holes. Los Angeles Police Department's forensic expert De Wayne Wolfer was in attendance during this time and it would be he who would produce a trajectory 'map' accounting for the directions taken by the bullets fired and the wounds sustained. He would say that Robert Kennedy had been struck in the rear of his right side about seven inches below the top of his shoulder, the missile lodging in his spine. Another bullet had hit him about an inch below the first, travelling in an upward and forward direction and exiting his chest. A third bullet struck him just below and to the rear of his right ear. Examination of the Senator's jacket showed that a fourth bullet had transitted the shoulder pad without hitting him, though Wolfer claimed this was the bullet which hit Kennedy's friend, Paul Schrade, in the forehead. Sirhan's gun held eight bullets. The fifth, in Wolfer's map, struck newsman Ira Goldstein in the left rear buttock, and the sixth passed through Goldstein's trouser leg, ricocheting off the cement floor and lodging in Erwin Stroll's left leg. William Weisel received the seventh bullet in his abdomen, and the eighth and final bullet, according to De Wayne Wolfer, struck a plaster tile and deflected to hit Elizabeth Evans in the head.

Wolfer gave the appearance of having worked out the trajectories to a fine art, and judging by the support it gave him, Los Angeles Police Department was extremely proud of his accomplishment. LAPD had declared it would conduct the most scrupulously careful and detailed examination of every aspect of the shooting since it was determined Los Angeles would not become another Dallas. It was a strange thing for a police department to publicise, since it gave the impression that its first priority was to prevent LA from becoming another Dallas, rather than direct its energies towards finding out who was responsible for the attack on Senator Kennedy. The Department decided it was a simple case. De Wayne Wolfer presented his trajectory map which, he said, accounted for the contents of Sirhan's gun: eight shots fired, eight shots accounted for. Only one gun had been fired: only one person was responsible. There was no conspiracy and they had their man.

At 1.44 on the morning of 6 June, Robert Francis Kennedy died of his wounds. The inquiry was now an investigation into murder. Wolfer announced it was an 'open-and-shut' case. They had their killer, the man who had been seen to shoot at Senator Kennedy and the others who had been wounded. There was no one else to seek.

Incredibly, for an 'open-and-shut' case, there were loose ends clearly visible everywhere which caused a great deal more than unease among those who had access to the detail of the investigation. There were those who, from the beginning, knew they had not heard the truth about the murder of Robert Kennedy. The autopsy report, all by itself for instance, was enough to tell them this. Dr Thomas Noguchi's autopsy report revealed that, without question, the bullet which killed Robert Kennedy was fired at point-blank range.* Noguchi placed the murder weapon as close as one inch from the edge of Kennedy's ear and not more than three inches. In the case of the other two wounds, the gun was between contact and one inch from Kennedy's back. These shots, clearly, could not have come from Sirhan's gun, which witnesses placed at a distance from Robert Kennedy varying between one-and-a-half feet, at the very nearest, to six feet, which was estimated by some. Added to this was the incontrovertible bullet-trajectory evidence. Dr Noguchi made it clear the bullets which struck Robert Kennedy's back were travelling in an upward and forward direction, which made it impossible for them to have come from Sirhan's direction, for he stood in front of the Senator and had any of his bullets hit RFK they would have been travelling front to back.

* This was the same Dr Thomas Noguchi who had carried out the autopsy into the death of Marilyn Monroe

When Robert Kennedy was shot, witnesses saw his head move in a forward direction before he keeled over and fell on his back, consistent with bullets fired from behind him. The Wolfer trajectory map began to fall apart with the testimony of Paul Schrade, who was hit by a bullet in his forehead. He could not accept Wolfer's claim that the bullet which had hit him was the one which had transitted Kennedy's jacket shoulder pad. Schrade pointed out that for this to be true he would have either had to have had his head on RFK's shoulder or else been nine feet tall. The trajectory map fell further apart when numerous witnesses said they saw bullet holes in the woodwork in the pantry. De Wayne Wolfer's meticulous accounting of the firing of eight bullets, all that Sirhan's gun could contain, was knocked sideways if but one additional bullet was found to have lodged in woodwork. Even just nine bullets mean that two guns had been fired in the pantry. Two guns represented two gunmen and two gunmen represented a conspiracy.

From the outset Sirhan Sirhan's appearance had given cause for concern, also, to those who were not prepared to accept the pat case presented by the Los Angeles Police Department. His peaceful eyes and smiling face betrayed indications that though his body was certainly present, shooting in the pantry, his mind was elsewhere. It was said he looked as though he was in a trance, and this gave rise to the notion that he may have been hypnotised. This idea was reinforced by his near-incoherence after the shooting and his inability to recall any memory of his attack on Senator Kennedy. A man on trial for his life can reliably be expected to speak up for himself and render his own version of events. Not so Sirhan. He had no recollection of shooting at Robert Kennedy whatsoever.

Claims that Sirhan was seen in the company of another man and a woman were resisted by LAPD investigators as best they could. This presented them with problems since so many people had seen them together, but they simply stonewalled the witnesses who rendered accounts in the statements they gave, or else ignored them. This was high-handed, to say the least, when witnesses gave detailed descriptions of them and some had even spoken to one of the couple. Of course acceptance that Sirhan was with others would have strongly supported a case for a conspiracy having taken place, and LAPD showed it was dedicated to accepting only a lone-gunman scenario.

But the existence of Sirhan's two companions is beyond any reasonable doubt. They constituted an important feature of what happened at the Ambassador Hotel that night, and the investigation team's decision to ignore them showed them to have been selective in the information they gathered.

Sirhan Sirhan was tried on a count of first-degree murder and, in his defence, his lawyers tried, with great single-mindedness, to establish a plea of diminished responsibility. In their anxiety to achieve this, however, they totally neglected the important loose ends which could have changed the nature of the trial and compelled the prosecution to answer for vital anomalies which existed.

These went completely unchallenged. The defence team accepted without question the evidence introduced relating to the ballistics data, when Wolfer claimed in the courtroom to have matched all the bullets retrieved to the murder weapon. The glaring fact that the gun to which he referred was not Sirhan's gun at all went unnoticed at the vital time. Dr Noguchi had been approached before the trial with a request to amend his findings to show the distance of the murder weapon from Robert Kennedy as one to three feet instead of one to three inches, which he refused.* The prosecution did not have to worry, however, for the defence cut short Noguchi's presentation of the autopsy details before the facts were told. Sirhan Sirhan was found guilty and sentenced to death. His lawyers had unwittingly played themselves completely into the hands of the prosecution, and it was small wonder Sirhan's mother complained he had had no defence. Fortuitously, California law relating to the death penalty was changed before Sirhan was executed and his sentence was commuted to life imprisonment.

Dr Noguchi was later pressured by the Los Angeles authorities not to speak of his autopsy findings and he refused. He was then dismissed from his job as coroner on the grounds of incompetence in regard to the Robert Kennedy autopsy. Noguchi bravely fought the Los Angeles authorities on this and went to court to challenge the allegations brought against him. He was successful: his name and reputation were cleared and the authorities were obliged to reinstate him to his former position. The sheer audacity of those who wished to

---

* Dr Noguchi was quoted in the *Los Angeles Herald Examiner* in an article published in 1974

WANTED

FOR

TREASON

THIS MAN is wanted for treasonous activities against the United States:

1. Betraying the Constitution (which he swore to uphold):
He is turning the sovereignty of the U.S. over to the communist controlled United Nations.
He is betraying our friends (Cuba, Katanga, Portugal) and befriending our enemies (Russia, Yugoslavia, Poland).

2. He has been WRONG on innumerable issues affecting the security of the U.S. (United Nations-Berlin wall-Missle removal-Cuba-Wheat deals-Test Ban Treaty, etc.)

3. He has been lax in enforcing Communist Registration laws.

4. He has given support and encouragement to the Communist inspired racial riots.

5. He has illegally invaded a sovereign State with federal troops.

6. He has consistantly appointed Anti-Christians to Federal office: Upholds the Supreme Court in its Anti-Christian rulings.
Aliens and known Communists abound in Federal offices.

7. He has been caught in fantastic LIES to the American people (including personal ones like his previous marraige and divorce).

(Plate 16) The infamous handbill circulated in Dallas on the day of the President's visit (*Courtesy National Archives*)

(Plate 17) Photographer James Altgens took this photograph of the motorcade just after the first shot was fired at President Kennedy. Note the heads of the secret service men turned towards the School Book Depository (*AP/Wide World Photos*)

(Plate 18) The famous Polaroid photograph taken by Mary Moorman at the moment President Kennedy was shot. Behind the fence in the background stood a sniper whose picture, arguably, was buried in the detail of this photo. A figure has emerged in enhancements (*Courtesy Mary Moorman, now Mary Krahmer*)

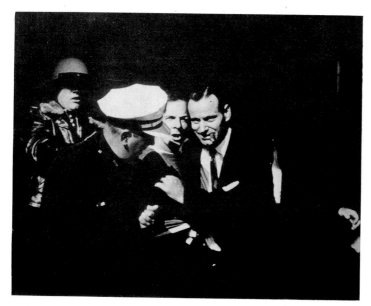

(Plate 19) Lee Harvey Oswald is arrested at the Texas Theater (*Courtesy National Archives*)

(Plate 20) Lee Harvey Oswald questioned by news reporters at a make-shift press conference in Dallas Police Headquarters late on the night he was arrested (*Courtesy National Archives*)

(Plate 21) Police Officer J.D. Tippit. Shot and killed (*Courtesy National Archives*)

(Plate 22) Jack Ruby. He shot Oswa in cold blood (*Courtesy Natio* Archives)

(Plate 23) Warren Commission exhibit 399, the 'magic' bullet (*Courtesy National Archives*)

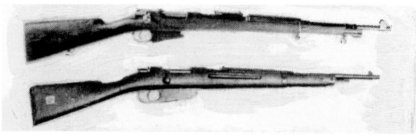

(Plate 24) A Mannlicher Carcano rifle (bottom) bears a superficial resemblance to a Mauser (top), it is true, but could experts not tell them apart? Could they, for instance, not read what was printed on them?

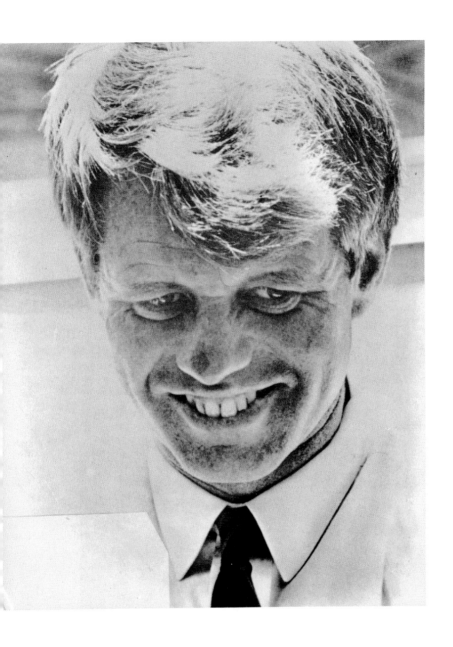

(Plate 25) Robert Francis Kennedy (Courtesy John F. Kennedy Library)

(Plate 26) It was while walking through the pantry area of Los Angeles's Ambassador Hotel that Robert Kennedy was shot and fatally wounded. He had forbidden a police presence at the rally (*Matt Flowers-Smith*)

(Plate 27) Assailant Sirhan Sirhan is tackled by two of those who accompanied Robert Kennedy, while others anxiously look in the direction of the wounded Senator. Sirhan nevertheless continued to fire his gun until it was empty. His head is just left of the cluster of hands (*AP/Wide World Photos*)

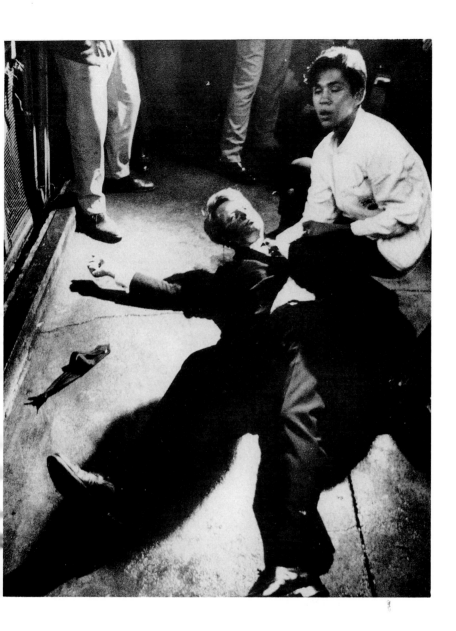

(Plate 28) Robert Kennedy lies wounded on the pantry floor. Young hotel worker Juan Romero holds his head and comforts him, 'Come on, Mr Kennedy. You can make it' (*AP/Wide World Photos*)

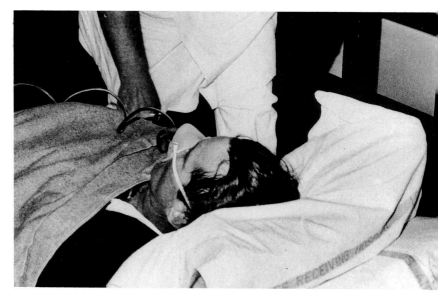

(Plate 29) The wounded Senator Kennedy is placed on a stretcher in readiness for his journey to hospital (*AP/Wide World Photos*)

(Plate 30) Sirhan Sirhan is led away after his attack on Senator Robert Kennedy (*Courtesy SE Mass. Univ. RFK Assassination Archives*)

discredit his unwelcome findings was breathtaking. As it turned out, their actions only served to highlight their determination to conceal those features of the assassination investigation which did not fit the case for which they had opted.

Taking the sum of the loose ends together, a strong case emerges for a conspiracy having taken place. More bullets were fired than could have come from Sirhan's gun, which indicated a second gunman, and Sirhan being seen in the company of others immediately before the shooting was another indication of more than one person being involved. Sirhan's curious behaviour added a unique flavour to the picture, suggesting he was under the influence of another, and the simplistic case for him being a lone killer at once becomes hard to swallow. From the facts known, the man who really killed Robert Kennedy was extremely close to him—almost hugging him—when Sirhan started firing, and he killed him at point blank range in cold blood.

It is plain that the role Sirhan Sirhan was given was that of a patsy, but the skilfully devised plan had him not only fulfilling the function of attracting the attention of all those in the vicinity, but at the same time providing cover for the shooting of the murder weapon by letting off every round in the gun he brandished. Those who looked for the second gunman looked long and hard at the only man who openly displayed possession of a gun and who stood slightly behind and to the right of the Senator when the shooting started. Thane Eugene Cesar was a uniformed security man provided by the Ace Guard Service, and he and maître d' Karl Uecker had led the Senator through the pantry. Upon seeing Sirhan firing a gun, Karl Uecker heroically threw himself at the man, placing his head beneath his arm in a headlock, and wrestling Sirhan's arm down to the adjacent steam table, where he struggled to loose the gun from his grasp. Cesar, by his own admission ducked when the shooting started and stumbled, ending up on the floor. His clip-on bow tie was seen—and photographed—lying on the floor a few inches from the mortally wounded Senator (see plate 28).

At some point the guard drew his gun, and one witness, Don Schulman, claimed he saw the gun being fired. Cesar's 'issue' gun being a .38-calibre weapon and Sirhan's a .22, bullets recovered in the pantry area would have been expected to reflect the fact that the guard had fired if, indeed, he had done so. No .38 slug was reported found, though it has to be said that it was entirely possible for bullets to have remained undiscovered. In fact, the bullet retrieved from Kennedy's body was so badly distorted that De Wayne Wolfer admitted it could not with certainty be identified as being of .22 calibre. It would be odd, however, in a professional killing, as this clearly was, for a second gunman to betray his presence by using a weapon of a different kind to that used by Sirhan. Of course there was nothing to have prevented Cesar from carrying two guns, one to show and one to use. Cesar's 'issue' gun was superficially examined by an officer after the shooting but no more. Test bullets were not fired from it and Thane Cesar was completely cleared of suspicion. Certain facts surfaced later to throw doubt on whether the police had acted hastily in dismissing Cesar from their inquiries.

Cesar had admitted to having owned a .22 calibre gun similar to Sirhan's, though he said he had sold it some months before the assassination, in February. Sergeant Phil Sartuche was given the task of checking this statement out, and he said it was correct. In fact it was a lie, for the person to whom he sold it produced a receipt for leading RFK researcher, Theodore Charach, to see, which bore a date about three months *after* the time of the shooting. The man who bought the gun, Jim Yoder, recounted it was later stolen from him. He reported the theft to the police but the gun was never recovered. One question which at once springs to mind is why, if a researcher could find Yoder, couldn't Sergeant Sartuche? Since Cesar supplied Yoder's name to the police, presumably a prompt inquiry on the part of the police would have exposed the untruth and the gun could have been sought. (Questioned again during a 1974 inquiry, Cesar amended his position to being *uncertain* whether he sold the gun before or after the RFK shooting.)

Cesar also said, when questioned by researcher Dan Moldea, that he had worked for the Ace Guard Service for six months or more before the shooting. Another researcher, Betsy Langman, discovered from the Ace Guard Service files, that Cesar had joined them only about a week beforehand.* Adding to all this that Cesar admitted to being a right winger and no supporter of RFK, there was ample evidence to warrant much deeper investigation into the guard. Some have suggested he might have shot Kennedy by accident in returning Sirhan's fire, though the evidence does not support accidental shooting. The wounds sustained by Robert Kennedy are not consistent with such gunfire. The killer was extremely close to his victim, and his proximity supports that the shooting was purposeful.

Donald Schulman, already mentioned as claiming he saw Thane Cesar fire his gun, made interesting statements to reporter Jeff Brent immediately after the shooting:

> I was standing behind Kennedy as he was taking his assigned route into the kitchen. A Caucasian gentleman stepped out and fired. The security guard hit Kennedy all three times. Kennedy slumped to the floor. The security guard fired back and I saw the man who shot Kennedy in the leg, he—before they could get to him, he shot a—it looked like he shot a woman and he shot two other men. They then proceeded to carry Kennedy into the kitchen and I don't know how his condition is now . . . he had—was definitely hit three times. The thing happened so quickly that—there was another witness standing next to me—and she is in shock and very fuzzy, as I am, because it happened so quickly.

Jeff Brent had one point in particular he wanted to clarify. He asked Schulman if he meant it was the security guard firing when he had spoken of firing in his statement. 'Yes,' was Schulman's answer. Schulman stated that RFK had been hit three times, and in this he was correct, a fourth bullet having missed which transitted his shoulder pad. Others asked how many times the Senator had been hit either did not know or suggested twice. Not so Thane Cesar, however. When he was asked, in an interview for radio, he was the only other person to get it exactly right:

> *Interviewer*: Officer, can you confirm the fact that the Senator has been shot?
> *Cesar*: Yes. I was there holding his arm when they shot him.
> *Interviewer*: What happened?

---

* Ace Guard Service records show Cesar was given his first job for them on 31 May 1968. Also he had not, as he claimed, worked at the Ambassador Hotel 'several times before the incident'

> *Cesar*: I dunno–gentleman standing by the lunch counter there and as he walked up the guy pulled a gun and shot at him.
> *Interviewer*: Was it just one man?
> *Cesar*: No–yeah, one man.
> *Interviewer*: And what sort of a wound did the Senator receive?
> *Cesar*: Well, from where I could see, it looked like he was shot in the head and the chest and the shoulder, but . . .
> *Interviewer*: How many shots did you hear?
> *Cesar*: Four.

This was incredible accuracy. He even knew where the bullets went and accounted for the one which missed. To take his words literally, he was also exactly correct in describing Sirhan as having 'shot at' the Senator and not 'shot' him. The little blunder in answer to the question, 'Was it just one man?' does not escape note, either.

Returning to Schulman's spontaneous interview, he obviously did not have everything sorted out. He spoke of the Senator being hit in the leg which was not so, but otherwise gave the impression of reliability in his account, in spite of the fact that he was suffering from the effects of a shocking experience. Some time later he was interviewed again, this time by Theodore Charach:

> Well, I didn't see everything that night, but the things I did see I'm sure about. And that is about Kennedy being shot three times. And a guard definitely pulled out his gun and fired . . . He wasn't very far from Kennedy. He was just behind Mr Uecker and on Kennedy's right side, but there was another guard in front of Senator Kennedy and one on Kennedy's left side in the very crowded sardine-like conditions.

Schulman also recounted graphically what it was like during the moments the shooting took place and immediately afterwards. He spoke of 'extreme confusion, chaos, noise . . .' and told how '. . . everyone started to fight with each other in hysteria and duck, with the guard dropping to the floor, then getting out . . .'

Don Schulman's statements appear very enlightening and serve to describe the events in the pantry very well. In the light of his claims, it is hard to believe that the police did not regard Thane Cesar as a suspect in the murder of Robert Kennedy. They did not.

Leaving the wisdom of failing to investigate Don Schulman's claims against Cesar aside, there are two other important things which the police might have questioned the guard about concerning his behaviour on the night Robert Kennedy was killed. First, as has already been said, he ducked when the shooting started. He is reported as saying this himself. He ducked and then stumbled finishing up on the floor. Since a guard is not expected to simply duck when gunfire breaks out, is this not curious behaviour for someone appointed and paid to respond to an attack? Secondly, what was he doing at Robert Kennedy's right hand, holding his arm and leading him through the pantry? We know it would not please Robert Kennedy to be shepherded this way by a uniformed guard. Even Bill Barry, his bodyguard, though not far away, was not as close as Thane Cesar, presumably because he knew RFK would object. Perhaps the guard's presence was unknown to Kennedy, Karl Uecker being in front of Cesar—and, in fact holding Kennedy's wrist—obscuring the guard from the Senator's vision. But why was he there at all? The two questions are totally related and entirely complementary. If Cesar was close to Kennedy, leading him through the pantry area in order to give him protection, why then, when it was required, did he not act in the Senator's defence? Why did he duck? Further, when he had not been as close to the Senator all night, and we know that Kennedy would have objected to a uniformed chaperon, why was it he suddenly appeared and virtually led him to the point where he was ambushed? Cesar claimed William Gardner, the hotel's security chief, told him to accompany the Senator through the pantry, though an FBI summary of an interview with Gardner conradicts this:

> . . . the Senator did not want any uniformed security guards in his presence nor did he want any armed individuals as guards. Mr Gardner said that this is one of the reasons why he did not have any guard assigned to escort the Senator through the hotel during the visit.

Asked about his reasons for being there by researcher Dan Moldea in 1987, Cesar then said he was there for 'crowd control. Nothing else.' It still remains a mystery why he was there. By all accounts there were *two* other guards there already. Cesar himself recounts that after he ducked and stumbled to the floor:

> . . . I think it was Murphy, *one of the security guards* . . . helped me up, and he says 'Let's get out in front here and stop the pandemonium.' So I got up and went with him. [Emphasis added]

Since William Gardner had only eight uniformed guards at his disposal that night it would seem odd if he despatched three of them to the same place, specifically at the point where Kennedy—whom he knew did not want them in his presence—was going to be. The question remains, therefore, and is repeated: what was Cesar doing leading the Senator by the arm through the pantry?

Sirhan's companions on the night he shot at Robert Kennedy have been a source of intrigue and mystery to all who have studied the details of the tragic affair. He was seen at various times and in different locations within the Ambassador Hotel with a smart-looking young woman, and at times with the woman and also a tall man. The woman was eye-catching, not just because she was attractive, but because she wore a polka-dot dress. Witness Susan Locke saw the girl in the polka-dot dress in the ballroom and noticed she did not have a badge permitting her to be there. Lonny L. Worthy saw Sirhan standing next to the girl in the polka-dot dress in the bar. Booker Griffin saw Sirhan in the Embassy Room with a girl whom he described as having on a predominantly white dress which may have had another colour.

Sirhan and his companions apparently left the hotel and were seen re-entering by a witness at about 11.30. They entered by an outside fire-stairway on which Sandra Serrano, who later became an important witness, was sitting. Sandra had left the hurly-burly of the exciting proceedings in the now-hot ballroom to take a little fresh air, when the threesome ran up the stairs, the girl excusing herself as they squeezed past her to get to the door by which Sandra had just left. She would see them again and many other people would see them before the night was out.

Booker Griffin saw the girl three times that evening, the first and second time in the company of Sirhan, the second and third time with the tall man, also. Several people who saw them, including Booker, commented that they seemed out of place because they looked so unsmiling, so glum. They stuck out like sore thumbs in the happy, jubilant atmosphere. The three orientated themselves to the pantry area where they were seen by a number of others, including a member of the kitchen staff, Vincent Di Pierro. Sirhan and the girl had a coffee there just before Robert Kennedy arrived after completing his speech in the ballroom. Walking ahead of the Senator, Darnell Johnson saw a group of five people in the pantry, including Sirhan, the girl in the polka-dot dress and the tall man. Johnson said the man, whom he estimated to be six feet one inch in height, wore a blue jacket, and he was not the only one to recall this.

During the pandemonium which ensued after the shooting took place, the girl in the polka-dot dress and the tall man ran out of the pantry and out of the building. Booker Griffin saw them and remembers he called out, 'They're getting away!' One of the Ace Guard Service personnel, Jack J. Merritt, saw them and, he said, a second man running through the kitchen back exit. 'They seemed to be smiling,' he commented. George Green, who had seen the threesome in the pantry earlier, saw a man and the girl in the polka-dot dress running out of the pantry after the shooting when everyone else was trying to get in. Freelance photographer Evan Freed saw two men and a woman, the woman possibly wearing a polka-dot dress, running to the exit at the east end of the pantry. Richard Houston, standing outside the pantry, saw the girl in the polka-dot dress race out on to the terrace area. He heard her shout, 'We killed him.'

Police Sergeant Paul Schraga was in his car and near to the Ambassador Hotel when he heard about a shooting there on his radio. As the first supervising officer on the scene, he commenced setting up a command post in the hotel car park, in accordance with standard procedure. As he made his way towards the hotel entrance he found a middle-aged couple, the Bernsteins, running into the car park in a distressed state. They told Schraga they were beside the exit stairs when a man and a girl in a polka-dot dress ran past shouting with elation, 'We shot him! We shot him!' 'Who did you shoot?' the girl was asked. 'Senator Kennedy,' came the reply. Mr and Mrs Bernstein had then run out of the hotel.

Meanwhile, outside, still sitting on the fire-stairway, Sandra Serrano had heard bangs. She looked up and recognised two of the three who had entered the building about half an hour earlier now running down the stairs (presumably after their encounter with the Bernsteins). As they raced down the stairs the girl in the polka-dot dress said to Sandra Serrano, 'We shot him! We shot him!' 'Who did you shoot?' Serrano responded. Again came the reply, 'Senator Kennedy.'

Sergeant Schraga had put out an APB on the two suspects very promptly after receiving the Bernsteins' description. As the business of organising the investigation proceeded, Schraga was approached by a senior officer with the request to cancel the APB. When Schraga declined, it was cancelled without his approval. Sergeant Schraga wrote up, by hand, an account of his meeting with the Bernsteins and sent it by courier to headquarters. It disappeared. He later submitted two copies of a full report which he filed with the watch commander. Told that they were collected by officers from Special Unit Senator, the body set up to run the investigation, he contacted members of the staff, to be told they had never picked them up.* Paul Schraga became the Roger Craig† of the Robert Kennedy investigation. His efficiency ratings reduced and reduced. It was clear he had fallen from favour in pressing the information he was given regarding the fleeing man and the girl in the polka-dot dress, and in making efforts to find them. He left Los Angeles Police Department the following year. Twenty years later, he learnt from documents released by LAPD that he was on record for having stated in an interview with an investigating officer that he had changed his mind and that he had declared the whole 'polka-dot girl' episode the innocent product of the Bernsteins' hysteria. Schraga has confirmed he was not interviewed by an investigating officer and that he said no such thing.

The Schraga affair was only one instance in which the two investigating bodies, the Los Angeles Police Department and the Department of the Los Angeles District Attorney, revealed an apparent obsession with ridding the Robert Kennedy murder investigation of anything which led away from Sirhan Sirhan. Philip H. Melanson, in his excellent book, *The Robert F. Kennedy Assassination*, concludes that both LAPD and LADA conspired to cover up the real facts of the case by ignoring evidence, coercing witnesses and, at times, massaging statements made to them. According to Melanson:

---

* This time Schraga had kept a copy for himself, however
† See Chapter Six, and for a fuller account the book by Matthew Smith *JFK: The Second Plot*, Mainstream, Edinburgh, 1992

We must now discard the officially sanctioned illusions created by conspiracy and cover up and proceed to the disconcerting reality of the truth behind the assassination of Senator Robert F. Kennedy.*

In an interview given by Paul Schraga for the television programme, *The Robert Kennedy Assassination*, he made a striking comment:

> I think we have a structure in this country and I refer to them (*sic*) as a corporate war-machine, or you can refer to them as anything you want. I believe they did and will do anything that they need to–or that they want to–to preserve their status quo.†

Mr Schraga is clearly one of those–and there are many–who recognise the existence of the Consortium, call it by whatever name, as he says. The members of the Executive Group had not pussyfooted around in seeking a way to preserve their status quo. They executed Robert Francis Kennedy as they had done his brother before him, this time using new *modus operandi*. In covering their tracks they were just as successful as they had been when they murdered President Kennedy.

* Philip H. Melanson, PhD, *The Robert F. Kennedy Assassination*, SPI Books, New York, 1991
† *The Robert Kennedy Assassination*, produced by Exposed Films and Channel Four in association with the Arts and Entertainment Network, 1992

CHAPTER ELEVEN

More than Meets the Eye

'We move about in this lie with complete naturalness.'
Octavio Paz

THE MORE WE learn about the murder of Robert F. Kennedy, the harder it becomes to think of it as the consequence of a frenzied attack by a crazed lone gunman and, conversely, the easier to recognise it as the outcome of a meticulously planned conspiracy. The theory that Sirhan Sirhan, of his own volition and completely unaided, laid in wait until Senator Kennedy came into view and then shot him with the only gun used in the ambush echoes, at once, the imaginative tale sagely propounded by the Warren Commission in respect of the assassination of President John F. Kennedy in 1963. There are shades here of Lee Harvey Oswald in the unwitting role he was given to play in the execution of America's Chief Executive, whom elements of the Establishment which we have called the Consortium found unacceptable. The similarity between the two murders does not end there. In both, the authorities, for reasons of their own, assisted the conspirators, albeit unwittingly–though many would challenge this–by concealing the true facts and denying there was ever a conspiracy. In both, the authorities refused even to investigate the existence of a conspiracy.

In both, witnesses were ignored and statements inaccurately recorded. In both, preference was shown for witnesses whose testimony supported the case the authorities had opted to prove. In both, vital photographic evidence was confiscated and never seen again. In both, the heart of the physical evidence was challenged on the grounds of the literal impossibility for the accused to have accomplished the feat of shooting attributed to him. And in the background of both, the presence of agents of the CIA, just far enough from sight to be identified—as might be expected—is discernible, much in the same way as a phantom is discernible though not seen.

The instance of photographic evidence being confiscated in the Robert Kennedy case involved Scott Enyart, the 15-year-old boy with the professional camera who was mentioned in Chapter Ten. He took a series of pictures of the Senator making his last speech in the ballroom of the Ambassador Hotel, and followed him as he made his way through the pantry, leaping up on a table to get the height he required to continue taking pictures in rapid succession when the crowd blocked his view. Of the series of pictures he took, 18 were taken inside the pantry. The value of them to LAPD was made clear in this extract from a police interview with the boy:

> *Enyart*: . . . the shots started to be fired and I took pictures and kept taking pictures.
> *Officer*: While the shots were being fired?
> *Enyart*: While the shots were being fired.

Within minutes of the shooting, Scott was stopped as he left the hotel. What happened to the boy and his pictures is best described in his own words, as he explained in a television interview:

> I looked up to see a shotgun. I looked up to see guns drawn all around me. They took my wallet, they took my camera, they took the film out of my pockets. They took me and tossed me into the back of a squad car which was sitting . . . right in front of the entrance.

LAPD promised to return all Scott's films, but when he called at the Parker Center Police Headquarters the photographs were locked away in a security cabinet:

> I was not allowed to look at the film. They took a stack of prints and one of the detectives shuffled through them and separated it into two piles and

basically he gave me the photographs from one roll of film leading up to the assassination and then after the assassination. Everything that I'd taken in the pantry was gone. If the Police Department was right [about what had happened in the pantry] then my photographs only would have proved that they were right, so for them to destroy it (sic) only leads me to believe that something's being covered up.

Quite logical: a fair conclusion to draw. Scott Enyart's experience, linked to that of Sergeant Paul Schraga in having his APB on the polka-dot-dress girl and her companion cancelled by higher authority, indeed, provides a strong indication that, from the very beginning of the investigation, something was being covered up.

It was quite unbelievable that the statements given by witnesses who saw the polka-dot girl could simply be 'filed away'–buried–without any apparent investigation being carried out. This, however, was not the worst example of the police's anxiety to 'dispose of' witnesses and their statements. Booker Griffin, for instance, the witness who saw the girl in the polka-dot dress with Sirhan in the ballroom and, after the shooting, saw her again with her six-foot friend haring towards the exit, was given a bad time by the police. Griffin had been interviewed for television later in the day of the assassination. He had seen the polka-dot-dress girl three times in all, including once when he saw all three together. After subjecting Griffin to an interview in which they demanded ultra-scrupulous accuracy if his statement was to be accepted, LAPD completely discounted what he had said. Seldom can any witness stand up to such a rigorous demand. Seldom is any witness totally and utterly certain about what he has seen. LAPD, however, seemed entirely happy to throw the baby out with the bathwater and discount everything Booker Griffin had told them. They said he had probably really seen Kennedy staffer Judy Royer speaking to Sirhan on one of the occasions he reported, then he 'mentally projected' the description of his second sighting of the woman to the later sighting when she fled with a man. The matter did not even end with this attempt to discredit him. A document released in 1988 was shown to him in which the police asserted he had admitted lying to them. Griffin was angry and denied ever having made such a statement. He reasserted his account of the sightings. 'I know what I saw,' he said. When asked

173

by author Philip Melanson if the police had asked him to take a polygraph—lie-detector—test, he replied *he* had brought the subject up and the police had said it was unreliable. This was a strange response from the same department which had subjected two other polka-dot-dress witnesses to polygraph tests and had dismissed their testimony on the grounds they had failed.

Sandra Serrano was one of the two who 'failed' the test. She was shamelessly harangued by LAPD's Sergeant Enrique Hernandez, who treated Serrano in a way which would have been totally unacceptable even had she been the most difficult, unco-operative and hostile of witnesses. A recording of one of her interviews survived to be released in 1988. In some parts it is difficult to make out exactly what is being said, but those parts which are intelligible leave no doubt about what went on. The following are extracts. The symbol † denotes a few of the occasions when Sandra Serrano is heard protesting in the background:

Hernandez: I think you owe it to Senator Kennedy—the late Senator Kennedy—to come forward and be a woman about this. If he—and you don't know and I don't know whether he is a witness right now in this room watching what we're doing in here—don't shame his death by keeping this thing up. I have compassion for you. I wanna know why, I wanna know why you did what you did. This is a very serious thing.
Serrano: I seen (*sic*) those people.
Hernandez: No, no, no, no, Sandy. Remember what I told you about it? You can't say that you saw something . . .
Serrano: I know what I saw. (*Garbled*)†
Hernandez: Sandy, look:† I can, I can explain this to the [investigators] and you won't have to talk to them and they won't come to you. I can do this. But please, in the name of Kennedy . . .
Serrano: [Don't say in the] name of Kennedy.
Hernandez: (*Garbled*)†
Serrano: I remember seeing the girl.
Hernandez: (*Garbled*) . . . brushing it off with a smirk on your face, with a smile, when you know that deep inside . . .
Serrano: I remember seeing the girl.
Hernandez: No, no. [I have in my] notebook you have told the (*garbled*) saying a person told you '[We] have shot Kennedy' and that's nonsense.
Serrano: That's what she said.

Hernandez: No it isn't, Sandy. (*Voice rises*) Please don't (*garbled*) † I love † this † man, and if you don't † † change he will be [able to hear] right now and (*garbled*) he can remember it.
Serrano: Stop shouting at me.
Hernandez: Well, I'm trying not to shout. I'm sorry, but this is a very emotional thing for me, too. If you love the man, the least you owe him, the least you owe him, is the courtesy of letting him rest in peace.
Serrano: I'm not gonna say nobody told me ['We shot him!'] just to satisfy anybody else.
Hernandez: This didn't happen.
Serrano: It happened.
Hernandez: No. It didn't happen . . . Nobody told you, 'We shot him!'
Serrano: Yes.
Hernandez: No.
Serrano: I'm sorry but that's true. That is true. . . .
Hernandez: (*Garbled*) . . . bad for the heart . . . This is gonna make an old woman out of you before your time . . . something that's a deep wound that will grow with you like a disease—like a cancer.
Serrano: The results of this test [the polygraph], how far will they go?
Hernandez: Just between you and me.
Serrano: I don't want any of this stuff made public.
Hernandez: We're not dealing with publicity.*

The so-called interview lasted between 40 and 50 minutes.

Sandra Serrano was subjected to a polygraph test in appalling circumstances and was said to have failed it. She was verbally beaten into submission by Hernandez and, eventually, when she succumbed, agreed she had been lying. When the LAPD documents were released 20 years later, she was asked again about her testimony. 'I was just 20 years old,' she said, 'and I became unglued . . . I said what they wanted me to say.' She insisted her evidence was true as originally recounted to her interrogators. It is extremely unlikely that the videotape from which the above extracts were taken was ever intended to be released. It is believed that when the LAPD documents were made available a box of tapes was released in error. The tape makes an unbelievable record of police harassment, of which LAPD ought to have been thoroughly ashamed.

---

* These excerpts were derived from two sources: a sequence taken from the videotape, and printed extracts.

It is interesting to note that in the accounts of the various sightings of the polka-dot-dress girl, she makes no attempt to conceal her presence. Quite the opposite, if anything. She almost flaunts herself both before the assassination takes place and afterwards, too. She was clearly visible with Sirhan and with another man, and of all the things she might have worn which would have helped her to melt into the background, she wore a polka-dot dress. It was as though she intended to be seen. It seems, also, she intended to be heard. But assuming she was connected to a conspiracy to kill Senator Kennedy, and about that there can be little doubt, who in her right mind would run from the scene of the crime announcing her confession of guilt for all to hear? It was heard by four people. Richard Houston, standing near to the pantry heard it, Mr and Mrs Bernstein heard it and Sandra Serrano, outside on the fire-staircase, heard it. 'Who did you shoot?' she was asked. 'Senator Kennedy,' came the obliging reply.

At the same time, there was no hint nor suggestion that the polka-dot-dress girl – or her accompanying male – were involved in any way in the actual shooting of Robert Kennedy. We know that Sirhan played out the role of assassin and we know that, shooting from in front of the Senator, and some feet away from him, he could not have been the killer. The real killer was very close to Robert Kennedy and he fired in a completely different direction. We are left to speculate on the role played by the girl in the polka-dot dress and her companion, because the police, by their actions and lack of enterprise, obscured the function of the pair. On the face of it, it appears they were there to create a *second* diversion, to attract attention and to lay a false trail. The plot to kill Robert Kennedy was intricate, devious, and meticulously carried out. Not only had they planted a patsy, they had planned a 'belt-and-braces' exercise with a 'second-string' suspect in case the patsy was not convincing enough. There was no intention of making the murder of Robert Kennedy look like the act of a lone assassin: it was made to appear the work of a local political cell. It was advertised as a conspiracy, with trails leading to the wrong people. The police, however, were not having a conspiracy of any kind, and all their efforts went into concealing the indications that a plot existed, including ignoring the girl in the polka-dot dress.

Had the girl in the polka-dot dress and the man with her been apprehended, it is unlikely they could have revealed anything under interrogation which would have led in a straight line to the conspirators. They would have known nothing of the 'core' plan and the real plotters. On the other hand, there was always a small chance they might have known something which would have helped in the investigation—provided some kind of a clue—though because the design of the assassination was extremely professional, it was a small chance. The one great advantage which their arrest would have brought was that it would at least have been clear from the outset that we were looking at a conspiracy, albeit the wrong one. It can be argued, of course, that if their purpose was to create a diversion and lay a false trail, they were unsuccessful *because* of the ineptitude of the police. And it would seem a pity if researchers today, with much more to help them in this investigation that they have ever had before, became preoccupied with trying to reheat a cold trail and thereby allowed the diversionary tactic to succeed where it failed before.

It is sufficient to establish the purpose and function of the polka-dot-dress girl and more valuable to see if we can learn thereby something more of the overall plan and the people who conspired to carry out such a cold-blooded murder. A careful analysis of the accounts rendered by the various witnesses reveals that there may have been more than one girl in a polka-dot dress present at the Ambassador Hotel that night. This would actually have been quite a logical move on the part of the conspirators and, had the police not adopted a policy of turning a blind eye to indications of a conspiracy, would have served to extend the diversionary tactic, creating problems in establishing a precise description of the girl.

Any innocent woman in the hotel wearing a polka-dot dress would fairly promptly have been identified, since news of the polka-dot girl and her behaviour circulated quickly among the stunned Kennedy supporters. One or two girls were, in fact, questioned because of some vague similarity or other, but it was plain they were not the girl observed by the witnesses. Incredibly, the police, after discrediting or ignoring those who saw the girl in question, turned up with their own candidate. This girl, they claimed, was wearing a polka-dot dress on the night and she was the one they had all really seen. The young lady they identified was the attractive, blonde Valeria Schulte, a Kennedy volunteer worker. Miss Schulte, who had sported a huge Kennedy button that night, did not wear a white dress with large black spots, she wore a green dress with large yellow spots, and because the girl had one leg in a cast from top to ankle, she had found it necessary to use a crutch. Furthermore, said the police, the witnesses had simply perceived Miss Schulte's behaviour incorrectly on the night in question. LAPD was unbelievable. In putting on this crass performance, they were demonstrating defiant opposition to the truth and making a mockery of the honest citizens who had come forward to assist the murder inquiry with eye-witness accounts of a man and a girl whose association with Sirhan, and outlandish reaction to the murder of RFK, clearly made investigation of them essential.

The descriptions rendered by the various witnesses who saw the girl in the polka-dot dress, while broadly consistent, do vary enough for there to have been two different girls or even three at different stages of the evening. The girl's height was given as 5' 4", 5' 5", 5' 6" and 5' 8". While there is no marked difference between 5' 4" and 5' 5", 5' 5" and 5' 6" or even 5' 4" and 5' 6", there is a significant difference between 5' 4" and 5' 8". The former might be described as of average height, where the latter would be a distinctly tall girl. The girl's hair was reported as being 'long and blonde', 'long and brown', 'light coloured', 'light brown', 'dark' and 'dark brown'. Again, in most cases, the witnesses were clearly seeing the same girl, but at the extremes, there is all the difference in the world between 'long and blonde' and 'dark brown'. Two witnesses—only—mentioned that the girl had a somewhat peculiarly shaped nose. One witness spoke of her as of Nordic appearance, whereas Sirhan himself, under questioning, saw her as, perhaps, Armenian or Spanish. There could have been at least two girls wearing polka-dot dresses connected to Sirhan at the Ambassador Hotel that night. There was one instance, in fact, where two sightings conflicted with one another. Darnell Johnson, who went through the pantry ahead of Senator Kennedy and saw a group of five people there, including Sirhan, the tall man in the blue jacket and the girl in the polka-dot dress, saw the girl and the man look into the pantry when Sirhan was being detained awaiting his arrest. He had, therefore, seen the girl twice already when, at the point later on when Sirhan was being led away by the police, he saw her again in the Embassy Room. How could he when, in the company of the blue-coated man, she had long since fled crying, 'We shot him! We shot him!'? He couldn't, unless there were two girls in polka-dot dresses.

There is no doubt that careful plans had been made for the decoys to disappear without trace. If the plan involved two or more girls parading in polka-dot dresses it was a simple matter for one girl to 'disappear' by making a change of dress in the privacy of the ladies' room. The girl who fled announcing 'We shot him!' and the tall man who left with her gave the police a slim chance of apprehending them, which they blew. This author favours the two would not run far before going to earth, however. They bore all the signs they were specially created phantoms and, in the best tradition of phantoms, it was planned for them to disappear. And they did. Forever.

As has already been said, Dr Thomas Noguchi's autopsy report, all by itself, should have been enough to convince the Los Angeles Police Department that Sirhan did not kill Robert Kennedy and, therefore, that a conspiracy had taken place. Noguchi made it clear that the Senator had been killed by someone firing from very close quarters. The bullet which killed him was fired behind his right ear at a distance of one to one-and-a-half inches from the tip of the ear. The other two bullets to Kennedy's back were fired close together, the killer moving his gun but an inch between shots. These were fired so near that the muzzle of the gun might have been rammed into the Senator's back, and the missiles travelled in an upward and forward direction. The fourth bullet fired did not hit the victim. It missed, entering and exiting the right shoulder pad of his jacket. There was no way Robert Kennedy's wounds could have been caused by Sirhan Sirhan, who stood in front of him. He was shooting in the opposite direction to the path of the bullets which killed the Senator. Furthermore, witnesses said that, in any case, Sirhan was simply not close enough to have fired the shots described by the coroner. Most witnesses estimated the distance between Sirhan and the Senator at somewhere between three and six feet. Only one placed him closer, and even he, assuming he was correct, said he was no nearer than one-and-a-half feet. The man who killed the Senator was close enough to be holding him when Sirhan began firing. The five others wounded in the pantry were all the victims of Sirhan's bullets, but Sirhan did not kill Senator Kennedy.

Sirhan's gun had held eight bullets and all had been fired in the pantry. Had Sirhan's gun been the only gun fired and had his bullets killed the Senator, the police would have had a very straightforward job of accounting for eight shots, four at Kennedy and, not at all remarkable, four wounding five other people. As was seen in Chapter Ten, LAPD chose to place the cart before the horse in first deciding all the shots *were* fired by Sirhan and disregarding any evidence to the contrary, coroner's report included. Their expert, De Wayne Wolfer, riding roughshod over conflicting evidence and witnesses' statements, described the trajectory of eight bullets and stopped counting. For his trajectory map to be correct Sirhan's gun had to be able to take wings to reach the Senator and be capable of firing bullets which changed direction at least twice in flight when it got there.

In spite of De Wayne Wolfer's stonewalling, the evidence that more than one gun was fired in the pantry was there for all to see. Police officers, newsmen, the hotel staff and even the coroner Dr Noguchi, witnessed the presence of bullet holes in the pantry woodwork. If De Wayne Wolfer had accounted for eight bullets being fired it only required one bullet hole to be found representing a 'miss' and the presence of a second gun was established, and there was more than one hole in the woodwork. Despite the fact that they were ringed by police officers and frequently photographed, De Wayne Wolfer steadfastly ignored their existence. Incredibly, Wolfer himself featured in one of the photographs in which he was inspecting the woodwork. He argued that the holes found had been made by nails. In a deposition he made in 1971 he said, '. . . there were too many holes to photograph', and '. . . in charge of the crime scene . . . I recovered the bullets that were recovered'. If he did he must have been totally aware that more were fired than could have come from Sirhan's gun.

It was the doorframe and, in particular, the door divider which bore clear evidence that a second gun had been used. LAPD officers Rozzi and Wright were photographed together bending down to examine a hole in the doorframe approximately 18 inches from the floor. An Associated Press photographer took the picture which was published above a caption stating that the officers were examining a bullet hole. Dr Noguchi, during a visit to the scene of the crime, was also photographed pointing to two holes in the doorframe. These were not to be confused with the hole Rozzi and Wright were examining which was low down in the frame. Noguchi was standing upright and the holes he pointed to were at chest height. Three photographs of the doorframe taken by the FBI were released in 1976 in which four holes labelled 'bullet holes' were depicted. One of LAPD's own crime-scene photos showed circles drawn round four holes, one of which the FBI had labelled 'bullet hole'. The circle drawn contained the chalked inscriptions, 'W Tew' and '723', the name and number of Officer W. Tew from the Sheriff's Office. Hotel waiter, Martin Patruski, claimed, '. . . one of the officers pointed to two circled holes on the centre divider of the swinging doors and told us that they had dug two bullets out of the centre divide . . . I am absolutely sure that the police told us that two bullets were dug out of those holes.'

The centre divider in the doorframe, bearing the holes, was removed by LAPD for examination. About a year afterwards it was destroyed. LAPD claimed it was of no significance since it bore no bullets and was, therefore, not actual evidence. When challenged on this destruction they said it was 'too large to fit into a card file'. Neither was the centre divider the only point of dispute in relation to the physical evidence. Though LAPD records show they removed only two ceiling tiles in their hunt for bullets in the pantry, witness Lisa Urso told how she entered the pantry to find 'five or six' tiles laid out on the floor for examination.

To add to the mysterious disappearance of Sergeant Schraga's polka-dot-dress girl reports—and not to mention the Scott Enyart photographs taken in the pantry which were never seen again—evidence exists that destruction of documents relating to the investigation began as early as July 1968, the month following the assassination. On 2 August 1968, 2,400 photographs were burnt. When the tapes of interviews conducted by LAPD were later released, over 2,700 hours of recordings were missing. At least, they have not surfaced to the date of the publication of this book.

LAPD criminologist, De Wayne Wolfer stuck rigidly to his assertion that only one gun had been fired in the pantry, the gun fired by Sirhan Sirhan, and that no more than eight bullets were accounted for in the investigation. By doing so LAPD was able to advance the claim that there had been no conspiracy to murder Robert Kennedy. The Department supported Wolfer's pronouncements against all criticisms and made him *the* authority on the case. To LAPD, Wolfer's integrity was impeccable and his expertise and judgment unchallengeable. The tragedy was that Sirhan's lawyers chose not to challenge De Wayne Wolfer in the courtroom, for the jury might have had other ideas about his expertise and his reliability. In two other cases his evidence was completely thrown out. One judge said his testimony was 'negligently false, borders on perjury, and is at least [tainted] with a reckless disregard for the truth'. Yet this was the same De Wayne Wolfer whose word on the Robert Kennedy case had been made law by the Los Angeles Police Department.

De Wayne Wolfer's testimony that all the bullets he recovered could be matched to Sirhan's gun was later challenged by several ballistics experts, notably William W. Harper, a highly respected criminologist with 35 years' experience. Harper issued a sworn affidavit declaring a second gun had been used in the pantry. In his affidavit, Harper also declared Robert Kennedy was shot from behind, the others shot in the pantry were the victims of Sirhan's bullets, and it was extremely unlikely that any bullet from Sirhan's gun ever struck the Senator. His conclusion that two .22 guns had been used was drawn from a study of the physical evidence. During Sirhan's trial, Wolfer introduced bullet fragments recovered from RFK's body and from two of the surviving victims. He stated the bullets had been fired from Sirhan's Iver Johnson Cadet model .22, bearing the serial number H18602. Astoundingly, this went completely unchallenged by the defence team and the judge. Sirhan's gun serial number was H53725. Wolfer had officially entered as evidence bullet fragments he declared he had matched to a gun which was known not to be Sirhan Sirhan's. LAPD later passed this off as a clerical error. Enquiries made later regarding the Iver Johnson .22 serial number H18602 made at the Criminal Division of Identification and Investigation at Sacramento, obtained the startling reply that the gun was destroyed by LAPD in July 1968. This was after its use for test purposes but *before* Sirhan's trial. LAPD claimed another clerical error had been made here. They said the date of destruction was July 1969.

Assuming for one moment that this was the truth, it was at least another example of LAPD destroying important evidence.

De Wayne Wolfer also told the court that because the bullet fragments recovered from Senator Kennedy's neck were so badly damaged, he was unable to be certain that they came from Sirhan's gun. Sirhan's defence lawyers also, meekly, let this pass unchallenged. Four days after the assassination, Wolfer had announced that the bullet which transitted the Senator's right shoulder pad had gone into the ceiling. When his Official Police Summary of Trajectory Study was released, he had changed his mind and stated this bullet was the one which struck Paul Schrade in the forehead. This was patent nonsense since, as Schrade pointed out, it was impossible unless he was either nine feet tall or had had his head on the Senator's shoulder. Wolfer's change of mind about the bullet's destination was doubtless to keep the tally of bullets fired to a maximum of eight, so that the one-gun theory could be upheld. Wolfer was wasting his time. FBI agent William Bailey, now retired from the FBI and teaching at a college, told this author he saw, without any doubt or question, two bullet holes in the centre door divider when he took part in the Kennedy investigation. This eye-witness evidence alone takes the total beyond the eight-bullet, one-gun count. Bailey was aware there may have been other bullets to be found in the pantry, but he personally examined the two in the centre divider. He agreed that so many people—investigators of one category or another, hotel staff, news reporters, photographers, witnesses and sundry others—saw what were patently bullet holes in the woodwork, it is astounding that LAPD—largely in the person of De Wayne Wolfer—ever got away with its barefaced rejection of such evidence and the establishment of a one-gun case.

Recognition of the fact that the murder of Robert F. Kennedy was the consequence of a conspiracy at once begins to raise the spectre of a shadowy group conducting a vendetta against the Kennedy men. Criminologist William W. Harper had no doubts in his mind about this:

[There are] too many things about this that point in one direction, and I think that the Kennedy family should by all means be interested because, hell, the next time it'll be Ted Kennedy and then it will go on down the line—any of them.

If the assassination of John F. Kennedy on the streets of Dallas was a ruthless act, then the murder of his brother, Robert, matched it in its brutality. In the Robert Kennedy slaying the Executive Group demonstrated it was capable of harnessing frightening techniques straight out of the scientific horror novel in the way it manipulated Sirhan Sirhan to do its bidding. But then, there was a great deal about Sirhan that the American people were never allowed to know.

CHAPTER TWELVE

The Manchurian Candidate and the Kimche Reports

'There was truth and there was untruth, and if you clung to the truth, even against the whole world – you were not mad.'

George Orwell

THE NOTION OF a person being hypnotised and programmed to commit murder sounds as though it has come straight from the pages of a best-selling novel and, indeed, it was from the pen of writer Richard Condon that we first encountered the idea. His book, *The Manchurian Candidate* – later turned into a movie – was fascinating. The idea of one man being able to control the mind of another, to the extent he could make him kill to order was of the stuff of which nightmares are made. It was intriguing: it made compelling reading, but it was comforting to know it could not happen in real life. Well it couldn't, could it?

Unhappily, as the twentieth century has progressed, along with the wonderful discoveries, inventions and developments which have enriched so many areas of life, have come the discoveries, the inventions and the developments which have turned nightmares into reality: the unleashing of atomic energy as a means of destruction, chemical and germ warfare, flamethrowing weaponry. Both in times of war and in times of peace, those determined to thrust their ways and values upon others have expressed their ruthlessness in terms which have stunned, appalled and horrified mankind: Belsen and the Nazi death camps; the inhuman taking of hostages and the treatment meted to them; the dread stalking campaign of the terrorist. New methods of killing and torture have been devised, and old methods have been refined. The Second World War, and the Cold War which followed it, saw the formation of secret organisations on a scale never before known to man, whose activities have undermined and frustrated the aspirations of legal governments, and whose honed and polished techniques for controlling nations and individuals strike terror and dismay in the hearts of those who have experience of them.

It was as a consequence of learning about the use of hypnosis and drugs in mind-control experiments carried out by the Nazis during the Second World War that the CIA became interested in developing their own research, at first because they feared the Soviets were also involved in such experimentation and they felt the US must compete. Also, not many years after the end of the Second World War, during the time of the Korean war, the attention of the world was focused on the use of brainwashing techniques in the Far East, and it was then that the Central Intelligence Agency began to devote considerable attention – and money – to studying mind and behaviour control. It was Richard Helms who proposed to CIA Director Allen Dulles that a programme on the 'covert use of biological and chemical materials' should be introduced. This was in 1953, when agents had become fascinated by what was written about a strange and powerful new drug known as LSD. Dr Sidney Gottleib was placed in charge of the top-secret programme which was known as 'MKULTRA', in which the Agency was known to cross ethical lines in its experimentation, the details of which were mind-boggling. LSD was known to be administered surreptitiously to staff members in order that behavioural changes might be observed, and not surprisingly, things went terribly wrong. In one instance an agent to whom the drug had been given was discovered by his colleagues – who had been obliged to go and search for him – hiding, shaking and terrified, near one of the bridges across the Potomac in Washington. He cringed when cars approached him. In his LSD-induced paranoia, they appeared to him as grotesque monsters. The experimental dose, administered in secret, had had dire effects on the man.

Author John Marks told of another instance, the details of which were culled from statements made by veteran CIA agents and documents obtained under the Freedom of Information Act.* Dr Frank Olsen, an Army Chemical Corps scientist, attending a conference at a venue buried in a forest, along with others of his colleagues, had his after-dinner drink 'spiked' with LSD by Gottleib. The quality of contribution to the conference deteriorated so much it was eventually abandoned. Olsen, in particular, reacted profoundly to the drug and became depressed, telling his wife he had made a fool of himself at the conference. He went to his startled boss and told him he wanted to quit. As it happened, his boss had also been at the conference and knew his behaviour had been impeccable, and he was able to dissuade Olsen. As time went by Olsen questioned his own confidence and clearly was in need of help. Gottleib sent him to a CIA-funded doctor in New York in deeper than ever depression and suffering from paranoia. He feared the CIA were out to get him. When in New York, he wandered the streets under the delusion he was carrying out orders, tore up his money, and was eventually found sitting in the lobby of his hotel. His condition did not improve and, on a second visit to New York, his doctor advised hospital and he was to return to Washington to make arrangements. Booked into a hotel for the night, it was in the early hours of the following day that the agent accompanying Olsen awoke to see him plunge through the blinds and closed window of the room and fall to his death in the street below. The Agency moved in to keep everything quiet.

The CIA, in its programme on the use of drugs for behavioural change and mind control, sought data on disturbance of memory, discrediting by aberrant behaviour, alteration of sex patterns, eliciting of information, suggestibility, and creation of dependence, and it was prepared to break all the rules to obtain the information it required. It has to be borne in mind that the collecting of such data was one thing; the *application* of the data, once collected, organised and harnessed, was another. Such terms as 'depatterning' and 'differential amnesia' belong to a nether world, the contemplation of which most normal human beings would find utterly appalling, indeed unthinkable. To most people, such a world belongs in the imaginings of those who

* John Marks, *The Search for the 'Manchurian Candidate'*, London, Allen Lane, 1979

seek to entertain us by leading us into an unreal world from which we are happy to escape back to reality. To those involved in such horrific experimentation the nether world is reality, inhabited by its people who seek to achieve its objectives in espionage by the control of the human mind and behaviour. The use of hypnotism in such a quest must surely rank as one of the less horrific options. We are back to *The Manchurian Candidate* and, of a sudden, the ideas involved in post-hypnotic suggestion and the programming of a subject to commit murder while under its influence do not now seem so far fetched.

When Sirhan Sirhan was apprehended by those who, in horror, had watched him draw a gun and shoot at Robert Kennedy he was, according to Yosio Niwa, a cook at the Ambassador Hotel, smiling. 'I'll never forget that guy's face,' he said. 'I'll never forget. I was so upset. I told him, "You got mother or father?" . . . He was smiling, too . . . He was looking at me. I was so excited, upset. He was smiling . . . I don't know why.' In spite of crying out, 'Kennedy, you son of a bitch!', firing at Senator Kennedy, and mustering enormous energy to wrestle with Karl Uecker when he tried to disarm him, Sirhan appeared to witness Joseph Lahive 'very tranquil'. A strange appearance for a man to have in the circumstances. No ugly face, no grimaces, no snarls. His eyes were 'dark brown and enormously peaceful', according to George Plimpton, another witness. He displayed a 'trance-like' appearance, and when questions were put to him he was incoherent, reticent, and he spoke rapidly, or rather, he mumbled rapidly in a weak voice. He drew his breath in deep draughts.

This state was to wear off. 'During the initial interview he was . . . quiet,' said Sergeant William Jordan, who was with Sirhan during the first few hours after his arrest. 'He didn't wanna talk. He was very restrictive with his words, very careful about saying anything. My third interview with him he would almost volunteer to talk about various things.' It was Sergeant Jordan who noticed a change in Sirhan's eyes, also. What they were like before, Jordan did not say, but by the time of his arraignment he passed a comment to the effect that they were now clear.

During the period before the shooting, witnesses observed Sirhan behaving peculiarly. Author Robert Kaiser* interviewed teletype operator Mary Grohs, who had been stationed at a machine located near the pantry. She told Kaiser:

> Well, he came over to my machine and started staring at it. Just staring. I'll never forget his eyes. I asked him what he wanted. He didn't answer. He just kept staring. I asked him again. No answer. I said that if he wanted to check the latest figures on Senator Kennedy, he'd have to check the other machine. He still didn't answer. He just kept staring.

It appeared a police officer had questioned her about whether he smelled of alcohol. Grohs told Kaiser Sirhan did not smell of alcohol. Not long before his appearance at Grohs's machine, Sirhan had been observed acting and speaking normally. Moments before his attack on Robert Kennedy, he was seen with the polka-dot-dress girl in the pantry area where they both drank coffee. Waiter Vincent Di Pierro saw them together and his strongest memory was of his smile. 'That stupid smile,' he said. 'A very sickly-looking smile.' The girl also wore a smile. Sirhan turned to her as if making conversation, but she did not reply. She just smiled, reported Di Pierro. 'When she first did it she looked like she was sick also.'

As Sirhan turned to shoot RFK he was observed by waiter Martin Patruski. 'The guy looked like he was smiling,' he said. Sirhan's smile continued as he was taken to Police Headquarters. Whatever the cause, Sirhan's behaviour and appearance was distinctly odd starting at round about 10.30 pm and continuing until well after he had been arrested, taken to Police Headquarters, and interviewed. This was a period of several hours. Beforehand he behaved normally and afterwards he behaved normally. But of shooting at Senator Robert Kennedy, Sirhan Sirhan had no memory. At his trial, and ever since, during all his years of captivity he has maintained the same position: he has no recollection whatever of shooting off a gun at Senator Kennedy. Careful study of his behaviour has resulted in the not-unreasonable suggestion by certain researchers that he was under hypnotic influence during his period of disorientation, and was programmed to shoot at the Senator.

---

* Robert Blair Kaiser, *RFK Must Die!*, E. P. Dutton, New York, 1970

The question of who would want to kill Robert Kennedy is not difficult to answer. The CIA agents who were connected with the Bay of Pigs débâcle had been livid with both John Kennedy and Robert Kennedy since that event, and it was well known they blamed them for what had happened. The group of agents who allied themselves to the Consortium had had but one aim in doing so: to get even with the Kennedys. They probably rationalised their actions as the acts of men acting in the best interests of their country, but it was their burning hatred which fuelled their endeavours and kept alive their determination to kill those they saw as the country's greatest enemies. They had achieved their objective in assassinating John Kennedy; Robert Kennedy had been an intended target for at least as long as his brother. They had waited their time and taken advantage of the liaison offered by others who hated the Kennedys almost as much as they did. Membership of the Consortium afforded a distorted kind of respectability to what they were doing. As they saw it, they had saved the country from disaster by killing the second Kennedy.

It should not be assumed, by any means, that these agents *represented* the Agency. They were renegades, and did not represent anyone but themselves. To stress that the CIA *per se* did not have anything to do with the murders of John and Robert Kennedy is not to say the brothers were not widely hated throughout the Agency, however. It was probably easy for the renegades to obtain the assistance they needed. In any case, in the very nature of the animal, secrecy, combined with a practice of not asking awkward questions made it possible for expertise outside the experience of the renegades themselves to be illicitly obtained. And it was known that the Agency *did* have knowledge and experience of the use of hypnotism.

The CIA had a higher profile in the Robert F. Kennedy investigation than most people thought. The two LAPD officers who, more or less, took charge of the investigation on a day-to-day basis both had CIA connections and were probably agents under cover of the LAPD. Lieutenant Manuel Pena played an important role in the co-ordination of information, statements and other data relating to the investigation. He acted as a supervisor and was responsible for preparing LAPD's case for Sirhan's trial. Pena had officially retired from LAPD to take up a post with the State Department's International Development Office. His appointment was that of 'public-safety adviser' and it was in his remit to contribute to the training of police officers in foreign countries. The US State Department Office of Public Safety was well known as a front for the CIA. The training in which it involved itself included toughening up members of security units designated to clamp down on leftist activists.

Roughly six months after his retirement, Pena was back with LAPD. It was his brother who blew the gaff about Manuel's CIA connections, when talking informally off-air – in a commercial break – to television personality Stan Bohrman during a show in which he was participating. 'Nobody's supposed to know about that. It's supposed to be a secret,' he said. Police Chief Robert Houghton, in his book, *Special Unit Senator*, effectively corroborated what Pena's brother had let slip when he wrote of Pena as having, 'connections with intelligence agencies in several countries'. Working with Pena and dealing with 'background investigation and conspiracy aspects of the case', was Sergeant Enrique Hernandez.

In the case of Hernandez, nothing showed of his CIA connections in what was known about him. He gave the game away himself when, interrogating Sandra Serrano (see Chapter 11), he attempted to reassure her by telling her of his wide experience of conducting polygraph tests abroad:

> I have been called to South America, to Vietnam and Europe and I have administered tests. The last test that I administered was to the dictator in Caracas, Venezuela. He was a big man, a dictator. (*Garbled*) was the man's name and this is when there was a transition in the government of Venezuela and that's when President Bettancourt came in . . . but this is all behind. But there was a great thing involved over there and I tested the gentleman.

This is on the videotape released by the Los Angeles Police Department. It left the the the stamp of a CIA agent, probably specialising in polygraph tests for them.

Los Angeles Police Department had a great many officers who were capable of running the investigation into the murder of Robert Kennedy. No doubt in various capacities there were dozens of officers involved in the case, but it was an interesting choice for them to detail two officers with CIA connections to take on such special tasks. Why should these particular two men be singled out for conspicuous involvement? It would be interesting to know who actually assigned the two officers to the roles they played and whether there was any pressure brought to bear by the CIA. Pena and Hernandez were placed in a unique position to control the inquiry, to filter out 'unwanted' testimony and concentrate the inquiry on the more desired areas of interest. Had LAPD laid itself open to manipulation in declaring a policy of 'no Dallas here'?

It came as something of a shock to researchers that Army Intelligence had a specific link with the Robert Kennedy investigation. By 5.00 pm on the day of the murder, Army Intelligence had a man, Timothy Richdale, referred to as 'Military Intelligence liaison' on duty at the Emergency Command Center. It was revealed that Military Intelligence at San Francisco had data on Sirhan Sirhan relating to his background and his participation in activities supporting the visit of the Shah of Persia. Their interest, on the face of it, was inspired by Sirhan's befriending of Walter Crowe, a young man who became involved in leftist activities and was said to have embraced communism. Since Sirhan's notebook contained certain entries which were interpreted as left-wing and pro-communist, it looked, at first, as if the authorities were preparing to give Sirhan a 'red' background.

The Mayor of Los Angeles, Sam Yorty, made an outrageous entrance to the debate on Sirhan's communist background. Only hours after the tragedy had occurred, he spoke of Sirhan as, 'a member of numerous communist organisations, including the Rosicrucians'. Unhappily for him, Mayor Yorty had put his foot in it. To the Mayor's embarrassment he was corrected: the Rosicrucians were distinctly not communist. Sirhan, in fact, belonged to no communist group, nor was he a communist sympathiser. Undaunted, however, during the afternoon Yorty got round to a second press conference in which he made no secret of his opinion that Sirhan was guilty and spoke of the notebook he had kept. He called him 'a sort of loner who harboured communist inclinations [and] favoured communists of all types'. The following day, the day Robert Kennedy died, he announced that, 'Evil communist organisations played a part in inflaming the assassination of Kennedy . . .' Indeed, in a series of announcements, the determined Yorty flagrantly hacked at the roots of Sirhan's pretrial rights and was promptly served with an order

(Plate 31) View of the pantry area in which the shooting of Senator Robert Kennedy took place. Note the two doors (one open), with the centre post between, which showed bullet holes. The post was destroyed by the police (*Courtesy SE Mass. Univ. RFK Assassination Archives*)

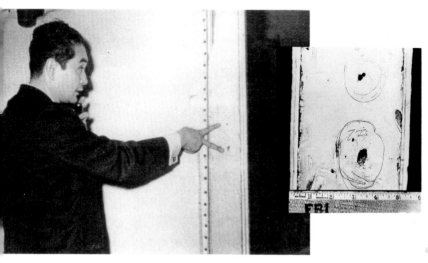

(Plate 32) Dr Thomas Noguchi, who conducted the autopsy examination on Senator Kennedy, is seen here pointing to two bullet holes in the doorframe. Inset shows enlargement (*Courtesy SE Mass. Univ. RFK Assassination Archives*)

May 18 9.45 AM-68

Pso 71-15 in 2m

my determination to eliminate
my determination to eliminate R.F.K. is becoming
more the more of an
please pay to the order unshakable obsession

plea   port wine   port wine   port wine

R.F.K. must die - RFK must be killed Robert
F. Kennedy must be assassinated R.F.K.
must be assassinated R.F.K. must be
assassinated R.F.K must be assassinated
R.F.K. must be assassinated R.F.K must
be assassinated R.F.K must be
assassinated assassinated Robert F.
Kennedy Robert F. Kennedy Robert
F. Kennedy must be assassinated
assassinated Robert F. Kennedy
must be assassinated assassinated
assassinated assassinated
Robert F. Kennedy must be assassinated
Robert F. Kennedy must be
assassinated before 5 June 68
Robert F. Kennedy must be
assassinated I have never heard
please pay to the order of of of of
of of of of of of this or that   HC

8   0 0 0 0 0 - ▢
Please pay to the order of

(Plate 34) A page from Sirhan's notebook. The repetitions suggested 'automatic' writing, performed while under hypnosis (*Courtesy SE Mass. Univ. RFK Assassination Archives*)

(Plate 35) Senator Edward Kennedy renders an account of events at
Chappaquiddick on television (*AP/Wide World Photos*)

(Plate 36) The bridge at Chappaquiddick. Onlookers watch Senator Edward Kennedy's car being examined after being hauled up from the water (*AP/Wide World Photos*)

(Plate 37) Kennedy's Oldsmobile displays extensive damage to the right side as well as the roof and windows (*AP/Wide World Photos*)

(Plate 38) Mary Jo Kopechne

(Plate 39) Police Chief Jim Arena

(Plate 40) Paul Markham

(Plate 41) Joseph Gargan

(Plate 42) Four of the girls who partied at the cottage as Senator Kennedy's guests arrive for the inquest into Mary Jo's death. Left to right, Susan Tannenbaum, Nancy Lyons, Esther Newberg and Rosemary Keough

(Plate 43) The Lawrence cottage on Chappaquiddick island, rented for the Edgartown Regatta week by Senator Edward Kennedy (*AP/Wide World Photos*)

(Plate 44) Lyndon B. Johnson

(Plate 45) Madeleine Brown with Steven, the son she claimed was Lyndon B. Johnson's child (*Courtesy Madeleine Brown*)

forbidding any more of his pronouncements. In any case, the 'red' background was dropped. It had been decided that even a communist conspiracy was not wanted. The authorities wanted no conspiracy at all.

In the days of the Cold War, communists were the first to be suspected where any treasonous act had been perpetrated or any crime had been committed against the Establishment and, at first glance, it looked as though both Military Intelligence and Mayor Yorty were following the well-worn trail. Arguably Mayor Yorty was, but there was much more to the interest being shown by Military Intelligence, which they expressed in hints of communist association. Sirhan Sirhan had a background in intelligence, details of which were not to be released to the people of America.

This author was alerted to the existence of three articles which appeared in the *London Evening Standard* in June and July 1968, copies of which he obtained from the British Newspaper Library. The articles were by Jon Kimche, a well-known British journalist who specialised in Middle-Eastern affairs. While this book was in preparation this author tracked down Jon Kimche and spoke to him about his sources for his reports. Kimche said he had used them for a long time and had found them extremely reliable. The first of the articles appeared on 13 June and ran:

BOBBY: RIDDLE OF TRIPS BY SIRHAN

Startling new evidence about the identity of the man charged with killing Robert Kennedy has been produced by an Arab government. The government has been making an intensive investigation into the background of Sirhan Bishara.

The new information, which is being communicated to the United States authorities, may open up an entirely new line of inquiry into the motivation and organisation of the attack on Kennedy. *It also indicates considerable variation in the accounts so far given of Sirhan's past and movements.*

His full name is given as Sirhan Bishara Sirhan Abu Khatar. *He was first brought to the United States as a four-year-old child in 1948 – not in 1957.* He returned to Jordan in 1957 and the records show that he was married in the Orthodox Church at Es Salt, 15 miles west of Amman on June 27, 1957, when he was only 13, to Leila Yussef Mikhael from Es Salt. Later that year Sirhan returned to the United States and three months later his wife was brought to him . . .

Rather more interest centres on three later journeys which Sirhan made, especially on the last two which, according to this investigation, were made in 1964 and 1966. In 1964 Sirhan, according to these records, returned to the Middle East for seven months, four of which he spent in Damascus. Where he was for the rest of the time is not stated. In 1966 he is said to have spent an even longer period in the Middle East, including a stretch of five months in Cairo. He returned to the United States . . . at the beginning of 1967.

The Arab government is convinced that its records are accurate but they are being sent to the United States so that they can be checked with the information assembled by the FBI. *There is an evident and increasing disinclination, however, for witnesses to talk and even those who spoke at first— such as Sirhan's father—have now adjusted their responses.**

Last week Sirhan's father cursed his son. Yesterday he was denouncing Kennedy and preparing to go to Los Angeles to stand by his son. [This author's emphases]

It was just a few weeks later that Jon Kimche reported that the Arab government quoted in his first article were now collaborating with two other Arab governments to piece together a picture of Sirhan's background and movements. (The three governments were Egypt, Syria and Lebanon, he told this author in 1993.) Together they came up with much more information. This *London Evening Standard* report was dated 18 July 1968:

Earlier details of Sirhan's journeys to the Middle East have now been fully investigated by the Arab governments concerned and they have filled in the missing details in the earlier report. These show that: Sirhan left the United States at the end of January, 1964, and travelled via Canada. From February 5 to February 21, he lived in the al Hamra suburb of Beirut with a Christian Arab family called Alquas al Mouishi.

He then went to Damascus and from February 23 to March 5, 1964, he lodged with Halim al Halibi in Ghouta. From there he went to the training camp at Qateneh, outside Damascus. With him at the camp were 10 other Palestinians and some Iraqis and others. The two officers in charge of the

---

* *This author's note*: This happened over and over again to JFK-assassination witnesses. RFK-murder witnesses in Los Angeles, also, became reluctant to talk. It is interesting that those connected to Sirhan, so very far away from the US, reacted in this way.

camp at the time were Lieut. Colonel Aziz al Marouf and an Algerian major known as Ahmed Belcasim. There are no details about the way he returned to the US. But the records show that Sirhan left again in April 1966. This time he signed on as a member of the crew of a ship going to Alexandria on May 22, 1966, and living for a week in Cairo in a small hotel.

After that he moved to the house of a Lebanese family. He stayed with them until he was taken to a training camp in the Ma'adi district of Cairo. On August 3 he was again moved to a camp in Gaza. There he stayed until the end of September before returning to the United States–again there are no details about the return journey.

It would seem quite clear that the three Arab governments did not have far to look for their information on Sirhan. Kimche's first report was published on 13 June, only a week after Robert Kennedy died, and the rest of the details reported were all available for his article of 18 July. This suggests that government representatives merely had to compare notes. It appeared they each already had detailed dossiers on Sirhan Sirhan. And from the information they provided it appears he was involved in clandestine activities in various Middle-Eastern countries and they had been watching him carefully.

When the background provided by the Arab countries is compared with the background given to Sirhan in the United States, discrepancies are noted. In 1966, notably between 3 August and the end of September, when Sirhan is reported by the Arab sources to have been in Gaza, he was reputedly working at Granja Vista Del Rio Farms in Corona, where he is said to have had an accident during the month of September. He continued in employment there, US records show, until December of that year. Since Sirhan could not have been in two places at one time, either the US sources or the Arab sources must be wrong.* If the Arab data was a fabrication it would create a riddle of enormous proportions. If the information was false, what would be its purpose? A superficial reading of the claims involved would first suggest that Sirhan was working for the Arabs themselves and the implication, therefore, would be that he had been acting for them in

---

* One of the dates quoted in FBI/LAPD records to support Sirhan's presence in the US was the day he was said to have opened a bank account, 5 April 1966. During his trial, in answer to a question, Sirhan said he did not have a bank account and did not understand the term, 'pay to the order of . . .' (See quotation from trial later in chapter)

killing Robert Kennedy. But that is patently absurd. If it were true, why would they advertise such a thing? Clearly the fact that three Middle-Eastern governments combined to release the Sirhan data supports he was *not* working for them. Similarly, no Arab government is going to provide evidence against a devotee to an Arab cause who, for the cause, albeit unwisely, has become involved in such a killing. They would simply have remained silent.

It has been suggested that the 'Arab sources' might have been putting Israeli disinformation about, but this is extremely hard to believe. To begin with, Kimche knew his sources well. He had used them over and over again and had found them reliable. Politics being what it is in the Middle East, Arab intelligence is well schooled on such matters and sources are not likely to be easily duped. Secondly, had the Sirhan data originated with the Israelis, there would have been an immediate outcry from the governments claimed to have been promoting the information. There was no outcry against the claims of the leading London newspaper, read regularly in London embassies and consulate offices, and the governments concerned continued to 'assist' the US regarding the information they had been sent. It is clear, therefore, that the three governments were not shooting themselves in the foot, so to speak, or betraying any Arab cause. Also, had they known that Sirhan was working for some government such as that of France or Russia or Britain they would have been extremely unlikely to have spoken up. Such countries would have seen the provision of such information as barefaced mischief. It was clear who Sirhan was working for. He was working for the United States government, for the CIA. The actions of the three Arab governments, Egypt, Syria and the Lebanon, may have been a covert—diplomatic—warning to the US not to palm the blame for Kennedy's death on to an innocent Arab cause. They were spelling it out: they were well aware who Sirhan was and, it seems, they were also well aware of what he was doing on his trips to the Middle East. They were not without their own 'eyes' and 'ears'. Since this author had had suspicions about Sirhan having been involved with the CIA before ever hearing of the Kimche reports, he finds it easier to accept the information put forward by the Arab sources. As for the farm work in Corona which Sirhan was said to have been doing at the time, it would not be the first time an agent had been provided with a double to preserve a second identity or to effect a cover.

The release to the public of the Sirhan information from the Middle East was likely to create all kinds of complications in the Robert Kennedy murder investigation. Any hint that Sirhan was a CIA agent would be likely to completely unhinge LAPD's assertion that there was no conspiracy, and the image of Sirhan as the unbalanced, volatile loner would be quick to evaporate. Kimche, in his 18 July article, gave the impression he was unaware of the significance of what he reported when he wrote:

> But more important has been the attempt to blanket the information about Sirhan's own earlier movements. Though these are now known and recorded in detail by at least three Arab governments – and presumably must be known by the FBI – there appears to be a desire not to bring this part of the case into court. (This author's emphasis)

But perhaps Kimche was only being diplomatic. If so, he would no doubt be content that his words were there to be interpreted. In a much briefer piece which appeared on Monday 17 June between the two reports shown above, Jon Kimche wrote, under the heading FBI PROBE MIDDLE EAST TRAVELS:

> The Federal Bureau of Investigation at home and United States officials abroad have been active over the weekend in seeking to penetrate the sickening smoke screen which is settling on the Robert Kennedy assassination – especially over Sirhan Bishara Sirhan's immediate past. They have been probing new information covering at least four foreign countries concerning Sirhan's movements. In doing so they are satisfied that Sirhan's constitutional rights for a fair trial will not be jeopardised. On the contrary, it is thought that timely action and revelation may protect his life more effectively than formalistic silence – especially if Sirhan shows any inclination to talk freely.

The FBI are here depicted as gallantly seeking to clear away the 'smoke screen' while government officials 'probed' new information in four countries in an attempt to find the truth about Sirhan and obtain a defence for him. This is both ironic and absurd. A smoke screen certainly appeared: it was dropped by those investigating the case, including the FBI. And the notion of officials seeking afar for defence evidence is ludicrous when the FBI could have told them that they needed look no further than the pantry of the Ambassador Hotel where, in the woodwork, there was all the evidence necessary to completely change the nature of the case against Sirhan. This evidence was consistently ignored by LAPD, and the FBI, which we know was also aware of its existence, and stood back and said nothing. As for Sirhan talking freely, if he was the victim of someone who controlled him by hypnotism, he was obviously oblivious of the fact and, therefore, could have nothing to say about that, nor could he speak of anything about which he had been programmed to remain silent, such as his CIA connections. He appeared, also, to have had his memory wiped of the identity of whoever had tampered with his mind.

In the third and final article, published on 18 July, before returning to his Arab sources, Kimche began with an item from the United States:

A MURDER LIST IN SIRHAN'S DIARIES

Curious moves have taken place before the trial of Robert Kennedy's alleged assassin starts in Los Angeles . . . Extracts from Sirhan Bishara Sirhan's diaries have been circulated to interested and important politicians and others. Apparently their aim is to show that the young man was mentally unbalanced and not responsible for his action. This is indicated, it is claimed, by names of other prominent American statesmen who were listed in the diary for assassination after Kennedy. A closer inspection, however, shows that these were all men directly involved in Middle-East politics and accused by the Arab spokesmen of being pro-Israel.

How far was this from the truth? Who would have the authority to circulate extracts from Sirhan's 'diary' to interested politicians and others? And whose consent would be required for such circulation? Adding together the liberties taken by Sam Yorty, the investigations abroad by 'officials', and circulation of the 'diary'—all of which took place shortly after the assassination of Robert Kennedy and long before the trial of the accused—there did not seem to be much going for the man who was given the role of the patsy in the case.

It comes as no surprise to learn that the CIA renegades were prepared to sacrifice one of their colleagues as the patsy in their plan to kill Robert Kennedy. They had done it before. Lee Harvey Oswald, also, was a CIA agent who happened to have all the background they sought for the patsy in the assassination of President Kennedy. In the case of the Robert Kennedy murder they required someone who was highly susceptible to hypnotism, and they found him in the person of Sirhan. He was a very suitable subject for hypnotism, having, himself, practised self-hypnosis and mind-control techniques. Hypnotised a number of times in prison by doctors acting for both the defence and the prosecution, details of the outcome of these sessions were examined in 1975 for John Christian and William Turner by Dr Herbert Speigal, a prominent New York psychiatrist and hypnosis expert.* Dr Speigal had no hesitation in declaring Sirhan a Grade Five subject, on a scale of one to five.† Sirhan, therefore, was extremely susceptible to hypnotism. Just as Oswald had a 'cause'–the cause of communism–Sirhan also had a 'cause'. His was the cause of Arab against Jew, and it was his support of this cause which, it was decided by LAPD, led him to kill RFK. When it is recalled that Oswald's communist background was provided for him by his CIA mentors, however, the authenticity of Sirhan's devotion to the Arab cause must also be brought into question.

If Sirhan Sirhan was not under the influence of hypnotism when he fired shots at Robert Kennedy, it is difficult to explain his behaviour and his reactions to what was to follow. He gave the impression of being in a trance, and has since been unable to recall what happened during those vital moments when Senator Kennedy was ruthlessly murdered. Those who practise hypnotism and are aware of the techniques involved in programming subjects to carry out post-hypnotic instructions confirm that it is entirely possible to create a 'Manchurian Candidate'. Interestingly, it is easier to create a robot who goes through the motions of shooting at someone than actually have him carry out a killing. Advanced techniques include the programmer programming himself out of the subject's mind, so that

* John Christian and William Turner were co-authors of the book, *The Assassination of Robert F. Kennedy*, Random House, New York, 1979
† Dr Spiegal revealed this to Philip H. Melanson, author of *The Robert F. Kennedy Assassination*, SPI Books, New York, 1991

he will be unaware that he has been programmed, and it is taken for granted that such a programme will provide for the subject finishing his assignment without any recall of what he has done. It would also seem that, in Sirhan's case, the programmer wiped his memory of any recollection of him having been connected to the CIA. It would have been devastating to have had the man accused of killing Robert Kennedy claim to be in the service of the CIA. Perhaps, like Oswald, he had been led by renegade colleagues to believe he was carrying out CIA instructions when, in his case, he collaborated in hypnotism sessions.

For those prepared to accept evidence at face value, Sirhan's possessions served amply to incriminate him. In his pockets were $400, a small fortune to someone like Sirhan, and big enough to be suspicious. Two spare .22 bullets and a used cartridge case were also found, as though Sirhan was making sure there would be no problems with ballistics evidence. Also in his pocket was an advertisement for a Kennedy meeting a few days earlier, which he attended. This tended to suggest he had been stalking his intended victim. He had bought a used car—a 1956 De Soto—only eight days before his attack on RFK and this served to strengthen the argument that he was 'in the money'. Strangely, he had in his pocket a key belonging to another car. The car was found and identified as a 1959 Chrysler Tudor which reputedly belonged to a man who worked in the kitchen of the Ambassador Hotel, Robert Grindrod. Sirhan's connection with this man does not appear to have been explained, though since Grindrod is believed to have been involved in activities which attracted the attention of the Secret Service—he was said to have been 'listed' by them—it could be believed that the mere placing of a key in Sirhan's pocket was only another red herring.

The really special piece of evidence against Sirhan was his notebook, sometimes erroneously called his diary. This was a most interesting item, though its true value as evidence has always been questioned. Sirhan had used the book for making notes in classes at Pasadena City College. He had not, as most people do, started at one end of the book and worked progressively, page by page. His notes were dotted on pages through the book. There were other notes, or doodles, too, which were also disordered, and it was the non-class notes which drew attention and demanded explanation. Analysed, they contained 'notes' on two main topics: money and what might be described as expressions of left-wing sentiments. He frequently writes 'pay to the order of', and comments, 'I have often wondered what or how it feels to be rich, rich, rich, rich, rich.' He writes:

> I advocate the overthrow of the current president of the . . . United States of America. I have no absolute plans yet – but soon will compose some . . . I firmly support the communist cause and its people – wether [sic] Russian Chinese Albanian Hungarians – workers of the world unite you have nothing to lose but your chains . . .

The curious thing about his communist rantings was that he was not a communist. A communist friend, Walter Crowe, had tried to interest him in communism, for he saw in him left-wing traits, but Sirhan was not interested and Crowe dropped the subject.

It would be expected that Sirhan's enthusiasm for the Arab cause would feature strongly in the writings in his notebook, but the topic was curiously neglected, references to anything Arab few, and anti-Israeli passion completely absent. What might be termed his third 'preoccupation' was with Robert Kennedy. He wrote 'Robert Kennedy must be sacrificed for the cause of poor exploited people', and 'Kennedy must fall'. Yet his Kennedy references, which dominate any consideration of the notebook entries, occupy only two pages. It was his extraordinary repetitions of 'RFK must die!' and 'RFK must be assassinated', however, which investigators found compelling, together with the statement, 'Robert F. Kennedy must be assassinated before 5 June 68.' A superficial reading left no doubt that Sirhan Sirhan had planned to kill Robert Kennedy and his status as a crazy, mixed-up, lone killer was well supported.

A superficial examination is, however, often misleading. The repetitions were distinctly odd and highly reminiscent of 'automatic writing': that which is carried out while in a hypnotic trance and at the behest of the hypnotist. Some of the entries were written in the third person, examples being, 'Sirhan must begin work on . . .', 'Sirhan Sirhan has been determined . . .', and 'Sirhan heard the order of . . .', which was odd given that other entries were in the first person, for example, 'I advocate . . .', 'I firmly support . . .', 'I am poor . . .', and others were straightforward statements. When Sirhan was shown the notebook he had no recollection of it. In court his lawyer questioned him on the subject:

> *Cooper*: Well, now, let me ask you this. You still don't remember writing this?
> *Sirhan*: I don't remember it. I don't remember writing it.
> *Cooper*: Do you remember writing this: 'Please pay to the order of of of of of . . . this or that'?
> *Sirhan*: No, sir, I don't remember that.
> *Cooper*: What significance does this have to you?
> *Sirhan*: Nothing to me. I don't have a bank account. I don't understand it.
> *Cooper*: Well, can you understand why you put the name of a racehorse in there, 'Port Wine'?
> *Sirhan*: No, I don't.
> *Cooper*: But you don't deny writing it.
> *Sirhan*: No, I don't deny it. It is my writing.

Sirhan, here, has no problems about identifying the writing as his, yet while examining his notebook in the presence of Dr Bernard Diamond, his defence-team psychiatrist, he commented that the writing was not his usual style. Furthermore, he seemed genuinely surprised at some of the entries in the book, stumbled over words when he read from it and asked if someone had dated the pages. He had dated the pages himself.

Sirhan was questioned about the gun he used and where he concealed it on his person, about which he could remember nothing. He was, however, in the company of the girl in the polka-dot dress and her tall companion just before he leapt out to shoot at Senator Kennedy, and by this time he was displaying signs of being in a trance. Everything which happened during the time he was in that state was lost to his memory. It would not be unreasonable to believe that either the girl or the man passed the gun to him.

As has already been said, a man on trial for his life can usually be relied upon to put on his best defence, regardless of bravado. Sirhan did not. He expressed the wish to die, and his defence was shattered by his total absence of memory of the event and of his damning notebook. To those who had eyes to see and ears to hear there was something quite eerie in this alone. It would seem that the perpetrators of the murder of Robert Kennedy had devised a scenario in which their 'Manchurian Candidate' was not only programmed to shoot at the Senator, but was programmed also to self-destruct: to accept the consequences of a murder he did not commit and even to want to die for it. Following a frustrating period of intensive questioning in which he learnt nothing from Sirhan, Dr Seymour Pollack, the prosecution psychiatrist, had it exactly right when he commented, 'Ah, what a crazy mixed-up case.'

CHAPTER THIRTEEN

So Far, So Good: A Retrospective

> 'The art of the police consists of not seeing what there
> is no use seeing.'
>
> Napoleon

THERE IS LITTLE doubt that the members of the Consortium were greatly concerned with the success Robert Kennedy was achieving at the polls. Not only this, what he was saying in his speeches – and the response he got from the people – also bothered them. There could be no question of allowing Robert Kennedy to reintroduce the power of the Kennedy family to the White House. That was unthinkable. Nothing had changed regarding the Consortium's attitude to that situation. A Kennedy had become President once and that was enough. It had been an unmitigated disaster. The power wielded by John Kennedy – the combination of the power and influence of the Kennedy family and the power of the Presidency – had been frightening to behold, and he had slipped beyond the grasp of those who would have been a constraining influence, immune to the influence of those groups from whose ranks the members of the Consortium had been drawn. He had become 'untouchable'. When it had pleased him he completely ignored the advice of the Pentagon, the military-industrial complex, the oil industry and big business. Those Consortium members already devastated by the incompetence and ineptitude John F. Kennedy had displayed at the time of the Bay of Pigs, and who had already sworn enmity to him, had been inflamed by his threat to 'splinter the CIA into a thousand pieces and scatter it to the winds'. But then, those who had become members of the Consortium had never intended that Kennedy should ever reach the White House in the first place. They had done their best to stop him. It had been that fluke hair's-breadth majority which had been their mistake. Such a mistake would never happen again. They therefore watched Robert Kennedy with growing anxiety.

There were additional problems with Robert Kennedy. His anti-Vietnam war policy was a clear threat to Consortium members, some of whom were growing more powerful and others richer and richer as a consequence of the continuing war. This, of course, provided a great incentive to remove him from the Presidential campaign, but this was not their only concern. His dangerous support for the black communities threatened changes which would undermine the established balance in American society. The blacks had already been generously treated when it came to their rights and, as they put it, privileges, but they had been kept well under control. Their orbit was limited and their influence on the country and its affairs 'contained'. Kennedy was seeking to raise their status, increase their power and with it their influence, and it was clear that such a policy would result in catastrophe if it were pursued. Robert Kennedy was a wild man, an exceptionally dangerous man. But now the Consortium had matters in hand. Robert Kennedy was a dead man. It was only a matter of time.

The Executive Group had learnt many lessons from the assassination of John F. Kennedy. The patsy, well chosen, given the right background, and completely fooled by his CIA handlers, had been convicted by his presence at the Texas School Book Depository and on circumstantial evidence. In spite of the fact that the plan had gone seriously awry, it had turned out well. But that must be improved upon. When it was considered how many witnesses had to be silenced, there had been an element of luck involved. Luck must not enter into it when it came to disposing of Robert Kennedy. It had been the fear of war which had loomed large in compelling government action to control the Dallas investigation. Next time it would probably be the fear of negro uprising, in the wake of the murder of Martin Luther King.

Robert Kennedy was picking up far too many primaries for comfort. California was as far as he could possibly be let go. After that he would become more difficult to reach, to all intents and purposes the Democratic Candidate. The venue at Los Angeles would be the Ambassador Hotel. Preparations in LA would have to be put in hand immediately. The CIA-agent members of the Executive Group had all the right connections in LA. They would be needed for the plan the Group had in mind. The nature of the operation would be totally different to what had happened in Dallas. It would be a much neater affair, more compact and with fewer loose ends. The man who killed Robert Kennedy would be among the guests before the event and, if he wished, could stay with them afterwards.

Robert Kennedy would be killed in a crowd. To find him surrounded by people would not be difficult. It happened all the time, and the fact that he refused protection would allow the best possible conditions for the successful accomplishment of what they had to do. The basic plan was to have their man close behind the Senator in the crowd, and for a diversion to occur in front of him, created by someone firing a gun at him. This would capture the attentions of all in the crowd, and it would be at that moment that Robert Kennedy would be killed. Whoever created the diversion would have to be dispensable. To find the right person would be the most difficult task demanded by the plan. The CIA members were being pressed to provide someone for that purpose. The man who actually killed Kennedy should not be exposed and, therefore, should not be in any danger. He should be totally protected by the commotion which should follow the diversion. The gun he would use should be small enough to be palmed, and should never be seen.

The creation of the shooting diversion was given considerable thought. The problem was finding someone who would effectively be committing suicide. Added to this was the enormous risk to the assassination team which would be taken in afterwards silencing the patsy. If the patsy was taken alive by the authorities the conspiracy would be exposed. To shoot him dead on the spot would be the next best thing to advertising a conspiracy. It was the weakest link in the chain. The members of the Executive Group turned over between them every device they could imagine for entrapping someone into carrying out the patsy's job but the trouble was they could not conceive of anyone witless enough to carry out the 'commission' who would be capable of doing it. And to find the patsy did not answer the problems relating to silencing him.

After considering the administration of various drugs without finding an answer to their problems, it was probably one of the CIA members of the Group who raised the subject of hypnotism. He knew an experimental programme into mind control had been carried out and he knew of someone who was knowledgeable of the results. Commissioned to explore the possibility to the full, the Group was presented with ample detail of what it was possible to achieve by hypnotism. The programming was likened to the 'Manchurian Candidate' programming of which everyone had heard. There was scepticism at first, but this gave way to serious consideration when details of the 1954 CIA 'Artichoke' programme were introduced and discussed.*

Essentially, there was no real difference between the objective of the 'Artichoke' programme and the Executive Group's plan, but the transference of the topic from fiction to the realms of reality brought the subject into sharp focus. It was possible, the Group was told, to programme an individual so that he would carry out actions at a later time, responding to a 'trigger' of some kind. The trigger could be almost anything, a word, an action, the appearance of an object, almost anything. The subject's reactions after carrying out the desired action could be programmed, and his memory could be erased of anything which would betray a connection to the programmer, including the identity of the person who had carried out the programming. It was everything they wanted. Their requirement now was for a subject who was distinctly susceptible to hypnotism.

The Agency members of the Executive Group took on the task of finding the patsy. Questions they asked their colleagues in Los Angeles produced the answer in the person of Sirhan Sirhan, a young Palestinian-born agent, home from missions he had carried out for

---

* The 'Artichoke' programme was a project conducted by the CIA in about 1954. It provided for a subject to be hypnotised to respond to a 'trigger' and carry out the assassination of a designated person. The CIA said it was never used.

the Company in the Middle East, and known to be interested in hypnotism. At the behest of the agents who met him and spoke to him he began to practise self-hypnosis. He joined the Ancient Mystical Order of the Rosicrucians, who offered advice on positive thinking and self-induced mind control. On the grounds of his status as an agent and his suitability as a subject he was asked to participate in a hypnosis programme 'for the Agency', to which he agreed. He was hooked. His willing participation was in an 'experimental pro- gramme' for his employers. How was he to know that through it he was being irrevocably bonded to a conspiracy to kill the man millions of people were confident would be the next President of the United States?

When Sirhan was programmed for his role in the Robert Kennedy murder, a decision was taken that accuracy of shooting, which presented certain problems, would not be required. It presented a much less complex task for the programmer if his response to the 'trigger' was simply to get as close to the Senator as possible and loose off every round in his gun. The trigger would be a word whispered to him while he drank coffee. It had to be a word he would not encounter in the normal way, perhaps a word specially made up. While Sirhan was causing mayhem in front of the Senator, the killer would do his work from behind. If any of Sirhan's bullets happened to hit the Senator, so much the better, but it did not matter. The noise of Sirhan's gun would cover the shots from the killer's gun. It was not remotely expected that Sirhan would escape from the scene of the shooting, but he would have no memory of his actions or what took place during the period he was entranced. The programme allowed for his hypnotic state to wear off after a given period.

A person was required to say the trigger word to Sirhan at the right time and a girl was obtained for this purpose. It was decided also that it would be appropriate for a man to accompany the girl as back-up and the pair would fulfil other functions on the evening in question. They would make themselves conspicuous in the areas frequented by Kennedy supporters – the man could be very tall or very short and the girl could wear something which would be outstanding – and they could introduce another diversion immediately after the shooting, create a smoke-screen, and lay a trail to a fake 'conspiracy'. It was decided that there would be nothing more diverting than for the girl to scream, 'We shot him!' as the pair raced out of the building, and there could then be no doubt about which direction the investigation would take. Confusion in identifying the girl in the conspicuous dress would be increased by introducing another girl in a similar dress to parade herself at points in the hotel during the evening. It would be necessary to dispose of the three people involved as soon as possible afterwards.

The actual murder of Robert Kennedy would be carried out by a specialist assassin who would be sought by one of the Group's Mafia liaison members. They had the contacts for men with the required qualifications and talents, and mistakes in hiring the wrong kind of specialist would not be made. The man engaged would arrive with the guests, listen to the speeches and watch the results coming in. During the period immediately after Kennedy responded to the outcome of the voting, he would prepare himself for action. This would be after midnight, people would be tired, many would have drunk well during the course of the evening, and if the Senator's guard was going to be down it would be at this point. Someone, not too far away, would be on hand to make sure the Senator lined up with Sirhan's position. When the shooting was over, the assassin could melt into the background, hang around for a while so that he was not conspicuous in making a hasty exit, and leave when he felt like it. There should be very little risk involved. Sirhan would take the heat for what had happened, and the law would dispose of him.*

Yes, this was a very neat design for murder. It required the minimum of people and involved a very simple plan. The only daring part of the exercise was the use of hypnotism, but this carried no risks. Nothing started working until Sirhan leapt forward firing, and if, for any reason, Sirhan did not leap forward to create the diversion, everything was ordered to be cancelled. There would, if necessary, be a postponement to the next appropriate occasion. But an Executive Group member had sat in on a session during which Sirhan was hypnotised and he had no doubts the plan would work.

---

* In fact, California law was changed in regard to capital punishment while Sirhan was in prison awaiting execution, and his sentence was commuted to life imprisonment.

In spite of certain problems which had arisen, the execution of Robert Kennedy had been carried out very successfully. It was uncanny how Sirhan responded to his 'trigger', and how he had carried out the actions he had been programmed to perform. Even the burly maître d', Karl Uecker, could not disarm Sirhan until his eighth bullet had been fired. The young man's strength had been superhuman. In some ways the most impressive part of the programming was his total absence of memory relating to the shooting, and his inability to recall the earlier hypnosis session in which incriminating entries had been made in his notebook. Clearly the doctors who hypnotised Sirhan afterwards in prison had no idea what they were looking for. They lacked the kind of experience enjoyed by the man who had been provided by the CIA Group members. He had a deviousness which belonged in a different league.

The police, with the collaboration of the FBI and LADA had, effectively, changed the nature of the cover-up. It had been expected that the investigation would reveal that there had been a conspiracy, and this had been taken care of by the introduction of leads which would take the police to the fake 'conspiracy', far away from the Consortium, and a dead end. The girl in the polka-dot dress and her tall companion had performed well, but the actions of the police had rendered that part of the plan totally redundant. The evidence relating to the direction of the bullets fired into Robert Kennedy, alone, had been enough to blow the 'lone assassin' idea, and the number of bullets fired in the pantry would provide overwhelming confirmation that a conspiracy had taken place. But the investigating authorities, in an incredible way, stage-managed the evidence so that it all revolved around Sirhan. It was astounding how effective their blanketing of conspiracy evidence was. The investigation could not have been better conducted. And this time there was no government inquiry.

Sirhan's escape from execution was a setback, but the Group was assured that his secrets were well and truly locked up inside him. The only possible danger would be if a top-flight expert began exploring his mind. But then, such an expert would have to know what he was looking for, and the risk of that was remote, while the willingness of the authorities to co-operate in such exploration was a risk even more remote. It was very impressive how Sirhan's mind, even though probed and prodded under hypnosis while the various doctors tried their hands at filling in the gaps in his memory, presented a stone wall to them when it came to the programme.

There was an incredible 'carry over' from the fear experienced by Dallas witnesses, which had been very helpful. Many of those in the pantry area and elsewhere in the hotel were unwilling to come forward with anything they had noticed that night. If anyone saw the gun in the hand of the assassin either they did not come forward, or the police buried the statement. The worrying part of this is that, regardless of the LAPD position and the official burying of the conspiracy, so many people, reading between the lines, appear to have recognised the existence of the Executive Group and the Consortium to which it belongs. They recognised that those who struck down Robert Kennedy were the same people who struck down the President. There would have to be a great deal of hard thinking before the Consortium exposed itself in such a way again. There would have to be a different approach to disposing of Edward Kennedy. He had now appeared on the Presidential scene.

What is presented in this brief chapter may not be hard fact, but the reader may be assured it is not fiction. The facts known of the murder of Robert F. Kennedy support that, in essentials, this is not far from the truth.

CHAPTER FOURTEEN

The Third Kennedy

'Just as I went into politics because Joe died, if
anything happened to me tomorrow, my brother
Bobby would run for my seat in the Senate. And if
Bobby died, Teddy would take over for him.'

John F. Kennedy

EDWARD MOORE KENNEDY heard the news about his brother, Robert, being shot from a television newscast at a hotel in San Francisco, 400 miles north of Los Angeles. He was taking part in celebrations there of the incoming results from the California primaries which they had been avidly calculating, and had gone to his room with his administrative assistant, David Burke, to catch the late news. As the picture came up on the television set he found himself watching scenes of mass confusion, and it took a little time to realise this was a broadcast from the Ambassador Hotel in Los Angeles, and that the reporter was describing the aftermath of the shooting. Leaving at once, the two men were given the use of an Air Force jet to take them to Los Angeles, where they were taken by helicopter to the Good Samaritan Hospital. Edward Kennedy was told on his arrival that his brother was not expected to survive.

It is said that there was a suggestion by some that Edward Kennedy should drop into his brother's shoes and run for the Presidency, but this was quickly modified to a request for him to add his name to the ticket as Vice-Presidential candidate. He declined, but it is interesting

213

to observe an atmosphere in which he might easily have been swept into that office on a wave of popular emotion had he chosen to go forward. An incredible momentum had existed in Bobby Kennedy's campaign which appeared to render it unstoppable. The single-minded rank and file had been roused and they had had no doubts that they were behind the next President of the United States. The campaign had created a rare feeling among RFK's supporters, the kind in which they had experienced kindling an ember until it became a roaring, all-consuming fire. It had become more than a campaign: it had become a crusade, a march of zealots. And following a volley of shots . . . nothing. The crusaders had been robbed of everything in a twinkling. They were bereft, empty. Those who looked to find a degree of solace in getting behind the third Kennedy were disappointed, but they understood why he refused. This was Bobby's year.

Looking beyond the emotionalism, there is no doubt that Edward Kennedy, sooner or later, would have been despised for climbing over his brother had he accepted the spontaneous invitation to run as Vice-President. It is unnecessary to speculate that he would have come to hate himself for it, too. He never even considered it. Kennedy, no doubt, was wanted by the party to breathe some kind of life into a lost cause. It is a curious thought that it would not have been impossible, with Edward running for the Vice-Presidency in that charged atmosphere, for the nominee for the Presidency, whoever he turned out to be, to have been swept into the White House in a classic case of the tail wagging the dog. As it was, Richard Nixon had a free ride for the Republicans. There was no serious opposition to him.

In the cold light of day, it became clear that Edward was certainly not ready for the Presidency at that time, and there were those who questioned whether he was Presidential material for any time. After a mere five years in the Senate, he was not seen as a candidate for the Vice-Presidency, either, though it is usually overlooked that, in fact, he had *twice* as much experience as Robert in terms of actual service in the Senate. Edward Kennedy's problem was that he had two strikes against him already when he entered politics. One was called Jack and one was called Robert. He also had to cope with the stigma of being the youngest in the family. In one famous family picture he, literally, was 'the little one at the end'. Jack Kennedy had been seen as an intellectual and a man of vision; Robert an intellectual and a man of action. Edward's intellect was different and because it was different it was not to be compared to that of his brothers. That was the penalty exacted in the family game, and it was remarkable how the family game was played in the Senate. And then, apart from all this, the background and reputation which was Edward's own did nothing to inspire his fellow senators. He had been expelled from Harvard for arranging for another student to take a Spanish-language examination for him,* and he was known for his free-and-easy, playboy image.

It was Jack who reminded us that Edward's behaviour had not escaped the eagle eye of his father. Joseph P. Kennedy had, he said, '. . . cracked down on him at a crucial time in his life, and this brought out in Teddy the discipline and seriousness which will make him an important political figure.' Edward had it all to do. There was no doubt he was overshadowed by his brothers, whom he looked up to and relied upon. The family also observed a strict hierarchical structure, in which there was to be no such thing as leap-frogging ahead of the others. Each had his place and each had his turn. Their mother, Rose Kennedy, was to say:

> We tried to keep everything more or less equal, but you wonder if the mother and father aren't quite tired when the ninth one comes along. You have to make more of an effort to tell bedtime stories and be interested in swimming matches. There were 17 years between my oldest and youngest child, and I had been telling bedtime stories for 20 years. When you have older brothers and sisters, they're the ones that seem to be more important in a family, and always get the best rooms and the first choice of boats and all those kind of things, but Ted never seemed to resent it.

No amount of pressure would have persuaded Edward Kennedy to accept the nomination for the Vice-Presidency in 1968. It was not done. It was not his turn. He could never have climbed over Bobby in such a way. He would have his own chances. For Edward it never became a matter of attempting to sweep away the aura and the influence which were his brothers' legacy. He would have his own day and he would have to work towards that under his own steam.

---

* He later applied and was readmitted to Harvard, where he graduated three years later, with honours, in Government and History

Edward Kennedy read law at the University of Virginia Law School. He did not achieve this without difficulty, for he first applied to Harvard and was turned down. In 1959 he was admitted to the Massachusetts bar, and three years later he announced he would run for the seat in the Senate vacated by John F. Kennedy when he became President, ignoring advice to run for the House of Representatives. His entry into the Senate was not auspicious: he made more problems for himself in the way he achieved it. He leaned unashamedly on political connections and had no hesitation in trading on his brothers' names. At those meetings where the chairman ignored the fact that he was President Kennedy's brother, he was apt to begin by joking, 'I'm certainly glad that you didn't introduce me as the brother of the President.' Edward Kennedy beat George Cabot Lodge* for the seat by 300,000 votes, becoming the Senate's youngest member when he took his seat in 1963 but, as journalist William H. Honan expressed it:

> As it turned out . . . the caper branded him spoiled and privileged rather than bold and self-reliant, since he swept to a thumping victory in the wake of disclosures about his lack of previous experience in elective office and suspension from Harvard, which, for anyone except a President's brother would almost certainly have proved disastrous at the polls.†

It appears that when Edward Kennedy woke up to the fact that his election success was little more than an embarrassing example of hanging on to his brothers' coat-tails, it had a profound influence on his attitudes to such things. From that time forward he contrived to avoid the acceptance of his brothers' help. He had learnt his lesson. In future he would stand on his own two feet.

From entering the Senate Edward Kennedy worked hard, primarily for the people of Massachusetts, earning himself a reputation for being the 'quiet Kennedy'. He studiously learnt his craft and demonstrated an impressive understanding of problematic issues and the political techniques for finding solutions to them. This became Edward Kennedy's strength: he learnt the ways of government through the Senate and was prepared to beaver away to obtain the

---

* George's father, Henry Cabot Lodge, was ousted from the seat by John F. Kennedy ten years earlier
† William H. Honan, *Ted Kennedy: Profile of a Survivor*, Manor Books, US, 1972

desired results rather than use barnstorming methods. He was affable, friendly, deferential to his elders, and this earned him much respect. His work must have impressed the people of Massachusetts, for when his re-election was due, he was sent back to the Senate with a massive 74 per cent of the vote. Edward was a liberal who, like his brothers, supported civil rights, and he campaigned for stronger controls on firearms. His views on Vietnam were not those of Robert, but he was an advocate of finding a solution. 'It is time to talk,' he said, 'it is time for peace.'

Perhaps his greatest preoccupation was with the abjectly poor of the world, the under-privileged and the hundreds of thousands who became war refugees. Though he travelled widely, it was his trips to Africa and Latin America which underlined his interest in the deprived. 'It is difficult to talk about democracy to a Latin American peasant who is wondering whether he will go to bed hungry tonight.' He studied the refugee problems in India – the consequence of the Bangladesh–Pakistan war – and Vietnam. 'The war has created a rootless people, it has destroyed the familiar ritual and traditions of village life, it has fostered apathy, frustration and even distrust and hate for our efforts within a significant cross-section of the South Vietnamese people.' While his brothers had great concern for people and their hardships, Edward's was for human suffering as it related to all the poor nations of the world. In this he was treading his own paths, finding his own way.

With such sober and serious interests, it should not be thought that Edward had forgotten how to laugh, however, how to poke fun and indulge in the humour with which all the Kennedy boys had been endowed. William H. Honan quoted Senator Gaylord Nelson's recollection of an instance in which Edward's humour rescued Bobby in a moment of need. It was when both Edward and Robert were sitting on the Labor and Public Welfare Committee and Bobby was caught napping:

. . . Bobby introduced a bill and some substantive questions were asked. Bobby wasn't too well prepared and couldn't answer the questions. Everyone was a little embarrassed for him. Then Ted threw his hands up in mock despair and said in a loud, disapproving voice, 'Well, that's par for the course!' It broke everybody up, but you know he was having fun teasing his brother.*

It was the same brand of humour which was expressed in the telegram Edward sent to Robert when Robert and John were both away from Washington at the same time: 'PRESIDENT IS IN ASIA. VICE-PRESIDENT IS IN MID-EAST. YOU ARE IN MICHIGAN. HAVE SEIZED CONTROL!' Humour was an important component part in the Kennedy brothers' make-up, and it had an enormous humanising effect on those who worked closely with them. The American people, too, liked to hear stories of their wit or pranks, which made them real people. Brock Bower told a delightful tale about Edward in *Life* magazine† which must have been recounted countless times by the unwitting victim:

> As when a lady ahead of him in an airport corridor was struggling with her heavy suitcase, had given up struggling, was shoving it along the floor like a small house. 'I shouldn't . . .' he whispered, full of mischief, but ran forward. 'Hurry, hurry, hurry, come on, we'll be late,' already striding ahead of her protests with the bag in hand. 'You know, you look like Senator Kennedy – Ted Kennedy,' she said, trying to keep up. 'You know,' said Ted, 'you're the second person who's told me that today.' She said how her whole family were going to work for Ted because 'I think he really believes all the things he says he does, and he really believes in what Bobby believed in.' Ted was very dubious. 'Do you think so?' Yes, she really did, and you know you really do look a lot like him, don't people tell you that a lot? Well, yes, Ted allowed, sometimes they do. 'Of course it's a good thing that you're *not*,' she said, 'because I couldn't let you carry that because you know, he hurt his back and can't carry and lift things.' 'Is that so?' said Ted. But he was very, very dubious. 'He probably wouldn't ask to carry your bag anyway, that Kennedy fellow . . .'

The back injury had been caused by a plane crash in 1964 when he had been lucky to survive. Paralysed, he lay unable even to call for help. Senator Birch Bayh had dragged him to safety, and he was hospitalised for six months with severe injuries.

> . . . it was my third vertebra that was hit worst and pushed sideways. Fortunately that's below where the nerves branch out to your legs. If it had

---

* William H. Honan, *Ted Kennedy: Profile of a Survivor*, Manor Books, US, 1972
† *Life* magazine, 1 August 1969

been an inch higher, it would have severed my spinal cord. I would have been crippled for life.

During his six months in hospital his re-election came up and it was the Kennedy family who stepped in to run his successful campaign. Edward Kennedy was at first confined to a Stryker frame, but time saw him walking again, albeit with the help of a cane, and he eventually recovered. Though the injury to his back continued to be a cause for concern, Edward Kennedy tried not to let it slow him down. He resumed sailing and continued to participate in the sports he loved and it did not prevent him from continuing his work in the Senate.

He had wanted his place in politics and was prepared to work for it. Called by some a 'compulsive politician', he accepted the tedium which went with his particular approach to Senate work and was content to wait patiently for his objectives to be attained. It was a more restrained attitude towards politics. He put in foundations and did his building from the ground up. JFK had called Edward the best politician in the family. He was steady, he was forward looking and he was formidable. There was no doubt he had his Presidential ambitions, and he was making his way to that goal in his own time and in his own way. He may not have been as insightful as John or as gifted with flair and tenacity as Robert, but he had his own talents and he sharpened them to use as his tools. He took upon himself the job of convincing those around him, perhaps even himself, that the success he earned was *his*: it had his name on it, and it wouldn't have mattered if his name had been simply Edward Moore. He had given up hanging on to coat-tails.

When Robert Kennedy was killed Edward was shattered, and withdrew from public life. In declining the invitation to run for the Vice-Presidency he said:

Over the last few weeks, many prominent Democrats have raised the possibility of my running for Vice-President on the Democratic ticket this fall. I deeply appreciate their confidence. Under normal circumstances such a possibility would be a high honour and a challenge to further public service. But for me, this year, it is impossible.

My reasons are purely personal. They arise from the change in my situation and responsibility as a result of the events of last month. I know that the members of the Democratic party will understand these reasons without further elaboration.

I have informed the candidates for the Presidency and the chairman of the convention that I will not be able to accept the Vice-Presidential nomination if offered, and that my decision is final, firm and not subject to further consideration.

I believe, however, that there are certain vital foreign and domestic policies our party must pursue if it is to be successful in the coming election and is to solve our nation's problems. I will be speaking out on these issues in my capacity as United States senator in the future.

Edward Kennedy had a great deal of thinking to do, and it was right that he should not be stampeded into making hasty decisions. He was advised to quit politics altogether and practise law, but it was no doubt the 'compulsive politician' in him which won the day. Robert had faced up to the possibility that there was someone out there waiting to shoot him and had not let that deter him. 'I know I'm going to get my ass shot off just like Bobby,' he is reported as saying, but he adopted the same attitude as his brother. He took certain precautions such as keeping out of motorcades in his election activities, which were soon upon him, but he carried on. In the first speech he delivered after Robert's death, he said:

> There is no safety in hiding. Not for me; not for any of us here today; not for our children, who will inherit the world we make for them . . . Like my brothers before me, I pick up a fallen standard . . .

But when the elections were over he made a move which was perceived by many as decidedly odd. He ran for majority whip. As William H. Honan put it:

> The press and professional politicians around the country were left scratching their heads trying to figure out why the most glamorous public figure in the United States suddenly aspired to carry the water bucket. Was this the case of a young man on the way down? Or was there some deucedly clever motive behind it?
>
> Some Washington observers came forward with the theory that Kennedy's decision to run for whip was part of a carefully devised plan to

build a power base from which to launch the second attempt at
Restoration.. . . . But the power-base theory stumbled over the fact that
majority whip – despite the colourful English nomenclature – is anything
but ringmaster of the Senate . . . The whip exists merely to do the
majority leader's bidding – counting noses, bargaining for votes, excusing
members from roll calls when their votes are not essential, and so forth.*

The kindest interpretation which could be placed on this move to run
for whip was that it was part of Edward Kennedy's effort to dissociate
himself from family influence and to stand on his own feet. There was
also the possibility that it was the outcome of bargaining in the family,
a price he paid for continuing at all in politics. But it could also have
been that he was apprehensive of the Consortium's actions in
removing the second of his brothers. It may have been that, for the
Consortium's benefit, he was advertising a move in the opposite
direction to the Presidency, for since there was no chance he would
court the nomination as whip, there was little doubt that that was
what it was.

The notion had once been mooted that after John F. Kennedy's eight
years in office as President he would be succeeded by Robert, and
after his two terms Edward's time would then have arrived. He would
have been 48 years old by that reckoning, and would have been
following 16 years of Kennedy administrations. The assassination of
President Kennedy had telescoped the time-scale, but had Robert
gone to the White House there would still have been eight years for
Edward's preparation. When Robert was killed, Edward was in no
state of readiness for that high office. In the Consortium's calculations, therefore, there was no hurry to deal with the younger
Kennedy. They had reasoned he might never become a problem. On
the one hand, he might decide to retire from politics; on the other, he
might not be acceptable to the Democrats for the Presidential
nomination.

Their ideas were quickly revised when Kennedy was pressed to run
for the Vice-Presidency. It was not that he would have represented a

* William H. Honan, *Ted Kennedy: Profile of a Survivor*, Manor Books, US 1972

threat as Vice-President, it was the leap forward into the Presidential arena which worried them, and any relief they felt at his refusal to run for the VP nomination was short-lived, for immediately after Nixon's success for the Republicans, Democrats began talking of Edward Kennedy as their 1972 Presidential hope. The Consortium had miscalculated the importance which would be placed on the third brother. He had been quiet for a while after his brother's death, and had been successful in obtaining the post of whip. They now saw, as he looked in one direction while heading for another, a subterfuge, perhaps. They now saw his persistence in staying in politics as tantamount to a declaration of his aspirations to the Presidency.

It was the time-scale which gave the Consortium members a headache. If there was the remotest chance that Edward Kennedy might run for the Presidency in 1972 they would have to act quickly. But if a third Kennedy was killed within the decade they would be faced with potential exposure. There could then be no disguising their vendetta against the Kennedys. That part of their operation would be completely out in the open and that could prove exceedingly dangerous. The members of the Executive Group began to pit their wits against this problem. It needed resolving long before the time the candidates for 1972 began to emerge. How could they drive a secure wedge between Edward Kennedy and the Presidency without killing him?

CHAPTER FIFTEEN

An Accident of
Great Convenience

'O, what a tangled web we weave,
When first we practise to deceive!'
                                    Sir Walter Scott

CHAPPAQUIDDICK IS A tiny island which lies 120 yards off the coast of a greater island, Martha's Vineyard, which in turn lies off the coast of Massachusetts. Of the attractions to Martha's Vineyard, none is greater than the annual regatta, at the time of which the population of Edgartown multiplies beyond belief, crowding the inns and hotels in the town and beyond, and creating an almost carnival atmosphere.

The Edgartown Regatta attracted the wealthy, among them the Kennedys who had been competing in the sailing event for many years. In 1969 the family was represented by Edward Kennedy and his nephew, Joseph Kennedy III, Edward taking a respectable ninth place on the first day, Friday 18 July. Senator Edward Kennedy wanted, first of all, his sailing, but then a degree of privacy on this holiday break, and he had rented a cottage on Chappaquiddick Island, which was a haven for those who could afford it. He arranged to entertain a dozen people at the cottage, including himself and his driver. There were four other men and six of his female staff.

They booked in at Edgartown hotels, with plans to meet at the cottage on Chappaquiddick for partying, including a cookout on

223

Friday night. The party certainly went with a swing, as the neighbours reported, if the noise from the cottage was anything to judge by. Joe Gargan was in charge of the cooking, and his leg was severely pulled that night because the barbecue facilities were insufficient and the steaks came slowly for the hungry guests.

If the stories circulated are to be relied upon, the Senator and Mary Jo Kopechne disappeared late that evening. Wherever they went, they were not driven by Kennedy's chauffeur, Jack Crimmins, who stayed on at the cottage. Crimmins said that at about 11.15 pm the Senator said he wanted an early night and took his car keys, but others reported the time they went as up to midnight. They assumed the Senator was giving Mary Jo a lift, they said. Mary Jo Kopechne had been one of Robert Kennedy's 'boiler room' girls – a team who 'boiled down' the news and other desirable data so that the Senator could assimilate it quickly and easily – and since Robert's death she had transferred her allegiance to Edward. The other staff girls at the party were sisters Maryellen and Nance Lyons, Susan Tannenbaum, Esther Newberg and Rosemary Keough.

Apart from the Senator and his driver, Edward Kennedy's close friend, attorney Paul Markham, was also at the cottage party. The other men were Edward's cousin, lawyer-banker Joseph P. Gargan, lawyer Charles C. Tretter and Raymond S. LaRosa, a Massachusetts Civil Defence officer. The cottage party was not a one-off event. There had been other parties at other venues, intended to express appreciation to the guests for their endeavours on the Senator's behalf. Sparsely populated Chappaquiddick was ideal for providing the privacy the Senator sought for his partying.

It was early on the Saturday morning that two anglers, a young man and a boy, who had crossed on the first ferry from Edgartown, were seeking a likely spot to cast their lines. Walking over Chappaquiddick's Dike Bridge they were startled to see an upturned car in Poucha Pond, which the bridge crossed to give access to the beach. Poucha Pond belies its name. The waters which had at one time been severed artificially from the tidal seawaters were now subject to vicious currents since the barrier had been demolished. The car was lying in about eight feet of water, and the anglers ran to raise the alarm. The police in Edgartown were alerted and Police Chief Jim Arena himself went quickly to the scene, anxious to save life if that were necessary or possible. He ascertained by a cursory examination of the marks on the unrailed wooden bridge that the vehicle had dived off the side into the pond. Borrowing a pair of swimming trunks from a resident, he swam to the car to see if anyone was still inside it. The strong currents created enormous problems for him and, eventually, he had to abandon his attempts in favour of sending to the fire department for the services of a scuba diver. Their worst fears were realised when the diver reported the presence of the body of a girl in the rear of the upturned car.

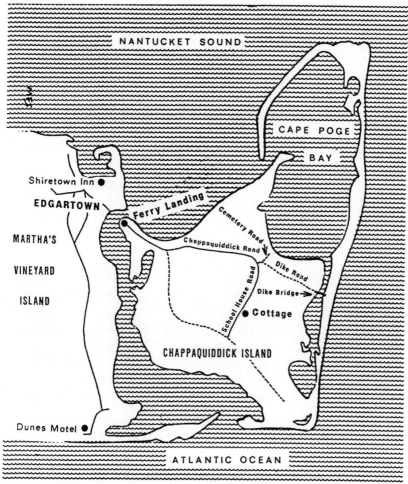

How could anyone leaving the cottage who knew the island take the road to the Dike Bridge in mistake for the road to the ferry landing?

The scuba diver touched the body and found it was in an advanced state of rigor mortis. The girl's head was fixed in a tilted-back position indicating her battle to obtain the last of the air trapped above her on the floor of the car before it had bubbled out, and her arms were stiffened in front of her as she had clutched the upholstery of a seat. So she was when she was brought to the surface. A doctor had by this time arrived and he confirmed that it was a straightforward case of death by drowning. A handbag was retrieved from the submerged car, the contents of which identified it as belonging to a Rosemary Keough, and this was the name at first attributed to the dead girl. It was soon established, however, that the name of the girl was Mary Jo Kopechne.

The number-plate and description of the vehicle lying upturned in Poucha Pond identified it as Senator Edward Kennedy's car. Kennedy had been seen earlier that morning on the ferry from Edgartown and he had spent some time at the ferryhouse on the Chappaquiddick side using the telephone, it was believed. He had returned to Edgartown before making contact with the police to report the accident. Senator Kennedy, in the company of his lawyer friend, Paul Markham, met Police Chief Jim Arena at Police Headquarters and, when asked to make a statement, expressed the preference for making this in writing. He and Markham closeted themselves away while they prepared the document. The complete statement was as follows:

On July 18, 1969, at approximately 11.15 pm, on Chappaquiddick Island, Martha's Vineyard, I was driving my car on Main Street on my way to get the ferry back to Edgartown. I was unfamiliar with the road and turned on to Dike Road instead of bearing left on Main Street. After proceeding for approximately a half mile on Dike Road I descended a hill and came upon a narrow bridge. The car went off the side of the bridge. There was one passenger in the car with me, Miss———, a former secretary of my brother Robert Kennedy. The car turned over and sank into the water and landed with the roof resting on the bottom.

I attempted to open the door and window of the car but have no recollection of how I got out of the car. I came to the surface and then repeatedly dove down to the car in an attempt to see if the passenger was still in the car. I was unsuccessful in the attempt.

I was exhausted and in a state of shock. I recall walking back to where my friends were eating. There was a car parked in front of the cottage and I climbed into the back seat. I then asked for someone to bring me back to Edgartown. I remember walking around for a period of time and then going back to my hotel room. When I fully realised what happened this morning, I immediately contacted the police.

The name of Mary Jo Kopechne had been omitted from the statement because the Senator said he did not know the correct spelling. In the eyes of the law, the only offence Edward Kennedy had committed was not reporting the accident when it happened. In his statement he admits his guilt and attempts to explain away the delay. In court the judge accepted the plea of guilty, and handed the Senator a two-month jail sentence which was suspended. But the matter was by no means ended. The public at large were far from satisfied with the simplistic, innocent explanation offered by Kennedy and the rumours started.

When the court appearance was over, Edward Kennedy moved to explain himself more fully in a television appearance. He said:

My fellow citizens:

I have requested this opportunity to talk to the people of Massachusetts about the tragedy which happened last Friday evening. This morning I entered a plea of guilty to the charge of leaving the scene of an accident. Prior to my appearance in court it would have been improper for me to comment on these matters. But tonight I am free to tell you what happened and to say what it means to me.

On the weekend of July 18 I was on Martha's Vineyard Island participating with my nephew Joe Kennedy – as for 30 years my family has participated – in the annual Edgartown sailing regatta. Only reasons of health prevented my wife from accompanying me.

On Chappaquiddick Island, off Martha's Vineyard, I attended on Friday evening, July 18, a cookout I had encouraged and helped sponsor for a devoted group of Kennedy campaign secretaries. When I left the party, around 11.15 pm, I was accompanied by one of these girls, Miss Mary Jo Kopechne. Mary Jo was one of the most devoted members of the staff of Senator Robert Kennedy. She worked for him for four years and was broken up over his death. For this reason, and because she was such a gentle, kind and idealistic person, all of us tried to help her feel that she still had a home with the Kennedy family.

There is no truth, no truth whatever, to the widely circulated suspicions of immoral conduct that have been leveled at my behaviour and hers regarding that evening. There has never been a private relationship between us of any kind. I know of nothing in Mary Jo's conduct on that or any other occasion – the same is true of the other girls at that party – that would lend any substance to such ugly speculation about their character. Nor was I driving under the influence of liquor.

Little over one mile away, the car that I was driving on an unlit road went off a narrow bridge which had no guardrails and was built on a left angle to the road. The car overturned in a deep pond and immediately filled with water. I remember thinking as the cold water rushed in around my head that I was for certain drowning. Then water entered my lungs and I actually felt the sensation of drowning. But somehow I struggled to the surface alive. I made immediate and repeated efforts to save Mary Jo by diving into the strong and murky current but succeeded only in increasing my state of utter exhaustion and alarm.

My conduct and conversations during the next several hours to the extent that I can remember them make no sense to me at all. Although my doctors informed me that I suffered a cerebral concussion as well as shock, I do not seek to escape responsibility for my actions by placing the blame either on the physical, emotional trauma brought on by the accident or on anyone else. I regard as indefensible the fact that I did not report the accident to the police immediately.

Instead of looking directly for a telephone after lying exhausted in the grass for an undetermined time, I walked back to the cottage where the party was being held and requested the help of two friends, my cousin Joseph Gargan and Paul Markham, and directed them to return immediately to the scene with me – this was some time after midnight – in order to undertake a new effort to dive down and locate Miss Kopechne. Their strenuous efforts, undertaken at some risks to their own lives, also proved futile.

All kinds of scrambled thoughts – all of them confused, some of them irrational, many of them which I cannot recall and some of which I would not have seriously entertained under normal circumstances – went through my mind during this period. They were reflected in the various inexplicable, inconsistent and inconclusive things I said and did, including such questions as whether the girl might still be alive somewhere out of that immediate area, whether some awful curse did actually hang over all the Kennedys, whether there was some justifiable reason for me to doubt what had happened and to delay my report, whether somehow the awful weight of this incredible accident might in some way pass from my shoulders. I was overcome, I'm frank to say, by a jumble of emotions – grief, fear, doubt, exhaustion, panic, confusion and shock.

Instructing Gargan and Markham not to alarm Mary Jo's friends that night, I had them take me to the ferry crossing. The ferry having shut down for the night, I suddenly jumped into the water and impulsively swam across, nearly drowning once again in the effort, and returned to my hotel about 2.00 am and collapsed in my room. I remember going out at one point and saying something to the room clerk.

In the morning, with my mind somewhat more lucid, I made an effort to call a family legal adviser, Burke Marshall, from a public telephone on the Chappaquiddick side of the ferry and belatedly reported the accident to the Martha's Vineyard police.

Today, as I mentioned, I felt morally obligated to plead guilty to the charge of leaving the scene of an accident. No words on my part can possibly express the terrible pain and suffering I feel over this tragic incident. This last week has been an agonizing one for me and the members of my family, and the grief we feel over the loss of a wonderful friend will remain with us the rest of our lives.

These events, the publicity, innuendo and whispers which have surrounded them and my admission of guilt this morning raise the question in my mind of whether my standing among the people of my state has been so impaired that I should resign my seat in the United States Senate. If at any time the citizens of Massachusetts should lack confidence in their senator's character or his ability, with or without justification, he could not in my opinion adequately perform his duty and should not continue in office.

The people of this state, the state which sent John Quincy Adams and Daniel Webster and Charles Sumner and Henry Cabot Lodge and John Kennedy to the United States Senate, are entitled to representation in that body of men who inspire their utmost confidence. For this reason, I would understand full well why some might think it right for me to resign. For me this will be a difficult decision to make.

It has been seven years since my first election to the Senate. You and I share many memories – some of them have been glorious, some have been very sad. The opportunity to work with you and serve Massachusetts has made my life worthwhile.

And so I ask you tonight, people of Massachusetts, to think this through with me. In facing this decision, I seek your advice and opinion. In making it, I seek your prayers. For this is a decision that I will have finally to make on my own.

It has been written a man does what he must in spite of personal consequences, in spite of obstacles and dangers and pressures, and that is the basis of all human morality. Whatever may be the sacrifices he faces, if he follows his conscience—the loss of his friends, his fortune, his contentment, even the esteem of his fellow man—each man must decide for himself the course he will follow. The stories of past courage cannot supply courage itself. For this, each man must look into his own soul.

I pray that I can have the courage to make the right decision. Whatever is decided and whatever the future holds for me, I hope that I shall be able to put this most recent tragedy behind me and make some further contribution to our state and mankind, whether it be in public or private life.

Thank you and good night.

Reaction came first in the form of telegrams—over 30,000 of them—supporting Kennedy, followed by volumes of letters. According to these his political future had a chance to survive. The supportive telegrams were followed by a very mixed press, however, which ranged from expressions of satisfaction in the Senator's explanation to criticism of a 'cold, heartless, political manoeuvre'. Taking the United States as a whole, the man in the street remained, at least, doubtful about what had really happened at Chappaquiddick. The man in the street at Edgartown who knew, intimately, the geography of Chappaquiddick Island, Poucha Pond and Dike Bridge had no doubts the Senator's story was a huge gloss. It included features found to be totally unacceptable and omitted satisfactory explanations for what had really happened.

For Edward Kennedy the nightmare was by no means over. It was just beginning. The people of Massachusetts may have rallied to his side in his hour of need, but the people beyond that state had not bombarded him with supportive mail. They had serious doubts about whether Edward Kennedy had a future at all in politics. The more they thought about it, the less they were convinced by his explanations. A number of things did not seem right. One of them was that there was something out of character about a Kennedy behaving in the selfish, cowardly way Edward Kennedy had admitted to. The press and the media in general did not let it go at that. Investigative journalists took up the challenge and began probing the events at Chappaquiddick and their reports kept the story alive long after Kennedy had resumed his seat in the Senate. Their efforts came to nothing, however, for whatever was still to be learnt was to be learnt from or through the people closest to the Senator and the tragedy which took place on the tiny island, and they closed ranks. But the absence of new facts led to the substitution of inventive scenarios which proved to harden the doubts surrounding the death of Mary Jo Kopechne and the disgrace brought upon the Senator for Massachusetts.

In the aftermath to the affair, the formal inquest into Mary Jo's death, which was held during October, was not open to the public, nor to the press. Thus the chance that disquieting doubts and rumours may have been dispelled by information surfacing during this procedure was lost. The documents containing the official details of what took place at the inquest were available only to witnesses or their counsel so that the accuracy of their statements might be checked. An application made for an autopsy to be carried out on Mary Jo's body was denied in accordance with the desires of her parents.

To one group of people the outcome of it all was not *entirely* what they had wanted, but it was the next best thing. It may not rid the Senate of Edward Kennedy, but he would never reach the White House. In that there was deep satisfaction on the part of those who had conspired to kill, once to rid the Presidency of a Kennedy, and a second time to keep another Kennedy out of that office. For the Consortium the 'mishap' at Chappaquiddick was an 'accident' of great convenience.

CHAPTER SIXTEEN

Investigation

'*It is far pleasanter to sit comfortably in the shade rubbing red pepper in a poor devil's eyes than to go about in the sun hunting up evidence.*'

Sir James Stevens, 1883

THERE WAS A lot more to the events at Chappaquiddick than came to light in the Senator's statement and television speech. As was mentioned earlier, the body of the girl removed from the submerged car was first identified, not as Mary Jo Kopechne, but as Rosemary Keough, another of the party guests, because her handbag was brought up in the search which was made. Little has been made of the presence of the bag in the car although it must be of vital importance to a complete understanding of what happened on the night of 18 July.

Rosemary Keough was asked how her bag got into the Senator's car, and she said she had left it there by mistake in the early evening when she had been taken on an errand in the car. She explained she had asked to be taken back from Chappaquiddick Island to her Edgartown hotel to get a radio for the cottage. She had been taken in the Senator's car and had accidentally left her bag behind. This is plausible to a degree, but it leaves many questions unanswered. In the first place, why would she be taken in the Senator's car? The group had a rented white Valient at the cottage, eminently more suitable for such a trip. She could have driven that herself, too. What is much more curious, however, is, assuming there was a good reason for her being taken in the Oldsmobile, and the bag had been accidentally left in the car, why was it not retrieved? Women are not easily parted from their handbags and are usually very unhappy without them. The Senator was at the cottage during the evening and the car stood at the door. Why did she not simply get into it and retrieve the bag?

In the bag two keys were found to the motel room shared by Rosemary and Mary Jo, which raises certain other questions. Since the handbag was left in the car until it was driven away by Senator Kennedy between 11.15 pm and midnight, when he was said to be driving to his hotel and taking Mary Jo to hers, would both girls not have been anxious to have sorted out possession of their room keys before the Senator set off? If Mary Jo really had been getting a lift with the Senator to her motel, how did she plan getting into her room? If she knew her key was in Rosemary's bag, why had she not taken possession of it and returned Rosemary's bag to her? Rosemary Keough must have known that the keys to their room were in her handbag in the Oldsmobile, too, and once they had set off she had no key. Neither, for that matter, had she her cosmetics or the other things ladies keep in their bags. Of course the simplest possible scenario to account for all these discrepancies might be that the bag had not been inadvertently left in the car at all and Rosemary Keough was also a passenger that night.*

According to lawyer Charles C. Tretter, one of Edward Kennedy's cottage guests, he and Rosemary Keough went walking at about 12.25 am. He says they saw the Valient driving towards the ferry crossing and, returning to the cottage wondering what was happening, found only Crimmins in bed and asleep, and then left for a second walk. This left all sorts of loose ends. There was the obvious question about Tretter walking out with a young woman after midnight. If Edward Kennedy was to be criticised for being in the company of a girl, why not Tretter? But this was not one of the burning issues. Tretter said they returned to the cottage and, finding no one there, went out

---

* It is interesting that Mary Jo's purse was left behind at the cottage, suggesting she intended returning there. Gwen L. Kopechne, Mary Jo's mother, in an interview given to the *New York Sunday News* (29 March 1970), said, 'I couldn't understand why she would leave it behind if she were going somewhere.'

walking again. Since they obviously thought there was something odd in seeing the Valient running around at that time of night, when there was, for instance, no ferry running, did they not think it odd there was no one around in the cottage? Where would Tretter and Keough expect the others to be? Why were they not alerted to something being wrong? After all, if Kennedy's statement was accurate Gargan and Markham would not be there but Raymond LaRosa should have been, and presumably Susan Tannenbaum and the Lyons sisters. Whatever the case, why did Tretter and Keough set off for a *second* walk, not to return, according to Tretter, until 2.20 am? Apart from other considerations, this was an excessive amount of exercise in which to be indulging during the middle of the night. If, in fact they *did* see the Valient heading in the direction of the ferry crossing, they were contradicting Kennedy's story that he, Gargan and Markham had made off in that car to *Dike Bridge* to attempt the rescue of Mary Jo. The ferry crossing was in the opposite direction to Dike Bridge. Was it not far more likely that Rosemary Keough was with the Senator—and her purse—and that Tretter was covering for her? This would not be to say Tretter was not out walking and saw the Valient.

Deputy Sheriff Huck Look claimed he saw the Senator's car as he drove home shortly after 12.30 am that night. Driving his Pontiac from the ferry, he swept round a bend on School Road as a huge black car approached him from the opposite direction. He saw the driver in his headlights and, he said, *a lady sitting in the passenger seat.* He could not, he said, distinguish between what might have been another passenger in the rear seat and what could have been a suit hanging up. But it was probably Mary Jo Kopechne that Look saw, since it was from the rear seat of the vehicle in Poucha Pond that her body was removed. Look had stopped his car when he saw the big black vehicle drive into what he knew was the entrance to an old cemetery. The car had stopped at once, hardly inside the opening and Look thought the driver had made a mistake and was seeking the right road. Huck Look had walked back to offer his assistance when the black sedan backed out on to the road at speed and made off at even greater speed—down the road which led to Dike Bridge. The Deputy Sheriff was skilled at recognising the make of cars and reading number-plates. Even in the dark he read off some of the numbers, which later corresponded with

235

numbers on the Senator's number-plate. When he heard of the events at Dike Bridge next morning he felt guilty that his presence at the opening to the old cemetery might have caused the driver of the car to use greater speed than he would otherwise have used and, therefore, that he had contributed in some way to the accident. On reflection it would seem that, the occupants of his car clearly having been picked up in the headlights of the Pontiac, the driver dived knowingly into the cemetery opening to avoid any further recognition, and when, to his horror, Huck Look stopped and began to make his way back to him, he backed out and drove off as fast as he could to avoid the Deputy Sheriff. To anyone acquainted with the geography of Chappaquiddick, the idea of a driver with any familiarity of the island taking the road to Dike Bridge by mistake for the ferry road was absurd. It is believed Edward Kennedy was entirely knowledgeable of the island's small network of roads, and while it can be argued it is always possible for a driver to make an error, it would hardly be *that* error a knowledgeable driver would make. The bridge was an access to the beach, in a totally different direction from the ferry. Another pertinent question was how had he managed to drive off the bridge? Yes, it was narrow, but not *that* narrow. It was 12 feet wide. It had no guardrails, it is true, but Edward Kennedy's car was the only car to have fallen from it in it's 20-year existence. The Senator claimed he had approached the bridge driving down a hill, which was meant to explain why he did not pick up the bridge in his headlights, and it had, therefore, come to him as a shock. There is no hill approaching the bridge, and headlights from cars normally pick it up some 300 feet away.

In his statement to the police, Edward Kennedy said he had returned to the cottage after failing to rescue Mary Jo, climbed into the back seat of a car and had then asked to be taken to Edgartown. This did not square with his statement that he took Gargan and Markham back to Poucha Pond to search for the girl,* nor did it square with the time sequence, for the ferry had stopped running a long time before this. How was he to be taken to Edgartown without a ferry? In his later

---

* Kennedy maintained that Gargan and Markham went back with him to Poucha Pond, diving in to attempt a rescue of Mary Jo. When they got back to the cottage at 2.15 am, however, one of the girls who saw them said they were both dry.

statement, on television, Kennedy changed this to his impulsively swimming across the channel to Edgartown. He obviously had to explain how he got across when there was no ferry service, but to say that he swam seemed ridiculous to those who knew the waters.

Another strange event might possibly explain how the Senator crossed to Edgartown in the middle of the night. Joseph P. Kennedy III, Edward's nephew, was offered a lift by someone he knew, who stopped to pick him up shortly before 3.00 am in Edgartown. He was alone, drenched to the skin, and, his friend claimed, was not very communicative. Asked where he wanted to go, he mumbled his reply and it was only by repeated questioning that 'Shiretown Inn' was picked up. That happened to be the same inn his uncle was staying at. Had Edward Kennedy arranged with his nephew to bring a launch for him to make his return from Chappaquiddick? And did he change his story to keep his nephew out of it? Was Joe's incoherent speech a cover for his reluctance to speak about where he had been?

Edward Kennedy's actions the morning after the accident also need some explaining. He appeared in the foyer of his hotel looking quite well and enquiring about newspapers. Hardly the action of someone who had almost lost his life the night before. Did he not want to consult a doctor about the water he had felt in his lungs? Who treated his injuries? Had he forgotten about Mary Jo? He said he had not slept at all that night but managed to appear quite fit next morning. It might have been thought that there were other, more important considerations than the newspapers when he surfaced, however. He went to Chappaquiddick, apparently to use a payphone there, made no attempt to speak to the Police Chief, who was involved in bringing up the body of Mary Jo Kopechne, and then returned to Edgartown before making any contact with the police. These were strange actions for a man who had driven his car into eight feet of water, knew there was a girl left in the vehicle, and had experienced the trauma he claimed.

Paul Markham and Joe Gargan had returned to the cottage at about 2.15 am, looking 'normal' it was said by one of the partygoers. Even if Kennedy had instructed them to say nothing about Mary Jo, as he said he did, would there not have been some little thing to indicate that something was sadly amiss? How could they act really normally? On the other hand, Joe Gargan was about soon after dawn and was reported as saying 'We can't find Mary Jo', as though there were no such secrecy instructions, and this was strange in the circumstances. Why did he say 'We can't find Mary Jo', rather than 'She must be drowned by now', or 'We tried to rescue her and failed'. '*We can't find Mary Jo.*'

It could be that this statement offered a vital clue. It certainly did if Mary Jo – and the car – were simply missing. That would also explain the Senator's peculiar actions next morning, if there was a rational explanation and a live Mary Jo expected when he reached Chappaquiddick. It would also explain the comment of one of his aides when the ferryman, Dick Hewitt, yelled a question in the Senator's direction at about the time he was using the payphone at the ferryhouse: 'Senator Kennedy, are you aware of the accident?' The aide replied, 'Yes, we just heard about it.' Just heard about it? What a strange thing to say. How could he say this if the Senator was also in the car when it plunged into Poucha Pond? Was it not more likely the response of someone who had just heard the worst?

All of this was supported by another outstanding and vital fact. If the Senator had gone back to the cottage telling Markham and Gargan about an accident in which Mary Jo was inside a car upturned in Poucha Pond, when all their efforts had failed to rescue her, their first act would have been to report the accident to the police. Markham was a lawyer and Gargan, now a banker, had been a lawyer, and both were familiar with the intricacies of the law, let alone such basic regulations as it being an offence not to report an accident. Had the events of that Friday night been as the Senator described, a phone call from Kennedy at the behest of Markham or Gargan, or a call from either one of the lawyers if Kennedy was too ill to telephone himself would at least have resolved all the legal problems which arose and would have kept the Senator out of court. That neither of them directed the Senator in the matter of that simple phone call nor made it for him supports very strongly that the events of that night were not as reported. It is more consistent with the car, and Miss Kopechne, having gone missing, and if this were true it would explain a lot of things. Was this what really happened on Friday night, 18 July? Could one reported fact which has not yet been mentioned here possibly provide the answer to the entire mystery? Sylvia Malm and her daughter, also Sylvia Malm, lived less than 200 yards from the

Dike Bridge. Just before midnight they heard a car race by their house heading for the bridge. It was 'going faster than usual', they said, and that made two odd things. The first was the fact that a car was driving down to the Dike Bridge, of all places, at that time of night, and the second was that it was being driven at speed. Did someone lie in wait for the Senator at Dike Bridge that night? Consistent with Huck Look's observations, did the Senator have a lady with him in the passenger seat, as well as Mary Jo in the rear? Was it Rosemary Keough? Did the Senator step out of the car at Dike Bridge and stroll along the beach, not alone but with Rosemary Keough, leaving Mary Jo in the car? Was it the case that when he returned, perhaps much later, he could not find the car or Mary Jo? If this scenario were true it would answer all the major discrepancies.

Charles Tretter's account of he and Rosemary Keough walking from just after the time Kennedy had left with Mary Jo until they observed the Valient making for the ferry crossing did not sit comfortably. It did not make sense that they saw no one but Crimmins at the cottage. It made less sense that they immediately set off for another walk which kept them out until 2.20 am, but this and the statement that they saw no one when they called at the cottage diverted any questions about Rosemary's whereabouts which might have been asked of the others. The two walks tidily accounted for the total time Rosemary Keough would have been away from the cottage. If she left with Edward Kennedy it would seem they planned to be together until long after the ferry had left and that an arrangement had been made for his nephew to bring a launch to take them both back to Edgartown. The launch picking them up at Poucha Pond would guarantee them their privacy, but they would want someone to hang around and take the Oldsmobile back to the cottage after they had departed. Was this Mary Jo Kopechne's job?

If a rendezvous had been planned, they would probably go out to one of the more attractive parts of the island, which could account for the car driving past Huck Look at some time between 12.30 and 1.00 am, when they were making for Poucha Pond and the launch. Did Kennedy and Keough stroll over the bridge and away along the sands, where they would be able to observe the arrival of the launch as it made its way in towards the bridge, leaving Mary Jo sitting in the car near the entrance to the bridge? Was the arrangement that they would return to the car to say good night, and Rosemary would collect her bag before they embarked on the launch, when Mary Jo would take the car back to the cottage? When she was alone was she overpowered by the occupants of the car Sylvia Malm had heard zooming down to the bridge shortly before the Oldsmobile had got there? It was entirely possible that the men in the car had observed the earlier liaison and had taken the only alternative route to reach the bridge first so that they could lie in wait for the Senator and his companions.

It would not be difficult to render Mary Jo unconscious and run the car off the edge of the bridge into Poucha Pond. Was it not the case that after the arrival of the launch, when Kennedy and Keough returned, they were utterly baffled by the disappearance of the Oldsmobile. After scouting around the vicinity, it would be their instinct to return to the cottage, reflecting that Mary Jo, for some reason, may have found it necessary to go back there. When she was not there was the alarm then raised and was it not then that Kennedy, Gargan and Markham, probably with Rosemary Keough, left in the Valient to scour the island for the missing Mary Jo? Was it that shortly after 2.00 am, they ran out of ideas and Edward Kennedy returned to Edgartown via the launch which the patient Joseph had waiting? Did Gargan, Markham and Rosemary Keough return in the Valient, to the cottage, and say nothing to the others? Joe Gargan could not sleep and, by dawn, he was up and it was then he reported, 'We can't find Mary Jo.' Had she turned up, dead or alive, anywhere but inside the Senator's car, she would simply have disappeared in the night.

If the Senator crossed the water with his nephew from Poucha Pond, it was a very much longer trip than the short ferry route. In this case he would probably make his way to his hotel room, leaving Joseph to moor the launch. Since Joseph was soaked through, probably from the spray, was Edward Kennedy wet through, also, and did this give him the inspiration for the claim that he swam across from the island? There was certainly no way he would have it known that his nephew had provided transport for him. But it will be recalled that shortly before 3.00 am, a sailing friend spotted the solitary Joseph, soaked to the skin, and offered him a ride back to the Shiretown Inn. This, no doubt, was timely, but it also appeared unwelcome, since Joseph said little and what he said was barely audible. This was probably his way of coping with a situation in which he did not want to answer questions.

It would not be difficult to believe that the Senator got no sleep that night. Room clerk Russell E. Peachey said he appeared fully dressed at 2.25 am, saying that he had probably been disturbed by the noise in the next room and that he couldn't find his watch. He asked the time and then went back to his room. In the time-honoured tradition of detective fiction, this gave all the appearances of being a device for 'fixing' with a witness his presence in his room at that time. This would fit a scenario in which the bewildered Kennedy, fearing something had happened to Mary Jo, was establishing that he was present in his room at the Shiretown during this night.

The next morning Edward Kennedy was seen in the foyer of the Shiretown at about 8.30 am seeking newspapers. He approached Mrs Stewart, the day clerk, asking about the availability of Boston and New York papers which the lady promised to obtain for him a little later, then he borrowed a dime to make a telephone call. Who he might have been calling with a dime from the Shiretown remains a mystery, since it seems the only telephone at the cottage was locked up in the studio reserved for the owner, Mrs Lawrence, from whom the cottage was rented. It must have been about this time that a group of the cottage residents – Joe Gargan, Charles Tretter, Paul Markham, Susan Tannenbaum and Rosemary Keough* – arrived at Edgartown off the ferry. By this time, also, the presence of the car in the water had been reported, and Police Chief Jim Arena was on his way to Chappaquiddick to see if there was anything which needed looking into. By shortly after nine o'clock Edward Kennedy with two companions had also crossed over to the island, and were seen at the ferryhouse using the telephone. They did not go down to Dike Bridge. It was at this point that Dick Hewitt yelled his question in the Senator's direction.

Edward Kennedy returned to Edgartown again before visiting the station and reporting his involvement. When, at about 10.00 am, Police Chief Jim Arena broke off from his operation at Dike Bridge

---

* Susan Tannenbaum, Esther Newberg, the Lyons sisters and Rosemary Keough were not told of Mary Jo's death until 11.15 am when Gargan told them, according to Charles Tretter.

and rang in to his office, he was told that the Senator was there. Arena asked to speak to him and the following is a fragment of their conversation, as it was reported:

> *Arena*: Do you know whether there were any other passengers in the car?
> *Kennedy*: Yes, there were.
> *Arena*: Well, do you think they might still be in the water?
> *Kennedy*: Well, no. Say, can I see you?*

Assuming the answers given by the Senator are reported accurately, and there is no reason to believe otherwise, Kennedy gave an amazing answer to the first question. He said, '*Yes, there were*', when asked if there were other passengers in the car, and then it seems realised the answer led to other questions. The trouble was that, like his answer to Arena's first question, the more he gave answers, the more the answers seemed to lead to other questions.

Of course the foregoing account of affairs at Chappaquiddick is conjecture. What else could it be? The principals have long since clammed up and will not assist with further investigations. What is written here is hardly inventive, however. In the face of an official story which appears improbable, the known facts have merely been stripped out and re-examined in a way which permits a more rational explanation to emerge. It is a pity the tragedy at Dike Bridge was not thoroughly investigated at the time it occurred. The root of the problem was that Police Chief Arena appeared to be content to accept the statements made, though it has to be said that when a US Senator steps forward and is prepared to accept the consequences for what he claims was the result of his own actions, there would seem to be small grounds on which to challenge what is said. On the other hand, Police Chief Arena had all the data available to him and did not even see fit to investigate what appeared to be obvious discrepancies – the purse belonging to Rosemary Keough, the curious walks she and Tretter claimed to take and the things they said they saw, the time problems, Huck Look's testimony, the swim the Senator claimed to make to

---

* Believed to be as reported by Police Chief Dominick Jim Arena.

Edgartown in the dead of night, to name but a few. Chief Arena appeared not to be interested in asking embarrassing questions.

It is also a great pity, in this author's opinion, that the family of Mary Jo Kopechne did not favour an autopsy being carried out on their daughter. The findings might well have compelled a full investigation into the tragedy. The Department of Public Safety conducted an examination of Mary Jo's clothing, and as part of this examination, they ran a test on her blouse which indicated the presence of blood on the left sleeve and the back of the garment. Analytic chemist Melvin Topjian, submitting this evidence, was asked whether anything other than blood might have caused the reaction in the test. 'In my opinion, no sir,' was his answer. Chief Arena appears not to have reacted to this, either.

Assuming that the scenario was as has been conjectured above, what was the objective of the attackers? The key may lie in the special trip Edward Kennedy made to the ferryhouse at Chappaquiddick landing while Police Chief Jim Arena and his team were involved in bringing Mary Jo's body to the surface. There was no obvious reason for Kennedy to have made this trip, but he had come for a purpose, there can be no doubt about that. He was conspicuous, and that must have hurt him badly on a morning when he was desperately troubled. The only reason for his visit to the ferryhouse seems to be the payphone there. Some have suggested that he may have had difficulty in finding a phone at Edgartown but this does not square with the fact that he used the phone, not much more than half an hour previously, at the Shiretown Inn with Mrs Stewart's dime. He had no difficulty then. It seemed more likely that he had been directed to the ferryhouse to *accept* a call, or that he had arranged to accept a call there, no doubt for privacy. Could the caller have been from the Consortium, making it clear to Kennedy that his Presidential aspirations were at an end? Did he tell Edward Kennedy that it would have been just as easy for them to have engineered his demise in Poucha Pond as Mary Jo Kopechne's? Did he, perhaps, threaten exposure of some other extra-marital affair of which they had evidence? Everything seemed to turn on that visit to the ferryhouse. On the return journey to Edgartown, Kennedy was subdued, according to the account rendered in Jack Olsen's *The Bridge at Chappaquiddick*:

Kennedy sat quietly, his head slumped, while the tall man with the receding black hairline spoke softly but emphatically, sometimes waving his arms to make a point. When the *On Time* [the ferry] nuzzled its nose against the landing on the Edgartown side, Kennedy jumped off even before the cables were hooked up. Hewitt and Ewing [the ferrymen] watched as the heavyset figure headed straight up the middle of Daggett Street, moving so fast that the tall, dark man was plainly having difficulty keeping up, and a photographer with a camera had to swing his body in a rapid arc to hold the vanishing image in his viewfinder. Two men strolling in the opposite direction jumped aside to keep from being bumped as Kennedy pushed doggedly on, his eyes fixed on the pavement and his deck shoes flashing in a style reminiscent of the Olympic walking event.*

Senator Kennedy was greatly disturbed by his trip to the Chappaquiddick ferryhouse. Is it merely a guess that he knew nothing of what was afoot, of where his car had gone the previous night and of Mary Jo's death until his trip to the ferryhouse? Is it mere conjecture that he had the full implications spelled out to him on the phone at the ferryhouse? Yes, Senator Kennedy was greatly disturbed by his trip to the Chappaquiddick ferryhouse.

---

* Jack Olsen, *The Bridge at Chappaquiddick*, Little, Brown and Company (Canada), 1970

CHAPTER SEVENTEEN

Aftermath

'*The frontier is wherever a man faces a fact.*'
Adlai Stevenson

THE QUESTION HAS been asked again and again: if Edward Kennedy was not in the Oldsmobile when it plunged from the Dike Bridge into Poucha Pond, if he had nothing to do with the events which resulted in the death of Mary Jo Kopechne, why did he accept full responsibility for the tragedy, attracting all kinds of criticism and bringing dishonour to his family? The answer appeared to lie in what transpired in the telephone conversation he had at the Chappaquiddick ferryhouse at about 9.00 am on the morning Mary Jo's body was found. If the scenario mooted in Chapter Sixteen is accurate, and all the known facts support it, there had to be a compelling reason for him not to go straight to the police to tell them Mary Jo had disappeared, along with his car, the previous night. He might have added that he and his companions had scoured the length and breadth of the tiny island searching for her, spending half the night combing the terrain before admitting defeat. One place they were not likely to spot the car was lying upturned on the bed of Poucha Pond on a very dark night, and it would never have occurred to them to look for it there.

When the car was brought to the surface, some of those who saw it and others who examined the pictures taken of it thought the damage excessive for a vehicle which had simply dropped off the side of the bridge. Besides the roof, which might be expected to be damaged, the panels of the right side of the car were very badly affected and, though the driver's window was rolled down, all the other windows except the one at the left rear were smashed. The car was full of broken glass. This attracted the theory that Kennedy had been drunk and had crashed the car, killing, as he thought, Mary Jo. To cover this up he rolled the car into Poucha Pond, not realising the girl was merely stunned, and thereby was responsible for her death by drowning. There is nothing to substantiate such a story, but it does, at least, serve to illustrate the impression made by the amount of damage the car sustained. One of the simpler questions asked was if the car bounced on to its roof why was the side so badly damaged or, conversely, if the car landed on its side how did the roof come to be dented? Another interesting feature was that the driver's snap-lock was down. Other things were as one would expect to find them: the ignition was switched on as were the lights and the automatic gear lever was set at 'drive'.

A blood sample was taken from Mary Jo's body which revealed an ethyl alcohol content of 0.09 per cent. In common terms this represented perhaps five or six drinks of 80–90 per cent proof spirit taken within an hour before her death, or even more taken within two hours prior to death. This gave rise to a mystery which was never resolved, for it was well known that Mary Jo did not drink or, at least, she drank little. Esther Newberg, one of the six girls at the cottage at Chappaquiddick, knew her well and testified at the inquest to that effect:

Newberg: Five or six drinks would have been completely out of order with the way she lived. And if a girl who didn't drink had that much to drink you would certainly be able to tell if she was more jovial than normal, and she was not.

Court: I am only telling you what a chemical analysis shows and the chemical analysis is practically irrefutable.

Newberg: Then I am the wrong person to be asked, because as far as I was concerned she was completely sober.

Court: And you saw her the time she left?

Newberg: Exactly the time she left.

If Mary Jo did not drink to excess in the period when she was in Esther Newberg's company, there were only two means by which the alcohol could have found its way into her system. One, of course, is that she immediately got drunk after leaving the cottage with Kennedy, which, assuming she found herself alone in the car by the bridge, might have accounted for the accident. Two things render this an unacceptable scenario, however. First it would have been completely out of character for her to have knocked back numerous stiff drinks in quick succession in any circumstances and, secondly, her body was found in the *rear* of the car, not in the driving seat and not in the passenger seat. Also, if Rosemary Keough was with them it would imply she was imbibing at a heavy rate, too, and there was no evidence whatever that she had been drinking to excess. If Kennedy had brought Mary Jo along to return the car to the cottage it was unlikely she would partake of any strong drink while out with the Senator. The other alternative is that Mary Jo was injected with a solution containing the ethyl alcohol by those who were seeking to discredit the Senator, and this would seem the more logical answer to the mystery.

It was at the inquest that evidence was presented regarding the presence of blood on Mary Jo's blouse. The benzidine tests conducted by Melvin Topjian and also by his supervisor, Dr John J. McHugh, of the Massachusetts Department of Public Safety, were positive:

Court: Would you instruct the Court as to what is this benzidine test?
McHugh: A test that indicates the presence of blood on the material. This test had shown positive over certain areas of the submitted white shirt.
Court: Could you tell us, and if you would examine the shirt and point to those areas so the Court is informed where on the shirt?
McHugh: Yes, sir.
Court: I think for the record you ought to state where it is, such as the back of the neck or the inside or something of that kind.
McHugh: If I might, I have it noted here. Let's see. Yes, sir. To continue, on gross examination of this item under visible and ultra-violet light disclosed the presence of reddish brown and brown washed-out stains principally on the back and left sleeve surfaces. Most of these stains gave positive benzidine reaction indicating the presence of residual traces of blood.

The next time the presence of blood on the shirt, or more accurately, the blouse, was mentioned was when Dr Donald Mills, Edgartown's local doctor who had conducted a superficial examination of the body when it was retrieved, gave evidence on the subject:

> *Court*: Expert evidence already introduced has indicated that the white blouse was subjected to chemical analysis and shows evidence of blood . . . are you able to express a medical opinion with reasonable certainty whether the presence of that blood is consistent with your diagnosis of death by drowning?
>
> *Mills*: Yes.
>
> *Court*: And what is that opinion, that it is consistent or that it is not consistent?
>
> *Mills*: That it is consistent.
>
> *Court*: With your diagnosis?
>
> *Mills*: With my diagnosis of death by drowning.
>
> *Court*: Could you explain to the court the reasons why you formed that opinion?
>
> *Mills*: In a drowning case when a person drowns there is what we call an exacerbation of blood or a putting out of blood from the lungs in the violent attempts to gain air and blood may and I believe usually perhaps more often than not, may be evidenced in the mouth and the nose of the decedent. Such blood might, in the efforts, the physical efforts to avoid drowning, might spread I suppose almost anywhere to the person's clothing.
>
> *Court*: Are you able, Doctor, to render an opinion as to how much blood normally is released from this kind of death? . . . Off the record. (Discussion took place without being recorded.) Can you render an opinion?
>
> *Mills*: A very small amount. I mean, less than half a cupful for example.
>
> *Court*: I am satisfied, Doctor. I have no other questions.

That the matter was let drop in this easy-going fashion was quite beyond belief. To begin with, it would have been expected that an autopsy would have been carried out on any case of drowning in circumstances where a submerged car was concerned: Dr Mills's 15-minute examination of the body was hardly satisfactory. Evidence of blood on the victim's clothing should have demanded both an autopsy and a searching investigation of the incident. The small amount of blood emitted from the mouth and nose by a drowning person could not with certainty account for bloodstains on clothing, especially on the back of the garment worn. Besides this, any blood emitted by a drowning person is likely to be carried away from the body by the water agitated by the throes of the victim. It would also be grossly diluted by the water rendering it unlikely to respond to benzidine.*

Dr Mills had been called out by the police to examine the body lifted from the car soon after scuba diver John Farrar had completed his work. The body was brought out of a police cruiser on a litter for the doctor to examine it, which he did there and then. Removing clothing as he had need, but not all of it, he conducted his brief examination, producing water when he pressed on the girl's rib cage and when he turned the body, first on one side and then the other, to look at her back. He found no visible signs of injury. 'Death by drowning,' he said. 'Not a question about it.' This was the only examination made of the body. Mills checked with the District Attorney's office regarding any necessity for an autopsy and was told by Lieutenant Killen, the DA's investigator, that as long as foul play was not suspected it would not be required.

It would not be long before District Attorney Edmund Dinis was at the throat of Dr Mills on the subject of an autopsy: 'I can't accept this man's findings at all. I can't accept anything he says. He has tried unfairly and untruthfully from the first day to shift the blame for not conducting an autopsy to this office.' Mills, in the meantime, was quoting Dinis as saying, 'I'm gonna keep my office out of it. I don't want another Lee Harvey Oswald affair, and if I get in it's gonna stir up a big Roman holiday in Edgartown.' It all revolved around the difference between a simple case of drowning and a drowned body being found in a submerged car. It also seemed to be a reflection of the need for a scrupulous examination of the body as compared to the, apparently, superficial examination conducted by Dr Mills at the side of Poucha Pond. Eugene Frieh, the undertaker who prepared Mary Jo's body for its flight to her home in Plymouth, was later to add fuel to the fire of the argument which came to rage round the dead girl's body when he rendered the opinion that the girl had died from

* Unlikely because a garment would hardly, in these circumstances, become deeply impregnated with the blood. Mary Jo's blouse was penetrated so deeply that when the tests were run, much later, there was, according to Dr McHugh, 'unusually strong' response to the benzidine

'suffocation rather than drowning'. He said he found the body contained 'very little moisture'.

When the evidence of the presence of blood on Mary Jo's blouse was combined with the revelation that a significant level of alcohol was showing in her blood sample, a girl known to be disinterested in drink, it should have been automatic for a complete investigation to be carried out, but District Attorney Dinis, uncharacteristically, did not press for this at the inquest. The inquest brought further discredit upon itself in the way it attempted to water down the impact of Deputy Sheriff Christopher F. (Huck) Look's important evidence. Look's story (recounted in detail in Chapter Sixteen), in which he described a large, dark car with a lady sitting next to the driver and, perhaps, another person in the rear on the road to the Dike Bridge, was disposed of by what can only be called gross legal chicanery:

Court: Now, at your closest point to this car how far were you from it?
Look: 25 or 30 feet.
Court: Are there any lights at that intersection?
Look: No, sir.
Court: Were there any lights either by your motor vehicle or that motor vehicle at that time? Were they on?
Look: Yes.
Court: And with reference to the motor vehicle you observed, were its lights on?
Look: Yes.
Court: Including its rear lights?
Look: Yes, sir.
Court: And what did you observe about the car at that time, if anything?
Look: That it was a dark car and that it was a Massachusetts registration.
Court: What did you notice, if anything, about the registration?
Look: That it began with an 'L' and it had a '7' at the beginning and one at the end.
Court: May I have the photograph of the car which is in exhibit?
(A photograph of Senator Kennedy's black Oldsmobile is handed to the Court. The registration number of the car, a Massachusetts registration, was L 78207.)
Court: Read the answer back, please.
(Look's answer containing the letter and the numbers was read aloud.)
Court: And did you also say, Mr Look, that it was a Massachusetts registration?
Look: Yes, sir.

Most courts comparing the number of the car in the photograph, which had been fished out of Poucha Pond, with the one described in Look's testimony would have had little difficulty in reconciling the two vehicles as one and the same. Look would have been in line for a compliment on his alertness and his adeptness in memorising that part of the registration details which he did. Not so this court. Judge Boyle asked Look if the car he had seen could have been dark green or any dark colour, and Huck Look, known for his punctiliousness and his precision when it came to matters of exact truth, agreed it could have been. Finally the judge demolished Look's testimony:

> *Court*: Well, you are unable to positively identify this car taken out of the water as the identical same car you saw the previous night?
> *Look*: In my opinion.
> *Court*: No, I'm talking about the positive identification.
> *Look*: No, I can't.

But just how many cars of this general description would be likely to be running about the tiny Chappaquiddick? How many vehicles of any description on the island were likely to bear a Massachusetts registration with a number beginning L 7 and ending in 7? Dick Hewitt, the ferryman, and his assistant could probably have made a stab at answering both of these questions since the ferry was the only means by which cars could cross from Martha's Vineyard. Not that the judge would have been remotely interested in hearing what they had to say. This, also, would have been less than one hundred per cent positive.

It goes without saying the outcome of the proceedings at the inquest could only be said to have been satisfactory to Edward Kennedy's position. This is remakable for another reason. Judge James Boyle, himself, had difficulty in accepting the Senator's account of events. In his findings he effectively called Kennedy a liar:

> I infer a reasonable and probable explanation of the totality of the facts is that Kennedy and Kopechne did *not* intend to return to Edgartown at that time; that Kennedy did *not* intend to drive to the ferryslip and his turn on Dyke [sic] Road was intentional.

Furthermore the judge said that if Edward Kennedy knew how dangerous the Dike Bridge was–as he must have done since he had driven the road on other occasions–'his operation of the vehicle constituted criminal conduct'. Exactly how much *would* it have taken to persuade the authorities to order a full-scale investigation into the tragedy at Chappaquiddick?

It is true that the Duke's County Grand Jury was convened in 1970 to investigate the affair. Foreman Leslie Leland announced:

> I just feel we have certain duties and responsibilities as jury members to fulfil. A great deal of time has passed since the girl died and it is time the public found out what happened.

Noble words sincerely expressed, but the public never did find out what happened. The members of the jury were instructed for an hour-and-a-half on the subject of the limitations of their responsibilities by Judge Wilfred Paquet, a Democrat and a Kennedy supporter, and the inquiry became a glorious non-event since a transcript from the inquest–which included Judge Boyles's devastating findings–was not supplied to it. It would be the next month before it became available. The information available to them being strictly limited, the frustrated Grand Jury was wound up. It never got off the ground, and that must have pleased someone. Leslie Leland had been receiving threatening phone calls: '. . . lay off, or else . . .'

Kennedy's guests at the cottage said little about the events of that Friday night and then fell into total silence, which completely stymied researchers and journalists. This tactic backfired to some extent, however, for it had the effect of bolstering the doubts about the Senator's story from the beginning. One of the group, Joe Gargan, did eventually talk to a former *Cape Cod News* reporter, Leo Damore, and Damore wrote a book which was published in 1988.* What Gargan said, however, did not change the basic story Edward Kennedy told. Gargan is said to have claimed that Kennedy wanted to tell the police that Mary Jo was alone when the car plunged into Poucha Pond, and that the Senator wanted him (Gargan) to pretend to discover the accident and report it. This, Gargan said, followed unsuccessful attempts by Kennedy, Markham and himself, diving

---

* Leo Damore, *Senatorial Privilege: The Chappaquiddick Cover-Up*, Regnery Gateway, US, 1988

into the water, to rescue the girl. The book claims Gargan and Markham refused.

While this account supports the view that there was more to the affair than ever came to light, it only serves to stir the same mixture around. Gargan is also reported as saying that Kennedy promised to report the incident immediately he reached Edgartown, which would serve to indicate that Kennedy was given the correct advice by him. A valid question is thereby raised as to whether the information volunteered was merely a justification and protection of Gargan's own position in relation to his knowledge of the incident. It may also be said that from the scant information gleaned from the other guests at the cottage, there would seem to be nothing to support his assertion that the three men ever attempted a rescue; rather there is more to indicate that none of them knew where either Mary Jo or the car were. It was Joe Gargan who, at the cottage at dawn on the Saturday morning, was reported saying, 'We can't find Mary Jo.' (See Chapter Sixteen.)

Late in 1988, the year Damore's book appeared, John Farrar, the scuba diver who brought up Mary Jo's body, spoke up to a television reporter on the subject. Always convinced that Mary Jo had survived, conscious, a long time after the car submerged, he said:

> There's no question that if the fire department had been notified within approximately one half to one hour of the time of the accident, we would have saved the girl's life.

On the same programme, Leslie Leland, the foreman of the Grand Jury, declared that had the existence of an air pocket been known to them, 'an indictment of manslaughter would have been brought in'.

Had the tragedy been thoroughly investigated, it would seem likely that a murder inquiry would have emerged; and had the police been seeking a murderer, Senator Edward Kennedy would probably have become the chief suspect. And, as the expression goes, he would have found himself between a rock and a hard place. A completely innocent man, how could he have convinced investigators that he knew nothing of what had happened to Mary Jo Kopechne until the next morning? If Rosemary Keough was with him that night, how could he explain his absence from the car without bringing her into it? To admit to having had two girls in the car with him would have ruined him altogether, from a political point of view.

Given that the cottage guest-list consisted of six men and six single women, there was already enough to give rise to suspicion of scandalous goings on, with hints that the tragedy might have been the outcome of a drunken orgy. When it came to the disappearance of Mary Jo and the car, how could Kennedy prove he had not dumped her in Poucha Pond for reasons best known to himself? The phone call which explained all to him did nothing to help him clear up the mess. Had he told that he knew of shadows who had set upon the girl and who ran the car off the Dike Bridge, who would have believed him? On balance it seemed he felt the story he told was the best option. This way he only took the blame for not reporting an accident and, at least, accidents drew sympathy, and there was a chance that sympathy might provide him with a chance to survive in politics.

Following the vote of confidence given to him by the people of Massachusetts, predictably the first time Edward Kennedy entered the Senate after the events at Chappaquiddick, he had the support of his fellow Democrats. 'Come in Ted,' majority leader Mike Mansfield announced, in a positive tone. 'You're right back where you belong.' Mansfield walked with him every inch from the entrance at the back to his front-bench seat, whereupon a number of his colleagues approached him to shake him by the hand. But for all this, Democrats were divided on whether he would survive politically. Some felt he had become a liability. 'How can any Democratic candidate even think of asking Teddy to campaign for him?' asked one. 'Every time he shows up, there will be someone in the crowd with a placard, "What about Mary Jo?".' 'Kennedy's finished,' said another. 'We haven't got a candidate for 1972.' *Newsweek** featured a lengthy article on Chappaquiddick entitled, 'GRIEF, FEAR, DOUBT, PANIC'—AND GUILT, which they concluded with a realistic quote from another Democratic senator:

> It's my feeling that he'll stay in the Senate—it's a club and they'll rally round him—and I think he'll come back less as the gay Lothario and the

* *Newsweek*, 4 August 1969. Senator's quote reported by Samuel Shaffer

guy on the white horse and more of a human being. He'll never be the same again. He'll go through life haunted by the ghost of that girl. Every morning he'll have to face himself in the mirror, and it won't be easy. But once the Presidential thing is eradicated, he will live better with himself . . . All the king's horses and all the king's men cannot bring him to the White House now. I think we have finally come to the end of Camelot.

His words have proved prophetic. The shape of US politics was irrevocably changed by the events at Chappaquiddick. Kennedy lost his post as whip to a competitor, and any hopes he might have had for the Presidential nomination for 1972 were buried in the tiny island lying off Martha's Vineyard. He was expected by many to make a determined effort to reinstate himself as a serious contender for the Presidency in 1979 but, again, questions about Chappaquiddick destroyed his chances. In a television interview with Roger Mudd the issue was brought to the consciousness of the American people once more. When Mudd shot a final question at the Senator, 'Why do you want to be President?' his answer was a shambles. It was about as competent as the answer he had given to the question, 'Do you think, Senator, that anybody will ever believe your explanation?' Chappaquiddick would never go away. Restoration, having been indefinitely postponed, was now cancelled.

In a quip made when he was campaigning in 1988 for Michael Dukakis, who was the Governor of Massachusetts, Edward Kennedy may have reflected upon his regrets. 'I have always maintained that what the country needed was a President from Massachusetts.' The Senator's consolation was that the people of Massachusetts continued to return him to the Senate in election after election. His popularity had fallen sharply elsewhere, however. The Consortium had, nontheless, achieved all they had set out to achieve in keeping Edward Kennedy from reaching the White House. Its work was sound. Just as surely as if they had shot him dead the power of the Kennedy family had, finally, been severed from the power of the Presidency. The age of Camelot had, indeed, passed.

CHAPTER EIGHTEEN

Cans of Worms and Blueberry Pie

*'That whenever any Form of Government becomes
destructive of Life, Liberty and the pursuit of Happiness, it is
the Right of the People to alter or to abolish it, and to institute
new Government, laying its foundations on such principles
and organising its powers in such form, as to them shall seem
most likely to effect their Safety and Happiness.'*

Declaration of Independence

THE DUST HAS not settled on the scandalous vendetta carried out against the Kennedy brothers, and it is to be hoped it will never settle before the perpetrators have been identified and brought to justice. Some have, no doubt, died by now, but others are still alive and the Consortium is still very much alive. In the search for those who have sought to change and control the government of the United States by violence, a great debt of gratitude is owed to those who have patiently, against all odds, researched and investigated the crimes involved, and also to those who have campaigned to restore truth and justice to America. Steps taken in a forward direction are usually small and before they can be achieved much arduous, painstaking, time-consuming effort is required.

The early researchers had to fight the stigma of being labelled anti-establishment, unbelievers and worse, sometimes odd-balls, muckrakers. But for them, however, the United States—and the world—would have gone on believing a lie, and the massive victory enjoyed by the forces of evil would have been matched by massive corruption which remained undetected. Some of those early stalwarts have now departed this life, but, thankfully, others are still with us and they continue their work. Their work has attracted a number of other men and women who have taken up the cudgels, among them young people who will make sure the progress is maintained.

Whilst there are basic rules which are observed by all researchers, each has his or her own methods for working. It does not matter as long as results are obtained. A negative result can often be as useful as a positive result, and all researchers know they must sift mountains of dust before they can hope to find their gleam of gold. It is the vital lead which is sought which can shed light on just one aspect of the mystery. Each chink contributes, no matter how small, to our understanding of the whole. And since the nightmare began, with the murder of John F. Kennedy in Dallas in 1963, our knowledge of what happened–what really happened–has increased by leaps and bounds.

One of the potent methods used by this author in his research is to identify patterns among the evidence. It is this technique which has brought him to the realisation that the assassinations of John Kennedy and Robert Kennedy were linked, that Chappaquiddick and the murder of Marilyn Monroe were part of the same diabolical plan, and that a vendetta existed. Combing the mass of data relating to these crimes, other patterns emerge, one of which might be described as the link between Washington and Texas, the Lone Star State.

As all who study the history of the United States know, after the war in which it secured separation from Mexico, Texas became an independent republic, and when it joined the Union, it preserved its independent spirit and became a symbol of adventurous endeavour. When Washington came to exercise control over Texas, there were those in Texas who, particularly since the discovery of oil in 1901 on Spindletop, struck back, asserting a degree of control over Washington. Texas was for Texas, with Austin its capital and Dallas the centre of enterprise which cocked a snook not only at the rest of America, but at the rest of Texas.

In an earlier chapter, where the composition of the Consortium was described, it will be recalled that some of the members were seen as coming from big business, the military-industrial complex and the oil industry. All of these were well represented in Texas, and it would not, therefore, be surprising if the Consortium members representing

258

all of these interests were Texans. Some saw another link with Texas. The mayor of Dallas in 1963, Earle Cabell, was the brother of Pierre Charles Cabell, the Deputy Director of the CIA who was fired by President Kennedy after the Bay of Pigs debacle. The fact that Dallas was chosen as the place for the assassination of John F. Kennedy was also seen as highly significant by many, while those seeking the reasons for JFK's murder did not overlook his declared intention to re-examine the oil depletion allowances, which ranked high among his worst sins to the oil men.

Texas connections were not hard to find. It would be hard to overlook, for instance, that Lyndon B. Johnson, John F. Kennedy's Vice-President was a Texan, and that he succeeded the assassinated President. The Consortium certainly advertised that they preferred a Texan to Kennedy. Deserved or not, a great deal of suspicion has fallen on Johnson as a consequence of this. Madeleine Brown would not say it was undeserved. Madeleine claims to have been Johnson's mistress for some 20 years and, on the morning of the day the assassination took place, LBJ telephoned her in Dallas from nearby Fort Worth, where the Presidential party had been staying overnight. She said that LBJ was livid. Something had upset him and during his conversation with her, she claims he told her, 'I'll guarantee you one thing. After today those sonofabitch Kennedys will not make fun of me again.' Madeleine Brown is quite adamant about this and her story is consistent whenever she repeats it.

Does this mean Lyndon Johnson had been tipped off that Kennedy would be killed at Dallas? It is extremely doubtful that he had any connection with the Consortium or that he could be seen as a conspirator: by all indications he suffered greatly from the Consortium's hidden pressures himself when he became President. But there can be no doubt that if Johnson had advance information that guns were waiting for Kennedy, he was party to it. Madeleine claims, also, that sometime after the assassination she asked Lyndon Johnson about the rumours and suspicions which were going around that he was involved in it. He became angry, she said, and told her it was the oilmen, with the CIA, who had killed Kennedy. Since 'oilmen' were likely Consortium members, as were CIA agents, this answer would be near enough.

Several mainstream researchers have drawn attention to the party which took place in Dallas the night before President Kennedy was shot. It was reputedly held at the home of oil baron Clint Murchison and, putting together the names quoted by the various researchers who have written about it, the guest-list was impressive. Richard Nixon was there, claims Penn Jones Jr. Nixon left Dallas only shortly before Kennedy arrived the following day and, questioned by reporters, denied at first that he was in Dallas at that time. Jim Marrs claims he was attending a Carbonated Bottlers' convention in the company of actress and Pepsi heiress, Joan Crawford.* Penn Jones Jr says that FBI Director, J. Edgar Hoover was present, also, and Madeleine Brown told this author she and Lyndon Johnson were there for a while. He had come over from Fort Worth and called before going on to Pat Kirkwood's place, The Cellar. She said that Chase-Manhattan Bank's John McCloy—later to be appointed a Warren Commissioner—was there, as was John Tower and oil billionaire H. L. Hunt.

Frankly, if only half of these people had been there it would have represented a very high-powered gathering. But was this merely a social gathering? It was reported in the social columns of the *Dallas Times Herald*, and from what Madeleine says she saw that night it was just that. Author and ex-CIA agent Robert D. Morrow,† however, appears to have other information. He states:

> Interestingly, on the eve of the assassination, Hoover and Nixon attended a meeting together at the Dallas home of oil-baron Clint Murchison. Among the subjects discussed at this meeting were the political futures of Hoover and Nixon in the event President Kennedy was assassinated.

If Morrow is right a group of those present retired to a room away from the social chit-chat to have a meeting. Madeleine Brown finds no difficulty in accepting that. It supports, to her, the mood Johnson was in when he left, and the comments he made. She now believes he knew Kennedy was to be assassinated when he left that house.

If such a meeting transpired that night, was it an incredible coincidence or was it timed with foreknowledge? Unhappily what we

---

* Jim Marrs, *Crossfire*, Carroll and Graf, New York, 1989
† Robert D. Morrow, *First Hand Knowledge: How I Participated in the CIA-Mafia Murder of President Kennedy*, SPI Books, New York, 1992

know does not provide us with anything which resembles hard evidence. We do not *know*, for instance, that Johnson learnt of the plot to kill Kennedy at that meeting. It is possible he was told beforehand. We do not know that any other guest had such knowledge, though the subject of the meeting, according to Robert Morrow, would seem a curious topic for discussion for the night before Kennedy was murdered. Morrow believes that Hoover had picked up information about the conspiracy which he did not share with the President's men. If this was so, would he share it at the meeting? If he did, with whom did he share it? Hoover was not renowned for sharing information with anyone unless he had a reason. And it would seem out of character for him to share such information with all and sundry at a gathering of this kind. After all, he would have been announcing his own treason to two future presidents. That does not make sense, but it does not mean he did not tell *someone*, in confidence.

Of those said to be at Clint Murchison's house that night, there were three whose futures would be profoundly affected by the assassination. J. Edgar Hoover was in an exceptionally vulnerable position at that time. It was doubtful he would survive in office. He had made it known to JFK that he had a file on his private life. JFK had made it known to Hoover that he, in turn, had a file on him. It was a stand-off at best, but Hoover knew that JFK was seeking the means of retiring him. When it came to Nixon, the assassination completely changed his chances for the Presidency. Had Kennedy survived, Bobby would have been waiting in the wings after his second term, and Edward after him. This would probably have wiped out his chances altogether.

But it was Lyndon Johnson who stood to gain most, and not just because he would become President. Rumour had it that Kennedy, concerned about the Bobby Baker affair and its proximity to the Vice-Presidency, had decided to drop Johnson from the ticket at the forthcoming election. Richard Nixon had said something about this while he was in Dallas: it was carried in the local press on 22 November 1963, the day President Kennedy was assassinated:

Lyndon was chosen in 1960 because he could help the ticket in the South. Now he is becoming a political liability in the South, just as he is in the North.

By all accounts Lyndon Johnson's political future was threatened on all sides by the growing scandal surrounding his close friend Bobby Baker. His accession to the Presidency may have come in the nick of time to rescue him from political calamity.

Johnson had been a survivor in politics from the time he had scraped into the Senate. His first bid failed, and when he tried next time his prospects looked doubtful. It was by an 87-vote majority that he beat his rival, Coke Stevenson, earning him the nickname, 'Landslide Lyndon', and attracting accusations of fraud. It appears that the votes cast in the district to which Box 13 had been allocated totalled 765 for Johnson and 60 for Stevenson. This return was locally announced. When Johnson was known to be in a corner and looked like losing by a short head, the figures magically changed: 765 became 965 for Johnson. One thousand and twenty-eight votes were cast in a box for which only 600 ballot papers had been provided. Johnson was elected on the strength of 87 votes from Box 13. Author Ronnie Dugger wrote:

> By every legal stratagem available to him, Johnson obstructed any investigation of Box 13. He went into state court to prevent officials of Jim Wells County from changing the late-reported figures. In federal court he sought to stop a judicial investigation. He resisted a court-ordered examination of the ballots in the south Texas boss counties, including the ballots in Box 13. He alleged fraud in other counties he said would give him a majority even without Box 13 – but he opposed judicial investigation of his own allegations. He was not going to stand back again. If votes were stolen for him, the other side had stolen more than he had – they'd stolen it from him in 1941 anyway, now it was his and he was going to keep it.*

Johnson survived, also, his connection with the Brown and Root company. Johnson had forged links with the owners of the Texas firm of contractors early in his career, and the firm won an uncommon

---

* Ronnie Dugger, *The Politician: The Life and Times of Lyndon Johnson*, W. W. Norton and Co., New York, 1982.

amount of government business after LBJ went to Washington. Brown and Root expressed their appreciation by way of financial support for Johnson, but the maximum contribution allowed by law was $5,000. Brown and Root found a way round the law, it was claimed, by having their associates, employees and subcontractors contribute the maximum amount, also. Internal Revenue investigated the contributions, finding that Brown and Root paid each of the associates, employees and subcontractors a bonus of $5,000 to coincide. The investigation was stopped by President Roosevelt but, after he died, it was taken up again, by which time the documentation had been lost in a fire. Johnson's relationship with Brown and Root was well known. In his book, Ronnie Dugger quotes Franklin Jones Sr, a lawyer in East Texas, who used to say, when referring to LBJ in the late fifties, 'Well, now, let's get down to the Brown and Root of the matter.'

The Bobby Baker scandal has been mentioned earlier in this book. Bobby Baker, who was Secretary to the Majority Leader in the Senate, was very much Lyndon Johnson's protégé. Sued by a vending machine supplier, Ralph Hill, for $300,000, it transpired that Hill had paid Baker to use his influence to keep his machines in government buildings. Baker, however, becoming aware there were healthy profits in the vending-machine business, used his influence instead to steer business away from Hill and into a company formed by his wife and brother. The family's company made enormous profits – California alone produced business worth over three million dollars – and when it all came to light, Bobby Baker was prosecuted. His close relationship with LBJ became a great embarrassment to the Vice-President, and the tightening noose of press attention could have engulfed him politically had Kennedy not been assassinated, making him President.

A further scandal threatened Johnson even when he was President, because of another personal friend, Billy Sol Estes. Estes was involved in grain and cotton-growing deals. In 1961 LBJ had supported him when suspicions arose about his cotton land acquisitions, but this did not stop an inquiry being put in hand. This, in turn, led to Agricultural Agent Henry Marshall being sent to investigate the affair, as we recounted in an earlier chapter. It will be recalled that Marshall investigated fully and reported early in 1961, and that he was found dead in the June of that year with five bullets in him. Without an inquest, he was declared a suicide. Years later, when his body was exhumed, it was found that he had received a blow on his head, and had suffered asphyxiation from carbon monoxide as well as having five bullets fired into his body. When Johnson became President, Estes, faced with criminal charges–though not murder–found the federal charges were not pressed. Not so a charge brought by the State of Texas, however. He was tried and convicted. Legal wrangles followed, but Estes was eventually jailed. Given a 15-year sentence, he was for a time paroled, though this was cancelled. In 1983 he was released and in 1984 was called before a grand jury which was looking into the death of Agent Marshall. Though Estes was hardly a man whose word could be trusted, and Johnson was dead by now, he did, in fact, implicate LBJ in the murder, though the truth of the matter remains uncertain. The least that can be said is that Lyndon Baines Johnson certainly befriended some strange people in his time.

Nor were these the only cans of worms which despoiled the blueberry pie of the American Establishment during this period. In 1973 Spiro Agnew, Richard Nixon's Vice-President, resigned in disgrace following charges of income-tax evasion and allegations of being involved in a 'kickback' scheme, and later Richard Nixon, himself, was impeached for his part in the Watergate scandal which rocked America. In his book, *Crossfire*, Jim Marrs draws attention to the discovery of an FBI memo in 1975 by Trowbridge Ford, an assistant professor in political science at the College of the Holy Cross, Worcester, Massachusetts. It was written in connection with an inquiry into organised crime in Chicago in 1947, and said:

> It is my sworn statement that one Jack Rubenstein of Chicago, noted as a potential witness for hearings of the House Committee on Un-American Activities, is performing information functions for the staff of Congressman Richard Nixon, Republican of California. It is requested Rubenstein not be called for open testimony in the aforementioned hearings.

The FBI said the memo was a fake, but continued examination of it suggests this is not so, and if it is genuine Richard Nixon employed Jack Rubenstein years before the assassination. Who was Jack Rubenstein? He changed his name to Ruby and moved from Chicago to Dallas. Jack Ruby, whose connections to the Mafia are well known, shot and killed Lee Harvey Oswald in the basement of Dallas Jail two days after Kennedy was murdered. What a small world it is.

John F. Kennedy having been killed in Dallas, it is not unnatural that those seeking his killers should look there first. When we talk here of his killers, we are not, of course, referring to those callous individuals who pulled the triggers: we are talking of the callous individuals who sent them. It would be easy to say that just as the killers of Robert F. Kennedy were not necessarily Californians and the perpetrators of the Chappaquiddick incident were not necessarily people from the State of Massachusetts, so the killers of JFK were not necessarily Texans. The members of the Consortium, after all, could have come from any part of the United States. There are tantalising hints that Texans were involved in the assassination of John F. Kennedy, however, which only supports what has already been said: that there is a likelihood that Texas was well represented in the membership of the Consortium. As we have also said, the oilmen were inflamed by the decision to reconsider the oil depletion allowances, the military-industrial complex was strongly linked to Texas and, if big business was represented in the Consortium, there were plenty of big businessmen in that state, also. And besides all this, the Kennedys were intensely hated in Dallas. On the other hand, it is unlikely that *all* the members of the Consortium came from the one state, by any means.

If Madeleine Brown's statement about the telephone call she received is correct—and there is no reason to doubt it—Lyndon Johnson was party to the assassination of President Kennedy just by knowing about it. Madeleine recalls another odd thing that LBJ said to her when they were discussing the Warren Report and the Warren documents sealed away until the year 2039. 'Remember Box 13?' he said. 'There'll be no information there to hang LBJ, that's for sure.' Even in macabre humour, why would he say such a thing? It could easily be explained away as a reference to how he had controlled the investigation through the Warren Commission, but is still a curious way to express it. If Madeleine Brown was bitter about LBJ and was simply trying to discredit him it would put a different complexion on her recollections. She does not give the impression she is bitter, however. Quite the opposite. She speaks with great affection of him, but in her mind has no doubt that he was a man ruthlessly determined to reach the White House.

It would be easy to argue that Madeleine Brown had cause to be bitter about Lyndon Johnson. She bore a son, Steven, whom she claimed was Lyndon's child. Lyndon never acknowledged the boy, however, though Madeleine says he took care of her financially. She has documents which she purports prove he provided a regular income for her (see over). When his mother told Steven, who served in the US Navy, that LBJ was his father, he filed a multi-million dollar lawsuit against Johnson's estate, but it failed. He died in 1990.

It is hard to see Lyndon Johnson as a conspirator or a member of the Consortium, there is no evidence of this, but it may be no flight of fancy that he learnt of the plot to kill JFK from someone at the meeting in Dallas the night before the assassination. Several members of the 8F Group were present that night, if sources are correct. The 8F Group, of which Lyndon was a member, met from time to time in room 8F at the Lamarr Hotel in Houston, two floors of which were occupied by the Brown and Root company. The members of the 8F Group were wealthy men who represented the upper crust of Texas society, and their meetings were the occasion of gambling for high stakes.

Interesting facts about other Dallas residents have surfaced to set tongues wagging. Leading citizen, oilrich H. L. Hunt, one of the richest men in the world, left his home in Dallas an hour after JFK was murdered and went to Mexico, where he stayed for a month. A known Nixon supporter, he was said to be concerned lest New Orleans District Attorney Jim Garrison tried to involve him in his assassination inquiries, though he never did. There has never been a single shred of evidence to link the Hunt family with the Kennedy killing, however. Namesake, Howard Hunt and Frank Sturgis, both Watergate burglars, were both said to be in Dallas on 22 November 1962, and this, also, has attracted attention. But the same applies: there is no evidence to link either of them to the assassination. They appear to be no more than, as we said, merely interesting facts.

JEROME T. RAGSDALE
ATTORNEY AND COUNSELOR AT LAW
1807 MERCANTILE BANK BUILDING
DALLAS, TEXAS 75201
May 18, 1973

Mrs. Madeleine Brown
218 South Windomere Avenue
Dallas, Texas

Dear Madeleine:

Thanks so much for breaking your plans and meeting with Jess and me
in Houston last week. I sincerely hope we did not inconvenience
you in any way.

Those of us that were close to Lyndon are saddened by his recent
death. It is fortunate that he died at the ranch; he would have
wanted it that way. It is unfortunate, however, that he died so
bitter and tormented.

As we discussed in Houston, you have my personal assurance that I will
continue with the financial arrangements that Lyndon provided for you
and Steve throughout the past. I know you were very concerned about
this and I simply wanted to relieve your mind.

As always, if you need additional funds for you and Steve's living
expenses, please do not hesitate to call me. Of course, I will
continue to make weekly home visits to verify you and Steve's welfare.

Sincerely yours,

Jerome T. Ragsdale

JTR:mm

Enc.

Madeleine Brown believes this letter is evidence of her relationship with Lyndon B. Johnson.

Taking the John F. Kennedy assassination by itself, it is not surprising that some researchers concentrate their efforts on Texas and the 'Texas connection'. The pattern which exists, however, is swallowed up in the larger pattern which connects that murder with the assassination of Robert Kennedy, the murder of Marilyn Monroe and the tragedy at Chappaquiddick. The overall pattern indicates the existence of a vendetta against the Kennedy brothers. The Consortium members do not all wear ten-gallon hats, however, nor are all the cans full of Texan worms. But the long view of politics and the background to the vendetta reveals, sadly, that America has seen too much of the blueberry pie eaten away by the worms, wherever they are from.

CHAPTER NINETEEN

Perceptions

'To the living, one owes consideration; to the dead,
only the truth.'

Voltaire

THERE ARE INSTANCES in life where truth, easy to recognise, is extremely hard to support with what we like to call, these days, hard evidence. Human thought is one example. It exists: we know it exists, but to attempt to support the fact with hard evidence is a daunting task. The best we achieve is to establish, by means of electrical impulses, the presence of mental *activity*. The fact that we cannot provide hard evidence for the existence of something does not make it cease to exist, however, just as the *absence* of evidence is not proof of non-existence. Many things in life which cannot be touched or counted or seen are perceived to exist. In perception there is an acceptable degree of evidence, often an indisputable degree of certainty.

In the case of establishing the existence of a vendetta against the Kennedy brothers, what is perceived carries enormous weight. Three brothers, one the President of the United States, one a Presidential candidate and a third with Presidential aspirations, all are stricken, two of them killed and the third permanently debarred from achieving his aspirations by a mysterious, damaging event. It would require a considerable stretch of the imagination to believe these were three unconnected misfortunes. They form a clear indisputable pattern. If one link between all three is the Presidency, another must be the avowed intention of the brothers to change the way of things in American government. A new concern for all men everywhere is evident in their policies, a new desire for *all* the people to experience the equality to which, in the Constitution of the United States, every American is entitled, a new compassion for the poor and the elderly and those unable to provide for themselves.

Inherent in the establishment of the existence of a vendetta is the establishment of the existence of a force which conducts the vendetta. In the case of the vendetta against the Kennedys, the nature of the force responsible is definable by the influence it wields, the power it exercises and the confidence with which it acts. By these criteria, it is perceived as a group, the membership of which may be identified by the interests best served by the consequences of its actions. Intelligence looms prominently in the membership: military and war-industry interests, the oil industry and big business all seemed to profit. This is not to say, by any means, that these groups were in any way represented *per se* by the members of the group. That would be a false and erroneous notion. What is being said is that membership seems to have been drawn from the ranks of the people who belong to these interests, which have profited most from the vendetta. We have gone as far as to call the group the Consortium, for it is otherwise difficult to make reference to a nameless organisation, and, because of its perceived operations, we cannot fail to identify it as selfish, lawless and ruthless. We argue the case for certain of its members being hived off to form an Executive Group, since, on the one hand, they were unlikely to trust outsiders with their planning and operations, and on the other, the involvement of the entire Consortium would have been unwieldly.

The existence of the Consortium has been recognised by others over a long period of time. Thomas G. Buchanan, in his book, *Who Killed Kennedy?* which appeared as early as 1964 and, therefore, must have been in preparation *before* the Warren Report was published, said:

I believe the murder of the President was provoked, primarily by fear of the domestic and international consequences of the Moscow Pact: the danger of disarmament which would disrupt the industries on which the plotters depended and of an international detente which would, in their view, have threatened the eventual nationalisation of their oil investments overseas.

There is no doubt that when it came to the murder of Robert Kennedy, many who had gone along with the Warren version of events, or had been agnostic, began to revise their ideas about the assassination of the President. The hand of the conspirators was partly exposed in the second Kennedy death. Police Sergeant Paul Schraga who, it will be recalled, tried without success to involve LAPD in tracking down the girl in the polka-dot dress, had no doubts about what was afoot:

I think we have a structure in this country and I refer to them [sic] as a corporate war-machine, or you can refer to them as anything you want. I believe they did and will do anything that they need to – or that they want to – to preserve their status quo.

Criminologist William W. Harper, who re-examined the ballistics evidence in the Robert Kennedy case, had seen the pattern being formed in the vendetta when he said,

[There are] too many things about this that point in one direction, and I think that the Kennedy family should by all means be interested because, hell, the next time it'll be Ted Kennedy and then it will go on down the line – any of them.

Jim Hougan, commenting in his book, *Spooks*, on the statement made by Virgilio Gonzalez, who was involved in the Watergate burglary, said:

If the Gonzalez affidavit is to be believed, the United States is a police state run by a dangerous consortium of CIA officers, private intelligence agencies and White House entrepreneurs.

L. Fletcher Prouty, the retired Air Force colonel who spent nine years in the Pentagon acting as Focal Point Officer with the CIA, first for the

Air Force and then for the Department of Defense, wrote of 'The Secret Team' in his book bearing that title.* In conversations with this author, Prouty acknowledged that we are both, in our different ways, describing the same organisation. In his book he refers to President Kennedy's perception of the Secret Team and pinpoints the problem when he asks:

> Can any President learn about, comprehend, and then believe what he has learned about this whole covert and complex subject? Can any President see in this vast mechanism, in which there is so much that is untrue and hidden, the heart and core of the real problem? Will any President be prepared to confront this staggering realisation when and if he does uncover it? *Is this, perhaps, the great discovery which President Kennedy made, or was about to make?* (This author's emphasis)

It would seem to have been realisation of the existence of the Consortium – or Prouty's Secret Team – that drove Lyndon Johnson to retirement. He had had enough. His moves after announcing he would not stand for a second term suggest he had found a new freedom when he threw off the shackles of the Consortium. President Richard Nixon, also, gave the impression he knew he was under the control of the Consortium when pressed by television journalist, Nancy Dickerson, on promises he had made to give the country the lift of a 'driving dream'. Nixon, an old hand at television appearances, hesitated, then thoughtfully and slowly said:

> Miss Dickerson, before we can really get a lift of a driving dream, we have to get rid of some of the nightmares we inherited. One of these nightmares is a war without end [Vietnam]. We are ending that war . . . But it takes some time to get rid of the nightmares. You can't be having a driving dream when you are in the midst of a nightmare.

Was 'nightmare' his way of alluding to the yoke of the Consortium?

The only time we have been given actual confirmation of the existence of a vendetta against the Kennedys – and implicit evidence of the

---

* L. Fletcher Prouty, Col. USAF (Ret). *The Secret Team*, Institute for Historical Review, Costa Mesa, California, 1973

existence of the Consortium—was when the Cuban-born CIA pilot betrayed the fact to Hank Gordon (see Chapter Seven). The reader will recall that Hank had been engaged to work alongside the pilot for a few days in preparing a Douglas DC-3 for take-off from Dallas's Red Bird Airfield on Friday 22 November 1963. The plane, we learnt, was purchased by an Air Force colonel for a Houston company, found to be a CIA front. Becoming friendly with Hank Gordon as they worked together, the pilot confided, 'Hank, they are going to kill your President.' Responding to Hank's surprise at his statement, he repeated, 'They are going to kill your President', and later in the conversation which developed added, 'They are not only going to kill the President, they are going to kill Robert Kennedy and any other Kennedy who gets into that position.'

The pilot's words came true the following day when John F. Kennedy was killed, and five years later his accuracy was again demonstrated at the Ambassador Hotel in Los Angeles when Robert Kennedy was assassinated. Since the murder of the third brother would have hacked at the roots of the security of even the Consortium, the tragedy at Chappaquiddick is seen as confirming every word the man had told Hank Gordon. In Hank Gordon a better, more reliable witness could not be wished for. He faithfully reported all he could remember and everything checkable about his statement checked out exactly. This included the number of the DC-3 and its sale to Houston Air Center. The accuracy of the story was again franked by the discovery that the Houston Air Center was a CIA front. This information represents the biggest crack in the conspiracy to come out of Dallas since the day the President died. It confirms the existence of the vendetta against the Kennedy brothers and the pilot's reference to 'they', translates into evidence of the existence of the Consortium.

The government of the United States did not acquit itself well in the so-called investigation into the assassination of President John F. Kennedy. The Warren Report was believed by the American people because they trusted the government of the United States. It was not that the people critically examined what Warren was saying and accepted the Commission's version of events. It never occurred to them that they should not put their complete trust in what they were being told. The early critics of the Warren Report were voices in the wilderness. Nobody listened to them for a considerable time. They were scorned, ridiculed and castigated for their attacks on the misleading and dishonest report. When the people finally awoke to the reality of the situation a rot set in which has gnawed away ever since at the very fibres of the people's confidence in the US government. Indeed, it might be said to have gnawed away at the foundations of the American way of life.

The formation in the mid-seventies of the House Assassinations Committee was the consequence of the disquiet of the people, but if the new investigation was set in motion to restore the confidence of the people, it did not, by any means, achieve that aim. The Committee took an unconscionable time to set itself up, and had a set target date for the publication of its report. The actual time devoted to new investigation, therefore, was limited to a few months. The Committee's chief preoccupation appeared to be the re-establishment of the Warren Report, but since evidence was submitted to it which supported the existence of a conspiracy to kill the President – which the Committee accepted with reluctance – the government may have been relieved it had no time to investigate it further. The United States government has consistently displayed a desire for everything connected with the assassination of President Kennedy to go away. It has had ample opportunity to set in motion an exhaustive investigation into the assassination conspiracy and has staunchly resisted doing so.

When JFK was killed, government agencies rushed to the assistance of the Warren Commission as it layed the blame on Lee Harvey Oswald and ignored the leads to a conspiracy. As time has gone by and more has become known, the clear impression left behind by both the FBI and the CIA is that they had information which they did not give to Warren, though this may well have been because they knew the information they had would be unwelcome. Military Intelligence certainly had a file on Lee Harvey Oswald under the name of A. J. Hidell which, it is believed, would have revealed he was a government intelligence agent. They withheld it. Its existence only became known when the House Assassinations Committee was in session in the mid-seventies but by then Military Intelligence had destroyed it. Dallas Police, having allowed Lee Harvey Oswald to be murdered while in their custody, did nothing to upset the Warren Commission. Indeed, the indications are they possessed knowledge which would have scuppered the Warren claims. It is not difficult to see the inspiration for the script Oliver Stone adopted for his film, *JFK*, which claimed the assassination was a coup d'état which had the blessing of the Establishment and that the Establishment conspired to cover everything up.* It is not impossible that we are saying the same thing. The question must be asked whether such 'Establishment blessing' derived from links between individuals associated with the Establishment and Consortium members. Could it be that they were the same people?

Robert Kennedy had been marked for assassination for as long as John F. Kennedy. Had he been killed in the years immediately following John's death, however, the existence of a vendetta would have been advertised loudly and clearly. The Consortium felt they had time to wait until the connection between the two murders was less obvious. After all, it was known that Robert did not intend entering the Presidential race until the primaries of 1972. It was because of the country's Vietnam war policy and fear of what another four years of Johnson rule might do that he changed his mind and decided to run in 1968. It was something of a last-minute change and it nearly caught the Consortium out. A last-minute candidacy is not the most effective way to enter into the running for a nomination, however, and, at first, it appeared the Consortium did not have much to worry about, for the Senator's chances looked quite slim. But when Lyndon Johnson announced his intention not to run in the forthcoming election everything changed overnight. It was then, no doubt, that the Consortium, watching Robert Kennedy's progress closely, decided it must bring its own programme forward and risk disposing of him at an earlier date than planned.

At John Kennedy's side throughout his Presidency, Robert Kennedy was as guilty in the eyes of the Consortium as John had been. He

---

* Oliver Stone was pressed in an interview in Europe to name the shadowy military man in *JFK* who enlightened Garrison at their meeting in the park at Washington. He identified him as L. Fletcher Prouty, to whom we refer earlier in this chapter.

was seen by them as the co-author of the Bay of Pigs disaster and approving of his brother's 'accommodation' of communism. He was equally culpable when it came to responsibility for the country's 'misfortunes' and the 'outlandish, ruinous, socialist policies' mooted during John's time in office, and about to be launched on the country in the second term JFK never had. In some respects he was an even more dangerous man than John F. Kennedy had been. The Consortium found Robert Kennedy's campaign speeches alarming and the people's response to them highly dangerous. He could not be allowed to survive beyond the time of the California primary results.

To the Consortium, Edward Moore Kennedy represented in some ways no less a threat than his brothers before him. On the face of it the chief threat from him was that he was a Kennedy, and his elevation to the Oval Office would have brought all the old problems arising from the marriage of Kennedy power to the power of the Presidency. Besides this, elected on a 'Kennedy ticket', there was no telling what Edward would turn the Presidency into, and there was every reason to believe he would be as troublesome as his brothers had been. Consortium members' fears were not allayed by those who tried to persuade them that Edward was more of a footsoldier than a general. They did not see him like that. He was a consummate politician: indeed, it was John who had said he was, 'the best politician in the family'. On another occasion he had said, '. . . my father cracked down on him at a crucial time in his life, and this brought out in Teddy the discipline and seriousness which will make him an important political figure'. Robert had not lacked praise for him either. 'Teddy will do well in anything he chooses,' he had said.

In view of the risks they had taken and the audacity they had displayed in killing John and Robert, there was no way the Consortium was going to allow the third brother a safe passage to the White House. Any star from the Kennedy firmament was totally unacceptable. Killing him, however, was now out of the question, since to kill all three of the brothers within a decade would leave not the slightest doubt in any mind that a vendetta existed. The hue and cry which would follow that would represent a suicidal risk. Chappaquiddick provided the opportunity to follow the course for which the Consortium opted: 'political disablement'. It had the same effect as far as they were concerned.

As was said earlier in this chapter, there are many references in literature to a secret government of the United States of one kind or another, and it is not unreasonable to believe that the various authors have encountered or perceived the same secret organisation, call it what we may. Perceptions often vary and no version can be dismissed because it is somewhat different from the next. Obviously and reasonably, different names have been given to it, among them the Secret Government, the Invisible Government, the High Cabal and the Secret Team. Where other writers have attributed a broader, more widespread and farther reaching, operation to what this author calls the Consortium, this should not be thought to be in conflict with his vision of the organisation. It should be remembered that the present study has been limited to the identification of that strand of Consortium activity which relates specifically to the vendetta against the Kennedy brothers. No attempt has been made here to plumb the depths of Consortium activities or measure the dimensions of its influence and control. This author, then, has no argument with those whose perceptions identify activities which extend into many of the structures and infra-structures of American life, society and government.

The study undertaken in this book reveals that the Consortium has existed from about the time John F. Kennedy assumed the Presidency of the United States. Some believe that it existed from an earlier date. One writer argues that it came into existence at the time the role of the CIA changed at the end of the Second World War. Another claims to trace it back to the thirties. Whatever the case, it is unlikely that it has ever been disbanded. Power, it is said, corrupts. When power of the kind seen to be in the possession of the Consortium is amassed, those wielding it are not likely to relinquish it. The power possessed by the Consortium is the kind of power which is born of greed, either for personal power or personal wealth, the one often bringing the other. Needless to say, therefore, there are no poor Consortium members. Members of the Consortium are likely to be people of enormous influence in their personal circles. If those who rub shoulders with them have any inkling of their affiliation with the dread Consortium they will only speak of it in whispers. It is dangerous to bandy such suspicions about. The members of the Consortium are members for life, of course. There are no resignations from this organisation. The group is extremely well informed: members are better informed than any congressman and, in spite of their breadth of interests, better informed than any senator, either. Their intelligence is provided by their CIA members, who have access to the Agency's sources.

If the question is asked, 'Why were the Kennedy brothers made the target of the Consortium's vendetta?' the answer is very simple. The Consortium could not control them. And more than this, the combination of Kennedy family wealth, influence and power, linked to the power, influence and aura of the Presidency created an irresistible, impregnable force which was greater than their own. It was for this reason that John F. Kennedy was removed from the Presidency by assassination and Robert Kennedy was killed to prevent him reaching the White House. It was for this reason, also, that Edward Kennedy was made the victim of the events at Chappaquiddick. At least he escaped with his life. The members of the Consortium were able to flex their muscles and these things were done. The Consortium was to be dreaded more than any elected government, more than the faceless moguls who have the country in their fiscal grasp, more than the invisible, covert, government which is the CIA. These governments are all represented in the membership of the Consortium, just as the oil barons, industry, commerce and the military are represented. They constitute a government above all other governments, and they are jealous of their privileged supremacy. The Kennedys were a challenge to that supremacy and they were ruthlessly destroyed.

NAME INDEX

SUBJECT INDEX